Is Fair Value Fair?

Financial Reporting from an International Perspective

Is Fair Value Fair?

*Financial Reporting from
an International Perspective*

Edited by

**Henk Langendijk, Dirk Swagerman and
Willem Verhoog**

WILEY

Published 2003 John Wiley & Sons Ltd, The Atrium, Southern Gate, Chichester,
West Sussex PO19 8SQ, England
Telephone (+44) 1243 779777

Email (for orders and customer service enquiries): cs-books@wiley.co.uk
Visit our Home Page on www.wileyeurope.com or www.wiley.com

Other Wiley Editorial Offices

John Wiley & Sons Inc., 111 River Street, Hoboken, NJ 07030, USA

Jossey-Bass, 989 Market Street, San Francisco, CA 94103-1741, USA

Wiley-VCH Verlag GmbH, Boschstr. 12, D-69469 Weinheim, Germany

John Wiley & Sons Australia Ltd, 33 Park Road, Milton, Queensland 4064, Australia

John Wiley & Sons (Asia) Pte Ltd, 2 Clementi Loop #02-01, Jin Xing Distripark, Singapore 129809

John Wiley & Sons Canada Ltd, 22 Worcester Road, Etobicoke, Ontario, Canada M9W 1L1

Wiley also publishes its books in a variety of electronic formats. Some content that appears
in print may not be available in electronic books.

Library of Congress Cataloging-in-Publication Data
Is fair value fair? : financial reporting from an international perspective / edited by Henk
Langendijk, Dirk Swagerman, and Willem Verhoog.
    p. cm.
  Includes bibliographical references and index.
  ISBN 0-470-85028-0 (cased : alk. paper)
    1. Financial statements.   2. International business enterprises – Accounting.
  3. Fair value – Accounting.   I. Langendijk, H. P. A. J.   II. Swagerman, Dirk, 1949–
  III. Verhoog, Willem, 1950–
  HF5681.B2 I67 2003
  657′.3 – dc21

                                                                    2002191094

British Library Cataloguing in Publication Data
A catalogue record for this book is available from the British Library

ISBN 0-470-85028-0

Project management by Originator, Gt Yarmouth, Norfolk (typeset in 10/12pt Utopia)
Printed and bound in Great Britain by TJ International Ltd, Padstow, Cornwall
This book is printed on acid-free paper responsibly manufactured from sustainable forestry
in which at least two trees are planted for each one used for paper production.

Contents

Part III   Supervision and compliance

Part IV   IAS and the users of financial statements

Part V   Fair Value Accounting

Part VI   *Capita selecta*: external financial reporting and law

About the editors

Professor Henk P. A. J. Langendijk (1952)

Professor Henk Langendijk studied Business Economics at the University of Amsterdam (1972–1976). He subsequently worked for a number of years in the accountancy field (at BDO and Arthur Andersen). From 1980 to 1988 he worked for the University of Amsterdam as a lecturer of finance and from 1988 to 2000 as a senior lecturer in the field of financial accounting. In 1997 he was appointed part-time Professor of Business Economics at the Nyenrode University. Langendijk was subsequently appointed Professor of External Financial Reporting at Nyenrode University in 1999 and Professor of External Financial Reporting at the University of Amsterdam in 2000. He gained his doctorate in 1994 on the subject 'The market for the statutory audit in the Netherlands' at the University of Leiden.

His recent research concentrates on the quality of external financial reporting, with a particular focus on creative accounting and fraudulent reporting. He has many articles to his name, which have appeared in international magazines such as *European Accounting Review, European Journal of Finance, Accounting, Auditing and Accountability Journal* and in Dutch magazines, including *Maandblad voor Accountancy en Bedrijfseconomie, Accounting, Bedrijfskunde, Tijdschrift Financieel Management, De Accountant* and *Accountant-Adviseur*. He has also written a number of books in the field of financial accounting and is a member of the Advisory Council of the Limperg Instituut. In addition, Langendijk is editor-in-chief of the magazine *Accounting*, editor of *Accountant-Adviseur* and a member of the VERA steering committee on financial reporting.

Professor Dirk M. Swagerman (1949)

Professor Dirk Swagerman attended the electrical engineering section of Patrimonium Junior Technical School in Amsterdam and was subsequently admitted to the higher general secondary education class of Ignatius College in Amsterdam.

In 1969, he enrolled at the General Political and Social Sciences subfaculty of the Municipal University in Amsterdam. He followed this with evening classes at the Contardo Ferrini High School. In 1971, he passed university entry and first-year examinations. Following Bachelor degree examinations, Swagerman chose to study Public Administration and in 1975 was awarded a Master's degree. The most important subsidiary subjects that he studied for his Master's degree were Research Methods and Techniques, International and European Law and, at the Faculty of Economics, Administrative Information Management, Internal Organisation and Public Finance.

He studied at the Graduate Business School of Michigan State University in 1978 and 1979 and was awarded a Master of Business Administration degree. After this, he successfully completed the SIOO postgraduate management consultancy training course, which led in 1997 to a Master in Change Management degree. At Stanford University, Swagerman followed the Senior Executive Program in 1989 and the Financial Management Program in 1999. In 1991 and 1992, he was awarded a Master of Business Telecommunications degree at the University of Delft.

Swagerman has spent a major part of his working life as a management consultant, focusing mainly on fields relating to the organisation and design of the financial function for all types of organisations in the Netherlands and abroad. As a certified management consultant, he is a member of the Netherlands Order of Management Consultants, the Royal Netherlands Institute of Engineering and the Netherlands Association of Public Administration.

Since 1994, Swagerman has been attached part-time to the University of Twente in Enschede, where he obtained his doctorate in Financial Logistics Management on 25 August 2000. He is also attached to Deloitte & Touche in Amsterdam and to the Eurac/Erasmus University Controller's training course in Rotterdam, where he lectures on Financial Management and Treasury Management.

On 15 November 2002 he was appointed as professor at the Economic Faculty and the Faculty of Business Economics of the Rijksuniversiteit Groningen (RUG).

Willem Verhoog (1950)

Willem Verhoog has been the Secretary-general of Royal NIVRA's Committee for the Continuing Professional Education of *Registeraccountants* (VERA) since 1 August 1976. Following the award of a teaching certificate at De Driestar in Gouda in 1971, he worked until 1974 as a teacher in Werkhoven and Alblasserdam/Kinderdijk. On the occasion of his 25-year NIVRA anniversary, he received a *liber amicorum* (with 25 contributions from professors) entitled 'How good is a timely word'. Verhoog is responsible for the development and progress of the continuing professional education provided by VERA. In this capacity he is also involved in the organisation of pan-European congresses such as Form 20F and MD&A, Recent Trends in Valuation/Real Options and US GAAP.

Since 1990 Willem Verhoog has been the editor-in-chief of *VERA-Actueel*, the monthly continuing professional education magazine. He is editor-in-chief of 30 NIVRA/VERA books, of the annual VERA series *Actualiteiten in Accountancy* and the VERA series 'Fifteen expert opinions on ...'. In 2000, *Strategic Finance in the 21st Century* was published as part of this series and has now been released on the international market under the title *A Vision for the Future* by the British publishing house John Wiley & Sons. A Chinese version was published in 2002 and a Russian version will be published this year (2003). In January 2003 another VERA publication will be released on the international market by John Wiley & Sons under the title *Recent Trends in Valuation: From Strategy to Value* (edited by Willem Verhoog and Luc Keuleneer).

Abbreviations

AICPA	American Institute of Certified Public Accountants
AcSEC	Accounting Standards Executive Committee
ARC	Accounting Regulatory Committee
AA	Accountant Administratieconsulent
AEX	Amsterdam Exchange Index
AO	Administrative Organisation
ASB	Accounting Standards Board
ARC	Accounting Regulatory Commission
BV	Besloten Vernootschap
CMG	Dutch listed computer firm
CPA	Chartered Public Accountant
RA	Registeraccountant
CIMA	Chartered Institute of Management Accountants
CESR1	Committee of European Securities Regulators
CFO	Chief Financial Officer
CNOOC	China National Offshore Oil Corporation
CICA	Canadian Institute of Chartered Accountants
DNB	Dutch Central Bank
DCF	Discounted Cash Flow
EU	European Union
EFRAG	European Financial Reporting Advisory Group
EBITA	Earnings Before Interest, Taxation and Amortisation
EBITDA	Earnings Before Interest, Taxation, Depreciation and Amortisation
ERP	Enterprise Resource Planning
EITF	Emerging Issues Task Force
FASB	Financial Accounting Standards Board
FAS	Financial Accounting Standards

FAR	Open reserve for general bank risks
FEE	Fédération des Experts Compatables Européens
IAS	International Accounting Standards
IASB	International Accounting Standards Board
IASC	International Accounting Standards Committee
IFRS	International Financial Reporting Standards
ICAEW	Institute of Chartered Accountants in England and Wales
IFRIC	International Financial Reporting Interpretations Committee
IOSCO	International Organisation of Securities Commissions
IPSAS	International Public Sector Accounting Standards
IFRIC	International Financial Reporting Interpretations Committee
IMF	International Monetary Fund
IFAD	International Forum on Accountancy Development
JWG	Joint Working Group
LIFO	Last In, First Out
MD&A	Management Discussion & Analysis
MIS	Management Information Systems
MAB	Maandblad voor Accountancy en Bedrijfseconomie
NATO	North Atlantic Treaty Organisation
NIVRA	Koninklyk Nederlands Instituut von Registeraccountants
NRC	Handelsblad – leading financial daily in the Netherlands
NOK	Norwegian 'Kroner'
NVB	Nederlandse Vereniging van Banken/Dutch Bankers' Association
OECD	Organisation for Economic Cooperation and Development
PCNA	Platform Committee of Registeraccountants and Actuaries
RJ	Raad voor de Jaarverslaggeving
RUG	Rijksuniversiteit Groningen
SEC	Securities and Exchange Commission
SIC	Standing Interpretations Committee
SOBI	Stichting Onderzoek Bedrijffs Informatie
SQL	Structured Query Language
SEK	Swedish 'Kroner'
TEG	Technical Expert Group
US GAAP	US Generally Accepted Accounting Principles
VERA	Voortgesette Educatie Registeraccountants
VAR	Secret reserve for general bank risks
VNO-NCW	Dutch Employers Association
VEB	Vereniging van Effectenbezitters (the Netherlands Association of Securities Holders)
XBRL	eXtensible Business Reporting Language

Introduction

Willem Verhoog

In an age that is characterised by internationalisation, the call for uniformity in rules is becoming ever louder. For the sake of comparability, intelligibility and transparency of financial information the aim is to produce universal standards. Were not the units of measurements, weights and money the most important impulses for the unification of states? The increasing demand for uniformity in rules is also observed in the practice of external financial reporting. On 7 June 2002, for example, the European Council of Ministers approved the regulation requiring that all European Union (EU) companies listed on a regulated market, from 2005 onwards, prepare and publish their consolidated financial statements in accordance with international accounting standards (IAS). In March 2002, the European Parliament endorsed the regulation, originally proposed by the European Commission in February 2001. Certain amendments were also adopted including clarification on exemptions for certain companies until 2007. In addition to this regulation, agreements have also been made concerning the supervision of the financial reporting of listed companies and the co-ordination of this supervision. This again means a step in the direction of uniformity, harmonisation and a single, so fervently desired, capital market in the EU. Steps will also have to be taken to create a new supervisory body with special powers, which will primarily focus on the enforcement of rules concerning external financial reporting.

Clearly, the new regulations will radically change the various methods of financial reporting. Furthermore, the accountancy and controller professions will obviously be profoundly affected by the new developments. That is the reason why Wiley is publishing this book by Royal NIVRA's Committee for the Continuing Professional Education of *Register-accountants* (VERA) in order to cover the subject of IAS in detail. More than thirty experts present their vision of the effects that IAS will have on the practice of financial reporting. The reporting world is constantly on the move. Following a long period during which financial reporting standards changed little or not at all, we are now faced with a period of rapid change in which not only new financial reporting standards are emerging, but discussions are also taking place about the benefit and the added value of the standards. We see this discussion manifest itself in the differences in approach to reporting standards on the North American and European continents, for instance, with regard to the way in which goodwill is treated.

In any event, we are confronted with many issues in the field of standards. In this book, the term IAS will be used to denote the accounting standards of the International Accounting Standards Board (IASB). The term IFRS will – with the exception of a few contributions – not be used. The listed companies referred to will have to adapt their reporting system to the new set of rules in the very short term. Searching for a common thread in these accounting standards, it can be said that the accountants' world is evolving towards fair value and thus market value. It is expected that historical cost (also current cost) as an accounting principle will become less important in the future. The critical question to be asked is whether full compliance with accounting principles generally accepted in either the USA or in Europe automatically leads to the presentation of a 'true and fair view' of the company's financial position and its results of operation. Clearly, the new accounting standards show a tendency towards 'fair value accounting'. Whilst fair value accounting may lead to more relevant financial reporting, it may also lead to significant fluctuations in financial results over time.

The areas of attention in this book include: valuation based on fair value, the treatment of goodwill, the reporting issues of new economy companies, of insurance companies and banks, supranational and national rules and regulations. The common ground and differences between internal and external reporting will also be covered. Furthermore, the differences between 'accrual accounting' and 'cash flow accounting' will be dealt with in various contributions. Here, cash flow accounting should be considered to include the calculation of company value as an element of fair value accounting as well as impairment calculations that are currently very relevant for the 'capitalised goodwill' item.

The themes included in this book are: the future of 'international accountancy', US GAAP, regulations and regulators, supervision and compliance, IAS and the users of financial statements, fair value accounting and *Capita Selecta* (external financial reporting and law, external financial reporting and new economy companies, international government reporting, management accounting versus financial accounting and merger accounting).

Fair value accounting, especially 'mark-to-market accounting' has become extremely relevant as a result of the developments at Enron and, more recently, at Worldcom. 'Special purpose entities', which are an important tenet of consolidation, are also very much the subject of discussion because of Enron. Generally speaking, the Enron case has accelerated developments right across the board in the accountancy profession, particularly with respect to external financial reporting and the role of accounting firms in this. The more recent Worldcom and Xerox debacles only emphasise the need for proper – that is, independent and unbiased – auditing of financial statements. The redesign of the financial reporting model is currently under discussion. It appears from the Enron case that the standard setting process is going too slow and does not always provide the best solutions for essential elements.

As a consequence, the harmonisation process between US GAAP and IAS can thus receive a new impulse, particularly because it is asserted that such problems would not have occurred quite so easily at Enron under IAS. It is important to note that 'substance over form' is an internationally accepted principle of accounting. This principle has always existed, both in US as well as European accounting practices. It appears that US accounting practice has developed more towards 'checking the box', that is, ensuring compliance with the law and regulations. In European accounting practice, the presentation of a true and fair view has always been the primary focus. In a time frame of the further globalisation of business, international convergence of accounting standards is needed. The future will show whether the Securities and Exchange Commission (SEC) and the FASB will draft more detailed rules or more substance rules and support the convergence of US GAAP towards IAS.

The book concludes with an epilogue. Although a summary of all options contained in this book does not do justice to the content and can in no way cover all aspects and nuances, we believe that we should provide brief impressions of each contribution. The sketches in Chapter 1 indeed provide no more than an impression of what each of the experts interviewed has discussed. The fact that the abundance of ideas, opinions, critical comments, explanations and analyses cannot be covered by what is otherwise an extensive series of impressions can, on the one hand, be regarded as a shortcoming but, on the other hand, as a luxury.

Nowadays we live in a world where financial reporting – especially the so-called accounting scandals – are the talk of the town. Even hairdressers and cabdrivers have very specific opinions about financial reporting and the people who are involved in the process of preparing, auditing and analysing figures. A means of creative accounting and fraudulent report-ing is 'fair value accounting' (e.g. Enron with their mark-to-market accounting of long-term energy contracts).

We provide many opinions by internationally recognised experts in the field of external financial reporting. In addition, participants in the social and economic process who are directly concerned with external financial reporting, give their opinion about international developments. This book is therefore vitally important for everyone who operates in the international arena where the external financial reporting of organisations plays a role. On behalf of the editors, I would like to thank everyone who has assisted in the preparation of this collection of interviews and would like to believe that after reading them you will share our opinion that external financial reporting has entered a new phase of development, which rightly deserves the attention that is devoted to it in this compilation.

Chapter 1

Is fair value fair?

*Expert opinions on financial reporting
from an international perspective:
brief impressions*

Willem Verhoog

*Willem Verhoog (1950) has been the Secretary-general of Royal
NIVRA's VERA committee since 1 August 1976. He is responsible
for the development and progress of the continuing professional
education of registeraccountants, provided by VERA.*

In order to make it easier for the reader, this synopsis will briefly cover the main message of the persons who are interviewed. The rapid changes that are taking place in society are a recurring theme running through the interviews. One of the repercussions of these changes is the increasing importance of external reporting: the strong trend towards harmonisation in reporting rules, the role of supervisory bodies with respect to external reporting and the considerable interest shown in external reporting by the financial press.

Because of Enron, Worldcom and Xerox, the quality of external financial reporting has been thrown into the limelight. As a result, even more pressure has been put on the designers (regulators) of new rules. Fair value accounting is regarded as a solution in this respect. However, it appears from the interviews that this is not regarded by everyone as the panacea for the quality problems that have arisen.

The quintessence of the interviews is presented in this synopsis so that the reader is provided with a probing overview of the opinions of the experts who have been interviewed.

THE FUTURE OF INTERNATIONAL ACCOUNTANCY

Elliott

The opening interview with prominent accountant Robert Elliott outlines the general situation in the field of international accountancy and underpins the expectations for the short and long term. Elliott expects that the accountancy profession will not undergo any fundamental changes in the coming five years, but that IAS will subsequently exert an influence. Technological developments will also have an affect on the audit. Users will increasingly demand and receive online information in real time. Due to the asymmetry in the information available to the management of companies on the one hand and that available to stakeholders on the other, considerable demand for reliable information remains. On top of this, administrative assistance also remains important for clients. Elliott points to the problem that intangible assets are as a rule not valued on the balance sheet. This is certainly a precarious situation. The date and the number of outstanding shares are actually the only reliable information and this does not make fair value accounting a recipe for the future.

The expectation is that the IASB will develop to become the international standard-setter and thus outpace the FASB. The rules will, however, have to be designed to meet the specific demands of the users. Elliott would like to see a strict supervisory body like the American SEC, which can to a certain extent guarantee the quality and thus the reliability of external financial reporting. He wants to see companies reporting their stock options in the notes to the financial statements. All of this must, of course, be embedded in proper corporate governance, and audit committees must be appointed that have authority. For the future, Elliott sees that the accountant must continually be able to provide assurance about the reliability of information and about the systems in question. In a world of real-time information, a journal entry is the correction of an error. This seems controversial, but it isn't.

Strauss

Norman Strauss points out that there are many differences in details between IAS and US GAAP, but that standard-setters are trying to reconcile financial reporting standards so that there is increasingly less and less distinction worldwide. For Strauss, the ideal situation in the future would be a single global organisation concerned with the development of standards. He advises that those companies applying the new standards must reserve enough time for their calculations because the information required cannot be obtained from the general ledger system. Companies would do well to put together professional teams to determine the relevant values and to allocate goodwill and book values to the various business units.

Where the reporting of financial instruments is concerned, Strauss informs us that the FASB has announced that it believes that all financial instruments should eventually be valued on the basis of fair value. The IASB is also concerned with standards for financial instruments. Strauss believes that it is difficult to determine the fair value of certain financial instruments.

REGULATIONS AND REGULATORS

Tweedie

IASB chairman Sir David Tweedie foresees an important role for the Board: to develop globally applicable standards and to ensure that the various (supra)national standard-setters (particularly including the FASB) co-operate. Tweedie observes that the integration process is hampered by differences in insight, such as that concerning merger accounting, the impairment test, valuation of intangible fixed assets and the treatment of goodwill. He is sceptical about the arrival of the European Financial Reporting Advisory Group (EFRAG), which he believes has introduced a political dimension. Putting this into perspective, however, he is happy that EFRAG members are people who know what they are talking about and have an international perspective. If the IASB and the EFRAG work together intensively and continuously, it will certainly be possible to get things done.

In the short term, the IASB will mainly concern itself with the modification of existing standards, particularly those relating to financial instruments, leasing and share options. In the first instance, the standards are designed for listed companies. A simplified set of rules that are derived from these must then apply to other companies. In the new standards, the concept of 'true and fair view', the so-called disclosure requirement, will be retained.

According to Tweedie, a supervisory body like the SEC would be a possibility for Europe, but a Financial Reporting Review Panel would be less expensive (fewer personnel) and could operate more effectively. Such a body examines financial statements in response to complaints.

Van Helleman

To advise the European Commission about the introduction of IAS and to maintain contact with the IASB, the new advisory body EFRAG has been created. This body will serve to both channel and present a European opinion about the standards. Johan van Helleman, Chairman of the EFRAG, points out that the IASB, which up until now has focused exclusively on the balance sheet, the profit and loss account, the cash flow statement and the notes, should also produce rules for the directors' report. On this point, IAS should be able to follow the European standards that also provide rules for the formulation of the directors' report. It is also possible that notes concerning the remuneration of directors, which according to the EU should be included in the external financial reporting, could be included in IAS.

Although Europe has opted for international standards, it also wants to have its voice heard via the EFRAG. The American influence will be considerable, however. This implies specific, detailed rules for external reporting with strict application and enforcement by accountants and an alert supervisory body with authority. In a nutshell, this means a new playing field for companies, accountants and supervisors, with new rules, 'even though the sport will essentially remain the same'.

Responding to the new situation also involves additional training, both at universities and via VERA. Accountants who believe they are sufficiently informed will quickly discover that their knowledge is superficial and inadequate. Companies must also prepare themselves well in advance for the transition: systems and business practices must be adjusted. Various pension schemes will, for instance, have to be closely re-examined and there will be a growing appreciation of the economic consequences of external reporting.

Van der Tas

The Standing Interpretations Committee (SIC) answers questions about the application and interpretation of IAS. Up until now, more than 30 interpretations have been published, with SIC 12 (Consolidation of Special Purpose Entities) having the most far-reaching effect. Following a proposal by the new IASB, the SIC was replaced by the International Financial Reporting Interpretations Committee (IFRIC) at the beginning of 2002. The IFRIC consists of 12 voting members (accountants, compilers and users from various countries) and an independent chairman who has no vote but concentrates on running the meetings in a purely technical sense. In addition, the powers of the IFRIC will be expanded. The IFRIC will also issue interpretations on subjects that have not yet been laid down in standards. The powers of this body have thus been brought more into line with its US, British and Australian counterparts. All interpretations must first be approved by the IASB.

IAS must be applied in full; IAS 1 forbids partial application. If a company wants to enjoy the best of both worlds, the accountants and supervisors will just have to make sure everyone follows the same line. If necessary, the auditor's report must be modified, 'because there is no point in striving for international comparability if everybody does as they like and interprets the rules according to their own insights and convenience', according to the Netherlands' IFRIC representative Leo van der Tas.

The IASB's rules are stricter than the Dutch Council for Annual Reporting guidelines that still leave certain options open which the IAS no longer accept. It is, however, unwise to oblige all Dutch companies to apply IAS. If a small corner shop is a private limited company, it must prepare and file financial statements, 'but to oblige all such companies to meet the IAS requirements simply doesn't bear thinking about.' A separate, simplified standard should be introduced for small companies, which are nevertheless in line with the rules for larger companies.

Van Hulle

In 1999, the European Commission presented a programme on financial services. The emphasis was on some 40 measures that should ultimately lead to an effective, integrated market for financial services in Europe. The programme also devotes attention to annual reporting and accounting. In an integrated and efficiently operating capital market, companies will be able to attract capital at the lowest costs. To this end, the information underlying the decision-making processes must be complete and reliable. As soon as the capital costs are no higher than strictly necessary, European companies can become more competitive, particularly in comparison with the United States.

The attainment of such an efficient capital market hinges on two crucial elements: financial reports must be comparable and standards applied by companies must be strictly enforced. For the latter element, recourse will be sought from the committee that supervises the securities markets, the SEC. The ultimate sanction – delisting – cannot be ruled out, and that can have severe consequences for investors. Publicity, too, is an important sanction, together with timely auditing of the information in the financial statements. Disciplinary sanctions can be imposed on the accountant who does not keep to the rules.

EU top civil servant Karel van Hulle reproaches Europe for having done too little to standardise annual reporting. 'We are now paying the price for that.' Now either US GAAP or IAS will have to be accepted. The European Commission opts for IAS. These standards can be given world-wide force provided they are meticulously worked out and every country can contribute to them. They will then gain wide support. In this respect, Van Hulle expects a lot from EFRAG: creativity, alertness and quality.

Van Hulle is critical of the specific American approach to rules and regulations as a result of their liability-driven litigation culture. 'That's the reason for the plethora of formalistic rules: conditions, provisos, exclusions and so on.' A European approach must offer a counterbalance to this: lay down the principles and leave the rest to the accountant's professional opinion. The Americans must learn to live with these cultural differences. 'In fact, it may offer them a good opportunity to get rid of that paralysing claims culture', according to Van Hulle.

Klaassen

Jan Klaassen is an official consultant to the Ministry of Justice on legislative issues in the field of annual reporting. A bill that attempts to impede arbitrage has recently been put before the Lower House of the Dutch Parliament. It takes the position that US or international rules must be adopted in their entirety or not at all. The latter must then be clearly motivated. Dutch legislation will continue to apply to all unlisted companies in so far as they are non-financial institutions. Where supervision is concerned, Klaassen believes that international rules require international supervision. Some subjects will continue to be organised at the national level, such as capital protection, but they can be fairly well organised 'separately from financial reporting'. In the Netherlands, the remuneration of directors will be reported in the annual report and accounts, in the future even per person. Directors and supervisory board members must also be able to justify why a top manager 'deserves' a top salary, according to Klaassen. A bill is being drafted which will give shareholders a say in directors' remuneration. 'The nature of the problem is that remuneration is partly a question of negotiation, and you cannot negotiate with a shareholders' meeting.'

There is a need for more supervision and perhaps the Authority for the Financial Markets can play a role in this report. Supervision via the disciplinary court is also possible, although this is not the right way of doing things. Ultimately, the company and not the auditor is responsible for financial reporting. The auditor can only be held responsible for an unqualified report issued in error. Klaassen also argues in favour of the introduction of certifying auditors.

Eeftink

Although the company remains responsible for the quality of financial reporting, the accountant can play a stimulating and supervisory role. The accountant is not the primary but rather the secondary party responsible for the quality of financial reporting and his or her opinion about financial statements must be properly substantiated. Accountants must therefore show clients how improvements can be made.

The Dutch auditor will have to insure that a company claiming to comply with IAS really has complied in full with these standards, and not only in broad outline as is sometimes the case with current Dutch reporting practice. The Dutch 'polder model' culture of tolerance and 'turning a blind eye' (the bitter fruits of which the country is now tasting in 2002) is unknown elsewhere. 'So if we are soon to adopt international regulations, we will truly need to mend our ways as to their application before an international supervisory body gives us a good chastising. Compliance is compliance. And that means a switch from our culture and Dutch views to an Anglo-Saxon perspective on rules.'

For the auditor, there will be less room for forming an individual opinion; the job will shift more towards 'auditing according to a checklist' and away from interpreting general principles and standards according to the situation.

There is a strong shift towards fair value within the established financial reporting model. This particularly applies to financial instruments, but also to other assets and liabilities. The now frequently discussed impairment test is also based on fair value. Besides the often applauded advantages, fair value also has its drawbacks. For example, the fair value model still lacks conceptual underpinning. Furthermore, its reliability also leaves quite a lot to be desired. The effect of prognoses and assumptions on the determination of fair value is sometimes quite considerable, thus creating a wide margin of inaccuracy.

Under the influence of fair value, the IASB is discussing the future form and content of the profit and loss account, or 'performance statement'. Eeftink expects a proposal for a performance statement in which all fair value changes will be included; such a proposal will not be popular with companies due to the high volatility of the bottom line. The further format of such a statement is still uncertain, but a subdivision between operating and financing activities is in any case expected. For accountants, the auditing of fair value information is sometimes difficult. Prognoses and assumptions will where necessary have to be tested against business plans and market data. More than in the past, the accountant will have to be assisted by a valuation expert.

Den Hoed

Uniform rules that are written in clear language – one which can be interpreted in one way only – are essential to international comings and goings. This therefore also applies to annual reports, according to Jean den Hoed, former financial director at Akzo-Nobel.

Introducing a rule is a doddle; enforcing it is another story. Everyone is equally convinced of the necessity of applying IAS properly in every country. As soon as deviations are detected, people – particularly in the United States – will respond sharply. The Americans will only accept IAS if the rules are applied equally all over the world. In the US, scepticism about IAS prevails, the belief is that Europe will not be able to make IAS compulsory in 2005. The Europeans will have to do everything in their power to offer a counterbalance to this belief.

It is vitally important that a single financial reporting system is introduced. Only then can one draw comparisons and take decisions on the strength of the same information. This is one of the conditions for the perfect equity market, in which everyone can access the same information at the same time. It is also important in terms of competition.

Enforcement must not become an updated audit. It would be more effective to perform a proper review of certain companies on a random basis, as the SEC does in the US. Once every five years, particular companies are thoroughly analysed. According to Den Hoed, supervision must take centre stage and be arranged at European level with the aim of preventing differences in method, approach, interpretation and the like.

Nevertheless, we must ensure that the rules do not block the view. After all, rules are a means and not an end in themselves. Ultimately, it's all about the insight that financial reporting should provide. The purpose of the regulations is to promote transparency and not to cloud things up with all manner of complicated procedures.

SUPERVISION AND COMPLIANCE

Koster

The effects of the introduction of IAS are underestimated. Companies will have to rigorously reorganise their accounts. The Authority for the Financial Markets (previously the Securities Transactions Supervisory Board), as an independent governing body, supervises the Dutch capital market and is, if asked to do so, also prepared to enforce IAS compliance, 'because we are closely involved with listed companies and IAS relates to them in particular,' according to Authority for the Financial Markets board member Paul Koster.

How far the supervision of external financial reporting should go is quite a different question. This should be seen in an international perspective. Although it is not yet clear what supervision in a European context will look like, the Netherlands will follow. It is vitally important that the Netherlands continues to follow international developments because it is essential that Europe avoids creating 15 different national interpretations of IAS.

Where the supervision of financial reporting is concerned, there are many possible lines of approach: for example, the testing of annual reports on the basis of risk analysis and thematic examinations in response to national and international trends in financial reporting. The Authority for the Financial Markets wants to establish a forum with representation from the business community, the accountancy world, the university world, investment analysts and others. Together with the agenda of the IASB, this forum will provide research subjects: for example, goodwill, consolidation or stock options.

The quality of the content of annual reports has improved slightly over the past few years. Koster believes that the report of the executive board must become part of a company's financial statement. Furthermore, he would like to see the cash flow statement be made compulsory for all companies. This statement should be given more of a prospective character, because information is far too often withheld from investors, while they are jointly responsible for financing. Koster therefore believes it would be a good thing if the accountants – and here he points to the major shortcoming of the annual report – could produce an opinion about cash flows. They will have to evaluate and elaborate upon particular scenarios so that they are not surprised by continuity problems. Accountants should have the possibility of forcing companies to make statements about realistic expectations. That is the reason why the supervision of annual reporting is so important. After all, the accountant then also receives support from the supervisory body.

Willems

The Enterprise and Companies Court judges disputes that can arise in a company: issues concerning accounting and reporting rules, employees' participation, dismissal of supervisory directors, right of inquiry and the like.

According to Huub Willems, Chairman of the Enterprise and Companies Court, the connection between accountants and misleading financial statements cannot be directly made. He outlines the dilemma whereby the judges state an opinion about financial statements in disciplinary or civil proceedings, while if the case was dealt with in the

Enterprise and Companies Court, this court could conclude that both judges have expressed an incorrect verdict about the financial statements. The Supreme Court of the Netherlands has determined that the mere circumstance that the disciplinary tribunal has judged unfavourably about the work of an auditor does not automatically imply that the auditor is liable according to the law of tort or for breach of contract. Willems does not like the American claim culture. 'And it certainly won't improve matters if that is where the emphasis comes to lie.'

The question is how the standards of a body governed by private law like the IASB fit within Part 9, Book 2 of the Netherlands Civil Code. Accounting and reporting legislation in the Netherlands is still Dutch legislation and is partly dependent upon judicial interpretation. International law does of course have precedence over national law, but then only if a special treaty has been ratified. That is not yet the case.

Although a supervisory authority like the SEC or the Financial Reporting Review Panel can fulfil a useful role, the judge has the final word if a conflict occurs and the case is submitted to the magistrate.

The process of accounting for one's decisions or plans has become increasingly important during the past few years, certainly now that shareholders are more and more often becoming involved in the discussion. The management of organisations are more and more often and increasingly emphatically being called to account for sound management. The Enterprise and Companies Court has played an important role in this respect: it has developed the principles of proper management.

Van Hoepen

The influence of Anglo-American culture on continental European, in general, and Dutch culture, in particular, is undeniable. That goes for external financial reporting as well. National regulations are being influenced by international (read: Anglo-American) rules. The guidelines of the Council for Annual Reporting are being 'converted' by stealth into IAS. The Council for Annual Reporting seeks to adapt its guidelines to IAS, given the Dutch situation. A striking example of this can be seen in the adaptation to the standard on Employee Benefits (IAS 19). In addition, further adaptation to developments, such as those in FAS 87 and IAS 19, will be necessary. Some specific Dutch circumstances, such as those created in the Pension and Savings Funds Guarantee Act, will not be so easy to incorporate into the framework of IAS 19, however. After 2005, the Council for Annual Reporting will need to guide the application of IAS in Dutch GAAP – or maybe even translate them one to one. Interpretations of certain points – given the unique Dutch situation – will always be necessary for application in the Netherlands. 'Even if there already is a Standing Interpretation Committee (SIC) within IAS, there is simply no way it can foresee all possible aberrations in all legal precedents.' The Council for Annual Reporting will therefore still have a role after 2005 and also for listed companies. However, steps must be taken to prevent the appearance of all kinds of national/contradictory interpretations of, what are in principle clear, international accounting standards.

Many disclosure requirements have been intensified so much that one starts wondering whether it is not too much of a good thing for many small and medium-sized enterprises and non-listed companies. 'Companies subject to US GAAP and which fall under the jurisdiction of the SEC cannot exactly be compared to the tobacconist "down the street" who has chosen to cast his business in the form of a private limited company.' The Council for Annual Reporting could play a role here by developing a 'small GAAP'. In addition, we also need rules for special lines of business for which there are not yet any IAS, such as the health care industry, housing corporations and such. Case law from the Enterprise and Companies Court will, apart from supervision developments, adapt to the guidelines.

Rien van Hoepen, among other things a lay appeal judge at the Enterprise and Companies Court, does not believe that an administrative body should be given both power of review and the authority to impose sanctions. There should be a division of powers: accounting and reporting legislation belongs to the judiciary, just like any penal sanctions. 'That must never be given administrative law standing.'

Vergoossen

Enforcement also determines the quality of external financial reporting. The underlying rules and regulations should be complete, clear and un- equivocal. They should also have legal status; the instructions must be compulsory. On top of this, there must be supervision of compliance with the rules. This is necessary to guarantee a consistent interpretation and application of IAS: with the set of core standards, the restructuring of the IASC and the projected 'IAS 2005', the first two criteria are complied with. Only the supervision has not yet been adequately provided for. Properly functioning supervision in Europe will not only be of overriding importance for the harmonisation at the European level, but will also be decisive for the worldwide harmonisation of financial reporting. The United States will only be prepared to recognise IAS when strict compli- ance with the standards is enforced in Europe.

The fact that the US capital market is by far the largest in the world and also the most liquid and efficient is partly because of the SEC, which is a very good stock exchange supervisor. It is also quite understandable that the Americans 'do not want to throw overboard what they have achieved.' They will therefore want to hold on to their own regulations for as long as possible. 'For the time being, they have more to lose than to gain.'

In May 2000 the international regulators' representative organisation IOSCO produced a resolution in which it recommended its members to allow IAS for so-called 'cross-border offerings and listings'. This was a recommendation and not an instruction, therefore. Furthermore, the recommendation explicitly allows members of IOSCO to impose extra requirements with respect to the financial information. 'As a matter of fact, the latter was required to win over the SEC.' According to Ruud Vergoossen, the practical significance of the IOSCO recommendation for the international harmonisation of financial reporting is very limited, also in view of the small number of companies to which it relates.

IAS AND THE USERS OF FINANCIAL STATEMENTS

De Vries

The Director of the Netherlands Association of Securities Holders, Peter-Paul de Vries, believes that financial reporting among listed companies in the Netherlands leaves an awful lot to be desired. It affords far too much room for interpretation. Investors and analysts are thus frequently left in the dark. Figures don't say very much in theory. Accounting principles, the relation between the key indicators and industry-level comparisons are all important for an interpretation of the figures. The insight provided by figures has become even cloudier since the year 2001 when companies adopted on a large scale the capitalisation of goodwill. That really made things worse. This is because goodwill is an 'extremely ephemeral balance sheet item'. Its valuation is highly arbitrary and the asset's value will not develop over 20 years on a straight-line basis to nil. Worse still, an acquired, properly maintained brand name might even increase in value, for example. This is therefore no way to achieve a clear reflection of reality, which is after all our objective. De Vries regrets that accountants have not taken up arms against this. This would have been appropriate within the scope of the prudence principle. As soon as companies get into trouble, they see a rapid decline in the value of their goodwill and in-tangible assets and their balance sheet position worsens. So 'if a company starts sliding down towards the abyss, it gets a severe beating on the way. That cannot possibly have been the intention of capitalisation.'

De Vries is also sceptical about mark-to-market. How can the value of intangible assets be established on the basis of fair value? Fair value is computed in a rather arbitrary manner. For example, the goodwill that was paid to acquire E-Plus, Germany's third largest wireless carrier, was capitalised in full in 2000, while it was clear on the balance sheet date that a major part of this value had already evaporated. At year-end 2001, the UMTS licences were stated at cost because they were not yet being used. Downward revaluation is also essential here.

At many companies, some of the air was released from the balance sheet at the end of 2001. Getronics, one of the world's leading providers of information and communication technology solutions and services, wrote down EUR 930 million from the goodwill paid for Wang and the write-down of CMG amounted to EUR 540 million. With this 're-evaluation', it is not only the necessity for a write-down that plays a role, but especially also the financial leeway provided by the balance sheet for this. At KPN, the charge on E-Plus at the end of 2001 was only possible due to an equity issue of EUR 5 billion.

De Vries argues for stringent enforcement such as that exercised in the United States by the SEC. In the Netherlands, everything is too per-missive. Seeking justice via the Enterprise and Companies Court is for many a much too hard and long process. 'Moreover, private parties are always at a great disadvantage, since they have not seen the underlying figures.' Supervision is vitally important to everyone – including the company itself. The SEC – currently under pressure because of Enron – operates more efficiently: 'Projected income is not accepted. An SEC sanction serves as a red flag for the financial markets. A company that is placed in the penalty box is stuck with a bad image for years. Another sanction is that a company which has been in violation must disclose in its annual report or in a prospectus the fact that it once overstepped the rules. That is an effective sanction. It ensures that investors are forewarned.'

The Enron affair has seriously harmed the confidence in financial statements and financial reporting. However serious this may be for the company in question, it is salutary for companies and markets. An absolute value is no longer unthinkingly attributed to figures. Investors and analysts keep a close eye on the quality of figures: is the income really shown correctly, are tricks used to spruce up results and which risks are taken in the field of derivatives. It is often asked whether an 'Enron' could also occur in the Netherlands. Not on that scale, but the bankruptcies of ICT companies LCI and Landis, which occurred shortly after the publica-tion of positive figures, do give rise to serious doubts about the financial reporting and the constructions used.

De Vries also wants companies to publish their quarterly figures. A three-monthly information system compels them to work quickly and stay alert. Problems can be placed under control more quickly. 'Moreover, companies in the year 2003 can simply no longer get away with reporting to their shareholders only twice a year.'

Van den Hoek

The supervisory board of a company oversees the policies of the management and the general state of affairs of that company. Internal and external reporting consists of more than just figures. Nevertheless, trends can be recognised in figures and they can arouse particular expectations. Here, the supervisory director must act as a sort of gyroscope to find the balance between the expectations and the reality. In short, the bottom line has got to tally. 'The Board of Directors is responsible for keeping disappointments to a minimum. If there are disappointments, it is also the supervisory director who is sharply rebuked by the public: he must pay better attention and take corrective action.'

The supervisory director does not have much to do with the actual preparation of the financial report, with the exception of the discussion about the accounting principles and the assignment of provisions. Paul van den Hoek, himself a supervisory director at many companies, attaches a lot of value to the directors' report. Compared to the American versions, Dutch annual reports sometimes look very 'meagre'. To make an impression on the SEC, US companies take care of their reports down to the last detail. This could serve as 'an example for us in the Netherlands. We must therefore catch up with the US GAAP, which are much stricter than the flexible Dutch rules.' Van den Hoek observes that it is therefore not surprising that the financial irregularities of the Dutch software and business services company Baan and the Belgian speech technology products firm Lernout & Hauspie were first exposed in the US. He is considerably more reserved about the treatment of goodwill as advocated by the Americans: 'Sometimes I wonder which interest is served with some of the new rules. Not every change is an improvement.' Nevertheless, the increasing uniformity in reporting is commendable in every way. Incidentally, Van den Hoek does not believe that separate financial reporting requirements are required for small and medium-sized companies.

Traas

Lou Traas, among other things chairman of the committee concerned with the reporting of insurance companies, is critical about their financial reporting. He misses uniformity, the lack of which in the Netherlands he blames on the fairly broad scope within which a company can choose how it wants to present its reporting. This does not make it any easier to compare companies' results. 'And comparison is not only becoming more difficult between companies – call it horizontally – but also between different years' annual reports from the same company – call it vertically – due to much switching between reporting methods in some areas.' As a rule, the system chosen is the one that enables the results to be presented in the most favourable possible manner. 'The user of the report has to be able to read between the lines.' Conceptually, the financial reporting of insurance companies is completely wrong as a result of averaging, according to Traas. He wants to eliminate the variations which currently exist. Quality could be improved by introducing 'comprehensive income' as this will create a solid link between the income statement and the balance sheet. Quality can also be improved by providing more information about solvency. 'It should be possible to answer the question of how big an insurance company's reserves are to absorb losses and to meet their current liabilities.' In order to properly assess insurance companies' results, Traas believes it is necessary to look at how much is represented by investment results, and what the nature of these is. 'Insurers suggest that you should not draw too many conclusions from fluctuations in investment results, since everything will be all right in the long run. But of course this is not so. It makes a considerable difference whether reductions in the value of the investment portfolio are the result of falling prices of structurally overvalued stocks (such as hi-tech shares) which will never return to their former values, or in Enron-type enterprises which disappear through bankruptcy, or relate, for example, to oil companies facing temporary pressure in the market due to a fall in oil prices. Movements in value should be clearly and openly described so that investors and analysts can ask the right questions and assess the quality of the profit. The opposite leads to totally implausible reporting. It is surely absurd – as happened in the past year – to report that a company has seen a major increase in earnings per share when, elsewhere, the annual report states that the investment portfolio has fallen in value by billions.'

Traas applauds the fact that globalisation is having an influence on the quality of financial reporting. However, the question is whether Europe will conform to IASB guidelines, which are fashioned along Anglo-American lines, without too many amendments.

Langendijk

Financial reporting expert and editorial staff member Henk Langendijk is not in the least happy with the quality of external reporting in the

Netherlands. The overly relaxed culture of tolerance and the self-satisfied 'polder' thinking have led to an unbecoming *laissez-faire* attitude in society. 'That same misplaced smugness is noticeable in the field of external reporting.' International experts in the field of accountancy consider the Dutch way of reporting to be 'highly flexible, extremely judgmental'. According to Langendijk's interpretation, this means 'double Dutch' in external financial reporting. And he continues: 'The law of elasticity reigns supreme in our annual accounting practices. There is an awful lot of latitude; there are a great many degrees of freedom which you can use, but also abuse. No wonder that the Netherlands has its share of scandals with financial statements that turn out to be not entirely above board.' Langendijk is not impressed by the Enterprise and Companies Court either – in its current set-up, it 'really serves no identifiable purpose'. He sees more in a supervisory body that can restore the public's faith in external reporting.

He is also in favour of adapting Dutch regulations to IAS. 'This will improve the quality of external reporting in the Netherlands.' The derogatory effect (Article 393, Part 4 of the Netherlands Civil Code) must be scrapped. This escape clause, which means that it is permissible to diverge from the detailed provisions of the law to give the required true and fair view, is 'asking for trouble'. And he continues: 'That article is a monstrous anachronism; it's more than half a century old and stems from the good old days when the world was still a happy and straightforward place and Mum knitted you a jumper for Christmas.'

Langendijk wants to move towards a system with a single method of valuation and a single method of estimation. Stringent rules must also be introduced for the profit and loss account. With IAS, there will be less latitude for earnings management. The Netherlands must introduce some kind of SEC. 'Such a body should bone and fillet the external reports of a few hundred companies every year and give their verdict on the quality.' In Langendijk's opinion, a communal supervisory body would be best in this respect.

Lakeman

SOBI chairman Pieter Lakeman is not very happy about the quality of financial reporting in the Netherlands, particularly during the past few years. Although annual reports contain more information, he doubts that this is sufficiently reliable. Companies that talk of nothing else but corporate governance and other high-principled ideals, do not appear to be particularly transparent in their annual reports. However, he does not consider that foreign accounting and reporting legislation and private accounting and reporting rules – which for him also includes IAS – are superior to Dutch legislation. His preference is still for Dutch law.

Lakeman believes that auditors in the Netherlands were until recently not subjected to enough critical examination. They are now 'gratefully back on their pedestal'. While lawyers and consultants have to compete for the client's favour, the auditor has effortless access due to the statutory audit and 'like an accomplished commercial traveller, sells a range of products that are often not related to the industry'.

Lakeman believes that the Public Prosecution Service as 'natural' enforcer has slipped up far too often. In his opinion, this is due to a lack of expertise. Subsequently, the Public Prosecution Service has been afraid of tackling new cases.

Lakeman argues that strict regulation is vital for accurate reporting. There must be clarity about depreciation and amortisation issues: 'I would consider it acceptable if the legislation or regulations used different amortisation periods for different types of goodwill. But these must be fixed so that everyone knows where they stand.'

No new kind of reporting is required for 'new economy' companies. These are just normal companies like all others, whatever 'Internet gurus' may claim.

Lakeman believes that the application of the impairment test in practice will lead to as much arbitrariness as the replacement value theory that was previously often used in the Netherlands. He is afraid that financial statements will lose their significance for users and become degraded to material for the writing of theses if the impairment test gains the upper hand.

FAIR VALUE ACCOUNTING

Hoogendoorn

Valuation based on fair value will become the standard for the 21st century, according to Martin Hoogendoorn. This will certainly have an influence on the treatment of financial instruments, commitments and provisions, and to a slightly lesser extent also on buildings, machinery, tangible and intangible fixed assets.

A different form of profit determination will also emerge, a kind of 'performance statement'. It is therefore better not to refer only to net profit, because there is no longer a traditional profit and loss account. Performance statements will consist of countless components, just one of which is the traditional profit concept. Furthermore, a difference will arise between consolidated and company financial statements. The profit in company financial statements will then be more prudently determined because of the realisation principle. An important question here is what can be distributed to shareholders and what can serve as a basis for the levying of taxes. A stronger link with the calculation of profit for tax purposes will arise here. As a result of the effect of exposure to market risks, currency risks, interest rate risks and the like, all kinds of unrealised value changes will emerge in the consolidated financial statements.

Hoogendoorn already notices a tendency to value a few isolated balance sheet items in terms of fair value, separately from the other balance sheet items and even separately from the entire financial position of the company. Fair value is already applied for quickly realisable investments; for example, listed securities and for real estate (valuation at appraised value). Valuation based on fair value will extend to non-financial items. One of the weak points of a partial application of fair value is the valuation of debt. Another question that needs answering is whether fair value will work in practice.

Oosenbrug

Alfred Oosenbrug, among other things Chairman of the Association of Actuaries and member of the Traas Committee, mentions in his contribution the fact that insurance companies and pension funds had seen as much as EUR 55 billion of their investments go up in smoke in the third quarter of 2001. Since they realised towering investment profits in the preceding 20 years, they were able to absorb the losses, however. Pension funds still have an average funding rate that is 20% higher than needed. Nonetheless, in times of prosperity much greater reserves must be built up and the pension funds did not do enough. Proper financial reporting could and should have revealed this earlier. Oosenbrug believes that financial reporting by pension funds 'is still in a prehistoric phase'. 'No-one had insight into or could have known what was actually happening.' The IAS insurance project focuses in particular on improving transparency in the financial reporting of insurance institutions by consistently valuing assets and liabilities on the basis of fair value.

The IAS Insurance project is far-reaching and goes back to the basics of financial reporting principles. The question is whether the wishes of the European Commission can be honoured; the IASB wants to complete the project before 1 January 2004. On this date, a final financial reporting standard must be ready. It is debatable, however, whether the planning is realistic. Not only is it open to question whether the necessary amendments in the field of legislation and regulations will then be ready, but at the same time it is doubtful whether the necessary fundamental changes in accounting systems can be implemented in the short term. Proper thought must also be given to all the steps that will have to be taken. At the moment, the figures presented by companies are 'completely incomparable'. Oosenbrug also expects a lot from the rendering of accountability on the basis of comprehensive income. Managers are afraid that the resulting volatility in the presented profit figure will not be properly understood by users of financial statements. Experience that has already been gained with the accounting for comprehensive income by pension funds, for example, demonstrates that there is absolutely no reason for such timorousness. Only managers who do not have financial developments under control have reason to fear the publication of the comprehensive income they have realised!

Storm

The treatment of both goodwill and capital gains indicates how differently insurance companies and other companies approach this subject. Former Aegon board member Kees Storm (who retired as chairman on 18 April 2002) is sceptical about the development of financial reporting by insurance companies. He also has his doubts about valuation based on fair value. There is still no framework created for this. It appears that there will probably be a single system in 2005, but that is deceptive: the underlying assumptions may after all be completely different. The discount rate is also highly subjective. The unsuspecting user of financial statements needs to bear this in mind. Other objections to IAS are that the reporting standards of IAS 39 are of no benefit to insurers. The fair value in the financial statements is conceptually not the most obvious reporting method. Furthermore, the proposed change is too comprehensive to be assimilated and introduced during the period up to 2005. There must first be total agreement about the issues concerning the fair value standard. Only then can such rules be applied to the financial statements. If the current proposals are introduced without any special provisions and without due care, the wrong signals will be sent to policyholders, shareholders and other stakeholders.

As long as no insurance standards have been agreed, US GAAP is the only option for a company like Aegon. If these principles are included in IAS for insurance contracts, harmonisation is within reach.

Storm discusses in detail the treatment of goodwill and the presentation of realised and unrealised capital gains in the profit and loss account. He emphasises the special character of life insurers and pension funds, which have different obligations with a longer life than is the case with investment institutions. Following this, he discusses the system employed by Aegon, which he also recommends is worthy of everyone's attention.

Bruggink

Bert Bruggink, head of the Control Directorate of the Rabobank Group, sees problems with the introduction of IAS in the banking world. The disadvantage of IAS 39, for example, is that the regulations are partial. Another drawback to IAS 39 are the provisions on hedge accounting. Bruggink considers that the proposals in question 'conflict with banking pragmatism'. He has mixed feelings about 'full fair value accounting'. On the one hand, valuation based on fair value can have a positive effect on risk management, but this does not apply where financial reporting is concerned. The principal objections attach mainly to those items where it is difficult or impossible to determine a market value. What is the market value of savings, of current account balances? Bruggink even expects that 'full fair value accounting' will result in a reduction in transparency and that, in fact, an organisation's performance will be less clear – at least, if the financial statements are used as the source of information. IAS are inevitable, however. 'Are we happy? Well, for internal use we have no problem, but for external use, in my opinion, it is a disaster.'

Good supervision is exceptionally important. Banks are satisfied about the existing supervisory structure, but the question is whether a single supervisory authority for stock exchanges, banks and insurers is such a good idea.

The regulations concerning banking transactions have not become any less complicated and this means that it has become more difficult to realise transparency. 'Volatility is increasing: things are based more and more on complicated models. You can say what you like, but Basle-1 was extremely simple. I could explain it to first and second year students in half an hour. You cannot handle Basle-2 in a single lecture. In a manner of speaking, it is a separate subject and even then it will be difficult to grasp all the principles. In other words, only a select group will be able to follow it and that has affected developments.'

Groeneveld

Valuation expert Joost Groeneveld does not believe that audits will become any easier with fair value. The market value of a company will fluctuate from year to year and if interim figures have to be presented, those fluctuations will only be greater. If the auditor has to express an opinion on the acceptability of the valuation, he will have to turn to a 'register valuator', for example. Groeneveld believes that the public's expectations of external financial reporting are too high. 'The need for the results and changes in net equity for the past year is completely different from that for information to base certain decisions on: financial statements are not meant primarily for that. Consequently, I prefer to see reporting in the context of accountability, of management. I think financial statements are more a result of policy than a factor informing policy.'

Financial statements are in principle based on realised cash flows: receipts and expenditures which have happened and not those which may occur in the future. That is because they depend precisely on policy which does not exist but which still has to be formulated, according to Groeneveld. In his opinion, 'fair value applications' are necessary for the operation of financial statements. A problem arises with full application, where the aim is to bring together book value and market value. Groeneveld therefore calls for the accountability in the financial statements and the quotations on the stock exchange to be kept strictly separate. Commercial value is derived from the future. In that sense, value is an expression of doing business.

IAS do not have to apply to every company in 2005. 'It is as if everyone will soon be walking round in Chairman Mao suits.' In theory, it is excellent that there will be a single set of rules, 'but if the suit does not fit, it will have to be altered.' Groeneveld sees a trial of strength for the audit profession here.

Finally, Groeneveld makes a number of comments about intangible assets and real estate that are worthy of consideration.

Swagerman

The interview with Dirk Swagerman covers various possibilities for the use of financial statements. On the one hand, financial statements can be seen as proof of good stewardship, on the other, as a tool for decision-making. There is a clear trend perceptible that financial statements are increasingly being used as a document for decision-making. The 'IAS framework' also anticipates this. The importance of the concept of a company's 'own nature' in relation to the financial statements will be further elaborated. If the straitjacket of financial reporting rules is too tight, a company's 'own nature' is inadequately expressed in financial statements. The company's specific characteristics can then be dealt with in the directors' report. More than is the case now, the directors' report will have to provide adequate information about future developments. Investors will then be better able to form an opinion about the company than they can on the basis of the historical information from the financial statements alone.

According to Swagerman, the introduction of external financial reporting based on IAS will contribute to increased transparency in financial information. The application of fair value accounting will, however, produce greater volatility in the results. Entrepreneurs may then be confronted with adjustments in results that are not the consequence of economic activities, but rather the use of fair value. The term 'accounting risk' can be used for this unpredictable change in value.

Swagerman believes that a broadening of reporting standards will take place in the future: elements of social entrepreneurship must be included in annual reports. In Swagerman's opinion, there will be greater emphasis on risk management. The application of risk management provides insight into the vulnerability of a company: this is more important than reporting the profit for the past period.

O'Malley and Hofsté

Tricia O'Malley (IASB) and Petri Hofsté (KPMG) observe that banks still have problems with IAS 39. Due to IAS 39 and the application of full fair value accounting in the balance sheet and profit and loss account, banks are afraid that they will no longer be able to manage their performance. Banks in the United States are, for example, still opposed to valuing financial instruments at fair value. It is possible that banks are not yet able to value all balance sheet items on the basis of fair value. More research may be required before the plans of the Joint Working Group (JWG) are implemented.

The existing regulations with respect to mixed financial instruments (FAS 133) are so complicated that experts have had to specialise in particular parts of this standard. This says quite a lot about (the lack of) transparency. The proposals of the JWG (fair value for all financial assets and liabilities) are therefore an improvement. These rules are, however, mainly directed towards efficiently operating capital markets and they do not work as well in countries where this does not apply. In addition, the incorporation of the unrealised results in the profit and loss account have not been properly elaborated in the JWG's plans due to lack of time. On top of this, the JWG proposals for the valuation of debt in terms of market value and credit risk are inadequately developed. If the credit rating of a company falls, the market value of its debt decreases, resulting in a gain in the profit and loss account. This goes against all economic logic.

The accountancy profession will change a lot because of all the new developments, and it is pretty obvious that this will be reflected in accountancy training courses. More attention will have to be paid to subjects like financing the accountant will have to work more closely with experts in the field of treasury and risk management. The question, however, is whether all of this will suffice to be able to value financial instruments on the basis of fair value. There is a risk that financial information will decline in quality on account of the gap between the standards and the extent to which accountants and the business community understand them.

CAPITA SELECTA

Beckman

Lawyer and expert in the field of accounting and reporting legislation, Hans Beckman thinks it is wrong for all kinds of rules to be imposed on the smallest companies. Reference is often made to (non-statutory) rules in the United States. But it is all too often forgotten that these only apply to listed companies and companies that are the subject of an audit. There is also a lot of misunderstanding about 'substance over form'. People often say that what accountants (or business economists) think is more important than what lawyers think. What is not recognised is that 'substance over form' is a legal rule that underlies both Dutch and community accounting and reporting rules. This principle also applies to US and IAS standards that have no legal basis. Since the Enron affair, some people have suddenly started saying that 'form over substance' applies in the United States. Beckman believes this is nonsense. The basic common approach in both IAS and US standards is that compliance to special rules produces a true and fair view and that such rules must be deviated from in exceptional cases. This rule also applies in the Netherlands. The freedom of interpretation nevertheless applies in relation to the level of detail. Accountants prefer to set their own rules, which are as detailed as possible. Lawyers recognise that the competent legal authorities must set the rules. These rules are more general in nature, so that the reality principle (= substance over form) becomes stronger and more independent. The development of IAS into a global standard is a good thing as long as there is a careful process of preparation, taking account of the differences in legal systems. A careful process of preparation also means avoiding a narrow, one-sided compilation by those involved in this process. Furthermore, the rules should be enacted under governmental authority. For this reason, Beckman applauds the fact that the European Commission has proposed an endorsement procedure for IAS standards. The rules thus obtain a public law character. There must also be a sound procedure for compliance to the rules.

With these developments, the financial statements can again become a legible document. Beckman repeats what he wrote on the subject in 1994. The illegibility of many financial statements is achieved by the apparent need to keep items off the balance sheet and by all kinds of modernisms in reporting theory. Among the latter, Beckman includes developments in the field of fair value accounting relating to financial instruments. Moreover, insufficient note is taken of the fact that financial statements are also an instrument within the scope of capital law and capital protection law. This could be remedied by confining IAS (and all kinds of modernisms) to consolidated financial statements. The community idea of limiting the planned compulsory application of IAS to consolidated financial statements is correct.

Continuation of the Council for Annual Reporting does not fit in well within the scope of the identified developments. Quite apart from the fact that this Council has included opinions in its guidelines that are in conflict with the rules of imperative law – with the consequence that auditors sometimes force companies to act illegally – it is also developing into a translation agency for IAS. Further consideration of the Council's continuation is therefore required, perhaps it should move towards becoming a source of information.

De Bos

Internet companies can be rather innovative with the space offered to them in the virtual world. Business economist Auke de Bos points to the problem of the definition of turnover with respect to Internet activities. 'Dotcom companies for example, often make barter transactions. If one company advertises at another and vice versa, has turnover been generated?' To answer this question it is necessary to formulate criteria to determine if, in the normal course of events, there also would have been turnover. According to the US guideline, companies can only recognise turnover from barter transactions if they can establish that such a transaction could have also taken place as a cash sale and therefore that it was also actually a cash sale. A further criterion is that the companies should have been able to sell the same advertising space to an unrelated party for cash during the past six months. The IASB has also recently published an Interpretation (SIC 31) on this issue. Another issue facing Internet companies is whether turnover should be recorded gross or net, and conditional sale.

If an investor evaluates an Internet company solely on its turnover, then the profit or loss reported doesn't really matter. New economy companies were often inclined to write-off costs as fast as possible and to capitalise as little as possible because the valuation of such companies was dependent on turnover or other indicators, such as EBITDA. 'The more that was booked in the profit and loss account, the better the results that could be shown. Furthermore, the classification of expenses could also be shifted around the various cost categories.'

Booking costs as much as possible in the profit and loss account strips the balance sheet naked. New economy companies show few assets: buildings are rented, motor vehicles are leased. The balance sheet of a new economy company does not offer much for scrutiny. There is little or no history, and thus an investor or a creditor has few clues to evaluate such a company. That is the reason why De Bos argues that intangible assets should be capitalised as much as possible. 'An asset is a resource with economic benefits that can be measured reliably. Many intangible assets satisfy this definition and should therefore be eligible for capitalisation. If the intangible stuff can be expressed on the balance sheet, the value gap can be closed up and a better picture of the economic reality can be drawn.'

Bac

The International Public Sector Accounting Standards (IPSAS) also exert an influence. As an expert in the field of government accountancy, Aad Bac discusses the phases in which IAS are adapted to become IPSAS. This also includes the specific areas of government that are not addressed by IAS. In principle, the government applies the accrual accounting method for national and local government's income and expenditure services. 'Given the methods applied, IPSAS could certainly play an important role for local authorities, provinces and water boards in the near future, relatively speaking.'

The financial reporting rules for central government have entered a transitional phase. The existing liabilities/cash accounting system is to be abandoned for a modified accrual system. A complete income and expenditure system is still a distant prospect. The rules on financial reporting by government agencies fall under public law. Changing these rules would automatically mean amending the law. That is something that a private organisation like the IFAC cannot enforce. Nevertheless, it does lobby extensively. Furthermore, international aid organisations, such as the World Bank, IMF, OECD, use IPSAS as a point of reference for proper financial reporting in the context of aid programmes.

Certain countries are keen to adopt fair value as the standard, but this would imply regular revaluations. What would be a reasonable book value for the Arc de Triomphe or a pyramid, the Dutch Parliament or the Louvre?

IPSAS do not go into the specific aspects of government, such as measuring aspects of policy (policy evaluation) or non-financial information. This will be reserved for the following phase in standard-setting, in which attention will focus on non-transaction-based cash flows, such as tax remittances. 'The point will be to resolve issues such as: When to account for taxes? How to allocate tax income to different years? Should such allocation be based on the year in which taxes are paid? That can take some time. Or should this be done on the basis of the assessment date, for example?'

Vosselman

Globalisation has had a strong impulse on accountancy. Although local colour will never fade away, the profession will become increasingly international. The issue is to determine the deciding factors of profit and loss. Internationally recognised analysis instruments, such as the Balanced Scorecard, have been developed for this. According to business economist Ed Vosselman, who has participated in projects that attempt to improve the knowledge infrastructure in the Netherlands, these generate not only information on profit, but also on the effectiveness of business processes and factors such as a company's delivery time, the reliability of deliveries, innovation and creative ability. One of these projects relates to the instruments available to accountants.

Proper valuation of intangibles, such as goodwill, may lead to a different classification of (knowledge about) intangible assets. Vosselman discusses the difference between explicit and implicit knowledge. This is an interesting issue for those that have to make decisions on the basis of available information. Both the academic and business world must develop adequate measuring, control and valuation tools for the assessment of intangible assets. Especially now that so many different parties are interested in information and transparency, the point is to design and tailor such tools to this end. Vosselman argues in favour of pragmatism. He considers traditional administrative organisation to be outdated. Contemporary, modern businesses are characterised by an advanced application of information and communication technology. And the relationship between ERP systems and administrative organisation are not done proper justice. Vosselman believes the influence of expertise, other than that possessed by accountants, to be an enrichment for the profession.

The profit concept is important for determining business activities and operations. 'That can take the traditional route, that is, income less cost, or it can run via cash flows. That only makes things more transparent.' Vosselman is sorry to see so little academic research in accountancy training programmes. 'Just compare that with the field of medicine. How could a physician possibly do a good job without regular input in the form of results from scientific research?' By paying extra attention to research, the quality of the profession will improve.

Blommaert

Professor of Financial Accounting Jos Blommaert believes that the existing accounting system is stuck in the days of the Industrial Revolution. 'You simply won't find the most important assets there. As a consequence, there is a big discrepancy between the value we see on the balance sheet and what companies are actually worth on the stock exchange or in terms of takeover value.' Whether the capitalisation of goodwill is then the best solution, is a question of a totally different order. A clear distinction is required here between acquired goodwill and internally created goodwill. The latter is much greater, but has not yet been taken on board, even though it has been found that it accounts for some two thirds of the total value of many companies.

Blommaert considers the big difference between what is shown on the balance sheet and what a company is worth on the stock exchange to be beyond belief. As a result, the balance sheet is no longer important for making decisions and assessing performance. He therefore wants to increase the relevance of financial statements. In his opinion, that is possible if reporting is based on fair value. This does, however, imply a lot of subjectivity in the valuation. But that cannot be avoided. 'To substantiate a concept like fair value, we must first of all develop instruments to measure fair value reliably.' Blommaert also considers the inclusion of companies in the consolidation and the 'group' concept. He believes that a certain amount of manipulation of figures in the context of consolidation, and in other fields too, is inevitable. In his opinion, too many rules can take away the pillars beneath the accountancy profession, leading to new problems. He also wants to see an end to the Dutch practice of equalising the equity and profit at consolidated and company level.

Part I

The future of international accounting

The model of Black and Scholes is like Newtonian physics before Einstein was born

An interview with Robert K. Elliott

Robert K. Elliott

Professor Robert K. Elliott (born 1941) is a partner in KPMG in New York City, a member of its Office of the Chairman, and a Trustee of the KPMG Foundation. He has worked for KPMG since 1964. Elliott was Chair of the Board of Directors of the American Institute of Certified Public Accountants (AICPA) for the year 1999–2000. He previously chaired the AICPA's Strategic Planning Committee and its Special Committee on Assurance Services ('Elliott Committee') and was a member of the AICPA's Special Committee on Financial Reporting ('Jenkins Committee'). He was also a member of the Auditing Standards Board and the SEC's Advisory Committee on Capital Formation and Regulatory Processes.

Elliott has received a number of awards, including the AICPA Gold Medal Award for Distinguished Service, the Journal of Accountancy *Literary Award, and the American Accounting Association Auditing Section's Distinguished Service in Auditing Award.*

He has been named in 'The 100 Most Influential People in Accounting' by the publication Accounting Today *each year since the inception of the list. Elliott has a BA from Harvard and an MBA from Rutgers. His publications, as author or co-author, include more than 80 books and articles.*

Robert K. Elliott can be regarded as one of the most important gurus in the field of accountancy; a man of very many talents, as can be seen from his curriculum vitae. One of his most important recent contributions to the profession is his thinking with respect to an increase in the number of audit products to deliver assurance. On top of this, he has broken new ground in the field of Internet reporting and Internet-related assurance products. Furthermore, while Elliott's ideas about the durability of reporting and the durability of auditing are vitally important for the accounting profession, his overall vision of the future of the accounting profession is vitally important for the readers of this book.

Do you expect the CPA profession will be the same as it is now in five year's time? What changes do you expect will take place?

Professor Elliott: 'I doubt that the CPA profession will look much different in five years' time because of the large installed human base. The profession has two functions. It creates value in its accounting role by producing decision-making information and in its auditing role it improves and gives credibility to the reliability of that information. These functions never totally disappear; it is impossible to imagine a future in which decision-makers do not need lots of high-quality information. Therefore, there is no question whether the functions of CPAs or RAs or their equivalent around the world will continue to exist.

'The audit function itself, the need for auditing, is built into the human wiring diagram so to speak. Human beings have a need to co-operate, but they also have incredible self-interest. These two aspects are sometimes in conflict and this leads to the moral hazard that is involved in any kind of purchase and sale transaction where the seller always has more information about the products and services than the buyer. The resulting information asymmetry leads to difficulties in contracting, and it turns out that an auditor can ameliorate the moral hazard in such a way that transactions can proceed more easily. In the past, auditing has primarily been applied with respect to financial statements because the monetary values involved are large enough to permit this. However, information technology is driving down the cost of auditing or providing assurance and, in my opinion, this means that it will be applied in more and more contracting situations in the future. Therefore, the function of auditing is rooted in the moral hazard inherent in contracting. This will never disappear unless human beings change completely, and this is not likely to happen.

'As the functions of both accounting and auditing are absolutely essential, the question now is whether the RA/CPA profession will fulfil these functions way into the future, or whether there is an opportunity for somebody else to take over the functions and perform them in a different manner. This is a little more difficult to answer. I think that our profession has what I would call "a right of first refusal" to offer such services to the public and to the decision-makers, but we could lose this right if someone were to come along with superior capital, technology, or information resources and was hypothetically able to produce ten times that much information and assurance for one tenth of the price with the aid of a different business model. I do not believe this will happen in the next five years, nor in the next 10 or 20 either, but the further you go into the future the greater the risk that somebody else will take over the function from us.

'On our side, the advantages we have in maintaining the function are the level of trust that we have with the public, the reputation for objectivity, integrity, and independence. The disadvantages that we have as a profession are that we are not capital intensive and we are, generally speaking, not at the top of the technology curve. A third disadvantage is that we are not very nimble; we do not respond very quickly to changes in the marketplace. Most people came into accounting because they were looking for something stable and conservative. They are willing to change, but perhaps less quickly than some others are, so if somebody comes along who is more nimble and more willing and able to change in response to customer needs then they could theoretically take the job, although not in the next five years.

'What we are going to have to do, assuming that we are going to move into this new setting, and assuming that we can make the changes necessary, is to completely change our mindset. Our mindset during the last 500 years has been to produce a sort of generalised, "one size fits all" product, a set of financial statements that are supposed to be for general purposes. We have trained the whole accountancy profession to produce these standardised statements, but in the future technology will permit the users of information to specify what they want, to set up their own template, to send out SQL (Structured Query Language) queries or XBRL (eXtensible Business Reporting Language) queries and get the information they want, at the time they want it, in the format they want it, and at the level of detail that they want. Therefore, the accountant is no longer going to be just a producer of "one size fits all" statements, but has to become the facilitator who provides for the right information that people need when they want it. This requires much more of a customer mindset rather than a producer mindset. It is a huge change that we have to make as a profession in addition to the technology issues.

'The way in which we have performed audits up until now is to come in after the fact with a team of young auditors who check everything out after the fact. They find the errors and they correct them. In the future, however, when the information is available online and in real time to the user who might be an investor, creditor, member of management, or anybody else who uses the information, we are going to have to provide real-time assurance that the information is correct and the only way to do this is to design systems that are reliable by design. The sources of errors must be identified and engineered out of the system, so the people involved must be much more technologically oriented than they are today. We therefore have to bring in new talent. In the big five accounting firms in the USA, before several of them split off their consulting departments, less than 20% of the new hires were accounting graduates. More than 80% were lawyers, MIS people, engineers, etc., so you can already see that the way in which we are recruiting talent has changed enormously and will continue to do so.'

What is your view on the independence of auditors nowadays?

Professor Elliott: 'Auditors are not totally independent today, never have been in the past, and I don't think ever will be. But they are objective. They are not completely independent because they accept a fee from the client, which no-one proposes to abolish, they know their client's people and they learn to trust them. An auditor auditing a set of financial statements has invested his or her reputation or the firm's reputation in the beginning balances that affect this year's income items. The auditor may get fees from other services to the client, such as tax and consulting services, and all of these represent actual, if small, impairments of independence. The question is whether these impairments are sufficient to bias the auditor's opinion with respect to the design or interpretation of the audit findings and rendering of the audit report. The answer to this question is that the system has for the most part worked well with that level of reasonable, but not complete, independence, because it is sufficient to assure objectivity.

'As an economy, we could purchase more auditor independence. For example, we could arrange that auditors never succeeded themselves, were paid from a public fund, and were prohibited from establishing any sort of dependency on the client. This would involve costs, and the more independence you want to purchase the higher the cost; it thus becomes a straight cost/benefit trade-off. What we find is that the level of independence is now sufficient for public purposes and the system works well. What has mainly led to questions about independence is the rendering of services other than the audit. I don't think there have been any questions about the auditor owning shares in companies because that would be a violation of the rules and the people involved would be punished.

'The question about independence mainly relates to non-audit services, and I submit that the vast majority of the other services performed by accountants for their clients are inherently not in conflict with the audit. Before my firm spun off its consulting practice about a year ago, I looked at our services and found that 96% were for the purposes of improving the quality of decision-making information. These services are consistent with, supportive of, and synergistic with the audit. As a result, these services do not create independence problems, while the other 4% either did not create independence problems or were rendered for non-audit clients. The question really comes down to whether you are receiving so high a fee that the client is buying an opinion, rather than an objective audit, and that depends on the total fees from all clients. A firm has to be in the financial position to say "No".

'Under recent disclosures in the USA, by virtue of an SEC rule adopted last year, public companies disclose their fees and there are some situations in which large companies are paying their audit firm as much as USD 100 million a year. This sounds like a lot of money, but these firms have turnovers of USD 10 to 15 billion, so it represents less than 1% of their total revenue. There have never been any cases demonstrating that the size of the fee or the nature of the services has biased the auditor's opinion. The more important question to me is why we still have audit failures. There are instances where auditors' opinions on financial statements are in error, whether intentional or not. As an auditor and as somebody who has been involved in the profession for a long time, I would say that the vast majority of these errors are related to questions of competence rather than independence. The auditor either didn't find the true facts, which has to do with the way in which the audit is designed, or found the facts and misinterpreted them, or reached the wrong judgement. If my view is correct and more audit failures have been caused by failures of competence rather than failures of independence, then the way to reduce audit failures if you only have a limited amount of resources to invest is to focus these resources on improving competence.

'I would also like to say something about accounting failures that are symbolic audit failures. I believe that GAAP financial statements are not properly able to describe modern companies. GAAP was designed to describe an industrial company that creates value by making things and distributing things. Every successful company today is involved in the production and distribution of information. Every product is now more information intensive than it ever was. You buy a physical thing and it comes with an instruction manual, a toll-free telephone number, a videotape, a CD-ROM, and a website. Even a company that makes things has to be nimble in the marketplace, has to have engineering talent, good relations with customers, research and development – intangibles that are not accounted for in our accounting system. All these post-industrial companies, even the ones that are making things, are supposed to describe themselves using an abbreviated vocabulary that was designed to describe an industrial company. There is a mismatch between what GAAP permits and what a good description would be. If people look back at an alleged audit failure, they may say that the rules were not followed exactly. But whether the rules were followed had nothing to do with the accounting failure, because the vocabulary is restrictive and impoverished. In summary, I believe that competency and the impoverishment of the accounting model have more to do with audit and accounting failures than a failure of independence.'

Everyone is talking about fair-value accounting nowadays. In your opinion, what will be the new role of the auditor in this respect?

Professor Elliott: 'When people talk about fair-value financial statements, they are basically talking about using current market values on the balance sheet. But such a balance sheet is still a "one size fits all" general purpose financial statement. One fair value is the cost of getting into a business, determining the reproduction cost, and establishing what the entry barriers are. Another fair value is the amount that could be realised by buying a company and breaking it up to sell off the pieces. Another fair value is the value of the human assets in a company, and that is not on the balance sheet at all. The first question therefore is: What is fair value?

'Secondly, even if we valued every item on the balance sheet at the fair value that the user thought relevant for his or her purposes, we are still confronted with an industrial balance sheet. It is still talking about inventories, plant, and equipment. The current value of the tangible assets of the enterprise no longer interests me very much. A company might have a lot of land and factories, so that might be worth talking about, but items such as inventory are disappearing as the supply chain is becoming tighter and tighter. Therefore, the real question is the fair value of the items that are not on the balance sheet. Many of these "intangibles" cannot be reduced to debit or credit entries on the balance sheet. One, for example, is good relations with customers: customer retention, customer loyalty, and customer satisfaction. You cannot put a precise monetary value on such things, but it may be possible to make comparisons across enterprises. Accountants do not claim that the net book value of a company is supposed to equal to its market value. Nevertheless, it's not too long ago that the aggregate market capitalisations of companies approximated the aggregate book value. These days, however, the market values of US companies are, on average, about five times their book value. We accountants can no longer just stand around with our hands in our pockets saying that book value is not supposed to equal market value. The further these values diverge, the more it becomes clear that investors are looking at other information. This other information, which has a major influence on stock prices, has not been produced by accountants, and it has not been audited by auditors. So our market share of decision-relevant information that goes into investment and credit decisions is decreasing. This imperils our future as a profession unless we can somehow get our arms around that decision-relevant information.

'One way of doing this would be to enter it on the balance sheet as a debit/credit entry and say it is fairly presented, but much of this type of information is very soft – meaning that the estimated values could vary substantially from the true values. However, we already have soft information on the balance sheet. Probably the only two exactly correct numbers on a balance sheet are the date and the number of shares outstanding. Every other number has some uncertainty around it. Even cash has some uncertainty because it may be in banks that fail, or may not be repatriatable, or may be in fluctuating currencies, or items deposited may not be paid. More and more uncertainty crops up as we go down the balance sheet to receivables, inventory and plant and equipment. With intangible assets, we have even more uncertainty. Basically everything on the balance sheet has some uncertainty. What we have said in the past as accountants is that there is a certain level of uncertainty about an item beyond which we will not put it in the balance sheet. We will put it somewhere else, such as in the footnotes. Take contingencies, for example. Under US GAAP, the rule is that if something is probable and estimatable it should be put on the balance sheet. If it is remote, forget about it. Otherwise, put it in the notes. As you can see, this is a pretty crude approach.

'The interim solution to providing fair value information about intangibles may be to provide supplementary information to the financial statements that helps investors and creditors value these items, but does not introduce excessive uncertainty into the traditional financial statements.'

What is your opinion about the current developments in standard-setting internationally?

Professor Elliott: 'If you look at a standard-setter like the FASB, you can see it is well funded and has a large staff, about 50 professionals with an annual budget of about USD 18 million. On the other hand, the IASC was poorly funded and had volunteer staff. Under pressure, particularly from the SEC, the new IASB is structured in a manner more similar to the FASB with full-time members and full-time staff. The board will meet for one week a month in London. However, two years from now, everybody will probably be saying that the IASB is a failure. The reason is that it is not likely to produce anything significant during the next two years. This is quite natural for a new board. But after this initial period, momentum will be gained and the IASB will eventually supersede the FASB even for US companies because the logic for global standards in accounting is unassailable. The differing accounting standards of different countries exist because of different social, political, and economic circumstances, and if they continue to need different accounting systems to support these circumstances, they can retain them as side systems. Nevertheless, the companies that are raising capital on the global capital markets are going to have to use global IASB standards.

'It may sound like the IASB is in the driver's seat. However, all accounting standards boards, including the IASB, are likely to become obsolete if their job continues to be to design general purpose, "one-size-fits-all" financial statements that no-one wants. When users are able to sit in front of a terminal and specify a decision problem that leads to an information template, which sends out queries and brings back, in real time, the exact information which they want, who cares whether some standard-setter says it should be in a balance sheet and what they said about it. I do believe, however, that there is a role for standards. Firstly, standards would establish the minimum set of information that a public company must collect and make available, and secondly, they would determine the data definitions. These are standard-setting issues, but involve a different set of skills than the ones that the IASB and the FASB and other standard setters now have. If accounting standard setters abrogate this role, an alternative could be ISO standards, for example.

'The question equally concerns the extent to which market regulatory bodies, such as the SEC, have enforcement powers and the way in which this enforcement is directed against various types of market participants. Almost every country has such a body, although the SEC is actually different than most because of its greater enforcement powers. Regulatory bodies should prevent companies from filing fraudulent financial statements and ensure that the financial markets are supplied with lots of high-quality information.

'The SEC has had a mixed history in the United States. On the one hand, it has fostered a financial market with a high degree of trust and reliability in which capital readily forms and is redeployed. On the other, it has basically poured concrete around the financial markets as they existed in 1934, before a number of great changes occurred. One is the democratisation of the stock market whereby many individuals in the United States, probably two-thirds of all the people, have beneficial interests in equities and securities, either directly or through intermediaries. Another is the globalisation of financial markets. Also the invention of the digital computer and the Internet. To a large extent, what the SEC does is to enforce rules that make it difficult to take advantage of these new capabilities. So that is the trade-off. When you lock things in place at a point in time, you pay a penalty even if you achieve trust in the fairness of the financial markets.

'Financial markets are global. Ideally there would be some kind of global control of the quality of information and fraud prevention. At the moment, there is no effective global agency to do this. It can't be done by the private sector or by the IASB. They can do helpful things, but they cannot effectively enforce. In my opinion, this cannot be done by the United Nations, nor the World Bank or the IMF. The IOSCO is not suitable because it has no power. The creation of a European SEC would perhaps be useful, but not as good as some agency that would have a broader footprint. In the meantime, I think it is worth noting that the UK has robust financial markets and yet does not have an SEC. Therefore, I think there are ways of producing trusted financial markets on a global basis that do not involve an SEC. However, it must be possible to reach out and punish those who fail to meet the standards, but I do not know how this can be achieved in a world that does not have an international governmental authority.'

For companies, sustainability reporting is becoming more and more important. What should be the role of accounting and auditing in this field?

Professor Elliott: 'I would identify five different sets of constituency interests that have an information interest in the enterprise. One of these is the shareholders and creditors and that is the interest that we, as accountants, have devoted ourselves to the most; the second is the vendors of supplies, materials and technologies; the third is the customers; the fourth is the employees; and the fifth is government as a surrogate for the people. In the case of the government, the interest is not contractually related. The government supplies me with stability, property rights and clean air, and water, but it is not contractually related in the commercial sense. Nevertheless, the government has legitimate information needs from the enterprise, including things like the enterprise's effect on the environment. We accountants have basically concerned ourselves with information flows from the enterprise to the investors and shareholders. But every other one of these constituencies has information flows to and from the enterprise. All of them represent areas where we can use our accounting skills, which involve figuring out what decision information needs are and then supplying relevant, reliable information to meet these needs. Such skills can be generalised to operate with all five of the constituencies. In my opinion, "green" accounting for investors and creditors, or whatever you care to call it, apart from environmental risk and liability information, is narrowly focused. It's also too often designed to bolster reputations so shareholders think the company's managers are nice guys. This is partly because we are only thinking in terms of the information needs of investors and creditors. In principle, however, there is no reason why we shouldn't also be concerned with the information flows to the other constituencies, including the government.

'Lots of the information that is available is quantitative and objective, and there is absolutely no reason we can't or shouldn't get involved as auditors either. In the United States, for example, my firm has an environmental group, mostly made up of engineers. These people can tell you how much particulate matter is going up the smokestacks, how much chemicals are in the water being discharged into the river, etc. This is objective, quantifiable information and there's no reason why our profession, realising that this information is useful to non-investor decision-makers, shouldn't be able to get involved. Since it costs money to gather information, there is a cost/benefit trade-off, but if the customers tell us if they are willing to pay us to do this, we should do it.'

Stock options in financial reports is a hot item in accountancy nowadays. What is the role that auditors should play in this respect?

Professor Elliott: 'Let me start by saying that stock options are probably a good thing, or to put it the other way around, there is no reason to prohibit stock options if willing participants think that they represent the best contracting relationship. There are lots of options, not just stock options; they are inherent in many, maybe even in most, contracts. Obviously, the reason for stock options, theoretically, is to better align the interests of management with those of the shareholders, although it is questionable whether this works. One of the problems is that an intelligent investor has diversified interests, whereas the holder of stock options in an enterprise may be very undiversified, so that may be a way in which the interests of management and shareholders differ. Nevertheless, stock options are basically a good thing because they permit contracting relationships to best serve the interests of all parties. But how do you account for them? You can use option pricing models and the like. The Black–Scholes model for pricing options is not perfect, but it is better than nothing at all. I would say that Black–Scholes is like Newtonian physics before Einstein was born. In the meantime, Newtonian physics does a pretty good job!

'In the US, option values are put into the footnotes instead of on the balance sheet itself. The decision to do this was a straight political compromise. The shareholders and the analysts are informed. In my opinion, it is a pretty effective political compromise. The information is made available, and it is audited. From that perspective, it matters little whether it is on the balance sheet or not. Many companies have rules about when stock options can be exercised and when they can't. These rules are self-imposed and to the extent that the shareholders think that they are good rules, they will reward the company in terms of its cost of capital. To the extent that they think the company is playing fast and loose with stock options, they will penalise the company in its cost of capital. I believe it is better not to regulate, but it is essential to make sure the information flows are adequate to investors so that they know exactly what is going on. Improvements can always be made, for instance by providing the information in real time.

'Corporate governance is also an issue here, but I think it is over-emphasised, because for practical purposes the real corporate governance, at least where public companies are concerned, comes from the marketplace. The share price of companies that are satisfying shareholders and attracting potential shareholders goes up, but it goes down if they are not satisfying and attracting them. This creates a market for management. The marketplace itself punishes managements that are not doing a good job and even if this doesn't happen that often, managements knowing that it might happen will conduct themselves in a way as to avoid this from happening. Merely the possibility that this can happen has a disciplinary effect on management.

'To improve corporate governance it is certainly important to have a good board. In the United States there are both inside and outside directors and the trend has been to have more outside directors. In many boards, the only insider would be the chief executive and chairman. An enterprise's audit committee must be also made up of completely independent directors. Such committees often consist of chief executives from other companies, so they are well versed about financial matters etc. Audit committees can be a good thing, although in many cases they are not because they spend all their time trying to beat down the audit fee instead of worrying about whether the auditors have identified and responded to all of the business risks. I believe that audit committees are getting better, especially when they think in terms of a broader risk management perspective. In practice, however, audit committees in the US might only meet three to five times a year for a few hours. That is not very much time to deal with complex information about an enterprise. All that they can do is ask interesting questions and hope that they get followed up.'

The audit profession is changing dramatically. What are the main challenges with respect to these changes?

Professor Elliott: 'Auditors should prepare for real time disclosure of financial information and help bring it about. The marketplace is more volatile than it has ever been, and that's not going to disappear. This volatility is caused by the speed at which things change. This in turn is underpinned by technology that permits the development of new products and permits them to come into the marketplace faster than ever and from any place in the world. A product that was the best thing on the market yesterday may be obsolete tomorrow. Therefore, we can no longer depend on quarterly financial statements because of what happens between those reports. Due to the lack of high-quality up-to-date information people guess and speculate, and subsequently the intrinsic value and the actual stock value begin to diverge. By reducing the volatility, the perceived riskiness of financial investments and thus cost of capital are reduced. If auditors come along at the end of the year and perform an "after the fact" audit, all they are going to be able to say to the people concerned is: "The information you were relying on all year was wrong, but don't worry, we corrected it." That service is of limited use, because the information has already been impounded in decisions for a year.

'If the information is available in real time, it is going to have to be assured in real time and that means that as a profession we have to develop the ability to create real time assurance. We will have to shift from "after the fact" detection of error to "before the fact" prevention of error. This involves evaluating the quality of information systems and providing opinions that the information systems produce good information by design. As a result, our strategy changes. We need to look at every error that appears and ask ourselves why it happened and how we can eliminate its source.

'Therefore, as auditors we will have to figure out how to redesign processes to get rid of errors. In my opinion, journal entries point to the existence of errors. I look at every journal entry as an error correction. For example, a journal entry to book periodic depreciation is only necessary because we did not book it in real time; a journal entry to reduce the receivables to collectable value is only necessary to correct the error caused by the fact that we did not reduce them in real time as the information became available. In summary, therefore, we must create a system that not only produces good real-time information by designing out sources of error, but also provides real-time assurance about it.'

Chapter 3

Current US accounting issues

An interview with Norman Strauss

Norman Strauss

Professor Norman Strauss CPA (1941) has recently retired as a partner of Ernst & Young LLP where he was National Director of Accounting Standards and a member of the Accounting and Auditing Committee. He has begun a new career as Ernst & Young Executive Professor in Residence at the City University of New York's Baruch College as well as joining the SEC Institute's faculty. While at Ernst & Young, Strauss was also the firm's representative on the FASB's Emerging Issues Task Force and the Financial Accounting Standards Advisory Council. He has previously served as chairman of the AICPA's Accounting Standards Executive Committee (AcSEC) and chaired or served on various other task forces of AcSEC, including those on the Conceptual Framework of Accounting, LIFO and Accounting for Stock Options. He was also a member of the FASB's Impairment of Assets Task Force and Cash Flow Task Force. Professor Strauss is continuing as Ernst & Young's representative on the Advisory Council for the International Accounting Standards Board. He is also a member of the Financial Reporting Committee of the Institute of Management Accountants. He has been published in the Journal of Accountancy *and elsewhere, and is also a frequent lecturer at the SEC Institute's conferences. Strauss received his BBA and MBA from Baruch College.*

Professor Norman Strauss has been acclaimed as the 'accountant's common sense champion'. Any change to corporate reporting rules will require approval by the SEC, which has its own political agenda of keeping accounting standards as transparent as possible. This is a nice goal, but with the SEC being a key player in all of this, a single accounting standard is still not imminent in his opinion.

Could you tell me something about the difference between international accounting standards and US GAAP?

Professor Strauss: 'The United States has been establishing accounting standards for many, many years; it has more standards on just about everything and with more detail than international standards. It is trying to work closely with the newly formed International Accounting Standards Board (IASB), which is picking up the standard setting from the old International Accounting Standards Committee. The goal of the US and of many other standard-setting bodies in the world is to have greater convergence and try to develop standards that are as close to-gether as possible. Some differences still exist: a simple example is the capitalisation of interest during the construction of a plant. In the United States, you have to capitalise interest during the course of construction, whereas the preferable treatment under international rules is to expense the interest as it is incurred. Another example is the difference with respect to the accounting for inventories. International rules might move in the direction of taking away the ability of companies to use Last In, First Out (LIFO) accounting, while US companies are permitted to use this form of accounting. There are many differences in details between IAS and US GAAP, but the goal of the standard setters is to try to come closer and closer together, so that there will eventually be fewer and fewer differences in accounting standards around the world.'

Will there always be two sets of standards?

Professor Strauss: 'I believe that there will be a continuation of the sep-arate standard setting for several years and I think it will be many years before the FASB literally goes out of business. I think the FASB recognises that it could someday put itself out of business by helping the IASB and it would probably be a good thing if we only had one standard-setter in the world. It will be a long time before that happens, but at the moment I think that everyone is optimistic that the IASB has a reasonable chance of being successful in the future.'

What are the practical difficulties of applying FASB's new standards covering the accounting for business combinations (FAS 141) and the accounting for goodwill and other intangible assets (FAS 142)?

Professor Strauss: 'The new accounting rules from the FASB will require many, very subjective evaluations and I believe that many implementation issues will arise. The new rules were adopted in the US effective from 1 January 2002 and AOL Time Warner, for example, has already announced that it may have a fairly large impairment charge as a result. Such companies are faced with difficulties because they have to use fair value information in order to determine whether they need an impairment charge or not. In order to perform the necessary tests, companies have to calculate the fair value of the assets and liabilities of their reporting units even though they are not planning to sell them, so it is difficult to conclude how precise these calculations are. I should add that the international standards developed by the IASB might move in the same direction as in the US, so they will become reasonably consistent.

'My advice to companies that have to apply the new rules is to allow a great deal of time to prepare the calculations because the necessary information cannot be obtained from the general ledger system. Companies are going to have to set up teams of experts to figure out what the relevant values are and they will have to allocate the goodwill and book values to the different reporting units.'

The IASB has put share-based payments on its agenda. What do you think the political consequences of this will be?

Professor Strauss: 'The FASB faced its rockiest road in history when it tackled the question of stock options and ultimately had to drop its plans to make the use of fair value a requirement. Instead, they made this optional and companies that choose not to use the fair value method have to put pro forma income disclosures in the footnotes to their financial statements. For the past four or five years, well over 99% of the companies in the US have chosen the footnotes disclosure option. The principal concern of companies about the FASB's rules with respect to the recording of charges based on fair value was that it would hurt the economy. Innovative, creative and hi-tech companies all use stock options, so they in particular felt that they would be hurt by such measures. Other companies, such as my firm at that time, Ernst & Young, believed that the values were not very reliable and that the information provided would not be that useful. When the FASB ultimately dropped its plans it was basically making a compromise.

'A few months ago, when the IASB put the subject on its agenda, I, as a member of the advisory council, and a couple of others from the US, cautioned the Board that this was a very difficult issue and that it would be better to leave it alone for now and concentrate on things that can be done without being too controversial. The IASB, however, felt that it was essential to go forward and tackle the controversial stock options topic, partly because there is so little guidance in this field in many countries. We also pointed out that if they did things differently, it would not be consistent with the goal of trying to realise convergence of accounting standards and that, in the spirit of international harmonisation, they should perhaps go in the direction of the United States. My expectation now is that the IASB will favour a fair value model using a "date of grants" approach somewhat similar to what Statement 123 requires to be disclosed in the pro forma footnotes. It will be a long process, involving the issue of a proposal, and we will have to see whether they get caught up in the same political fury as occurred in the US. It will be both an interesting challenge and interesting to watch it.'

In the future, do you think we will have one set of accounting standards for financial instruments based on fair value?

Professor Strauss: 'The rules on derivatives in the US are virtually incomprehensible and the FASB has announced it believes that all financial instruments should ultimately be carried at fair value. The IASB is also taking a look at what it thinks the rule should be on financial instruments and many of those serving on the accounting rule-making bodies believe that fair value is the best measure for financial instruments. On the other hand, many, including me, have concerns about fair value, especially because it is difficult to establish the fair value of particular financial instruments. A lot of unrealised gains and losses will be introduced into the financial statements, perhaps very many years before they are actually realised; showing a large unrealised gain may or may not be the most useful way of presenting a financial instrument to readers. In addition, showing the ups and downs of the long-term debt as a consequence of interest rate changes raises questions about the usefulness of the information. A lot of volatility would be created and financial statements would become confusing and less useful than they are now. There is some controversy in the United States about Enron at the moment. The question has already been raised whether some of the fair values that the company used for the energy contracts were appropriate. In general, I should say that once you get into the fair value world it is very hard to know what the values are. It's just like saying that your house is worth a million dollars; maybe it is maybe it isn't. You don't know until you sell it.'

Do you think that recent developments with respect to Enron will increase the likelihood that international accounting standards will be accepted in the US?

Professor Strauss: 'Enron is certainly getting a lot of attention in the press everyday and the importance of financial reporting is really being stressed to the public. I expect there will be a lot of initiatives to improve the process in the US because of Enron and over time this may lead to a greater knowledge of the need for a good international standards setting process and eventually to greater acceptance of the standards in the US.'

Part II

Regulations and regulators

Chapter 4

We have to produce one set of unified high-quality global standards

An interview with Sir David Tweedie

David Tweedie

In 1990, Professor Sir David Tweedie (1944) was appointed the first full-time Chairman of the (then) newly created Accounting Standards Board (ASB), the committee charged with the responsibility for producing the UK's accounting standards, and in 1995 he became a UK representative on the International Accounting Standards Committee (IASC). His appointment at the ASB ended in December 2000. Tweedie is a visiting Professor of Accounting in the Management School at Edinburgh University. He has been awarded honorary degrees by seven British universities, the ICAEW's Founding Societies Centenary Award for 1997 and the CIMA Award 1998 for services to the accounting profession.

Professor Tweedie was appointed Chairman of the International Accounting Standards Board (IASB) in June 2000, effective 1 January 2001. Sir David was educated at Edinburgh University (B.Com 1966, Ph.D. 1969) and qualified as a Scottish Chartered Accountant. He was appointed Technical Director of the Institute of Chartered Accountants of Scotland in 1978 and moved from there in 1982 to the position of national technical partner of the then Thomson McLintock & Co. In 1987, his firm merged with Peat Marwick Mitchell & Co. at which time he was appointed national technical partner of KPMG Peat Marwick McLintock.

He was the UK and Irish representative on the International Auditing Practices Committee from 1983 to 1988 and Chairman of the UK's Auditing Practices Committee from 1989 to 1990.

What do you think will be the role of the IASB as a global rule maker in the near future?

Professor Tweedie: 'The answer is very simple. We have to produce one set of unified high-quality global standards; the question is how we get there. What we really need to do is to form a partnership with the major standard-setters so that we all produce exactly the same standards. For example, we cannot force FASB, the US standard-setter, to reproduce our standards; we have to get them involved in this partnership. So we see ourselves as the crucible, if you like, leading to convergence. To do this, the IASB has been designed in such a way that it brings in the major standard-setters. You could argue that the Netherlands should be there too, but the countries that have been chosen are Australia, Canada, the UK, the USA, together with Germany, France and Japan. The choice was based upon the size of the economies and activity in standard-setting as much as anything else. Seven members of the board are the liaison members of these standard-setters; they attend the meetings of their national standard-setter and their job is to take our views back and bring the views of the national standard-setters over to us so that everybody knows what is going on at the same time. Ideally, the standard-setters will align their agendas so we all do the same thing at exactly the same time. We do not want to finish something, only to find that one of the partnership standard-setters comes up with a different answer a couple of years later; that does not solve the problem of unifying global standards.

'We have also tried to speed up the process by looking at the major differences between the various standard-setters. Clearly, there are some very obvious differences, such as in respect of business combinations. In this case, the Americans were the outliers, but they have now got rid of pooling and are in line with Australia and New Zealand. The international standard, the Canadian standard and the UK standard are all very similar. In the UK, 1% of our business combinations are poolings, but the question is whether it is worth keeping merger accounting just for the sake of that 1%. I can imagine, therefore, that poolings will disappear.

'There are also major differences with respect to impairment of goodwill – a method which was pioneered by the UK. The UK would have gone entirely for impairment, but the European directive would not permit this. In 1989, I proposed in an article in the *Financial Times*, jointly written with Graham Stacey, the technical partner of Price Waterhouse, that impairment was the way forward for the accounting of intangibles such as goodwill. That is why I am now very supportive of the Americans.

I don't actually agree with all the text of the US standard, but I think that the direction is right.

'There is a fair chance that the IASB will now also choose an impairment approach for goodwill. We cannot, however, follow the Americans if their standards are defective. In my opinion, the US business combination standards have defects; I don't think their impairment test or their approach towards acquisition provisioning is perfect. Everyone will have to make changes and standards will converge. Business combinations was one of the earliest standards to merit convergence and we will now have to examine income tax, pensions, etc. and resolve the differences between the various standards. Ultimately, people want international standards so that companies can go to any stock exchange in the world using these standards and users can understand the available information.

'Other major issues that we still have to resolve concern the capitalisation of interest, revenue recognition, the difference between liabilities and equity and share based payments (as we have seen with hi-tech companies, there is still a lot of work to be done in this field).'

What is your opinion about the valuation of intangibles?

Professor Tweedie: 'The US standard on intangibles is quite interesting; the proposals on goodwill that are being introduced are recognising a lot more in the way of intangibles. FASB are not allowing internally generated intangibles, but they are allowing purchased ones and they will allow them if they are either separable or based on a legal contract. The problem we find with internally generated intangibles is that unlike purchased ones, nobody has ever written a cheque for them.'

How do you see the future relationship with the European Financial Reporting Advisory Group (EFRAG), whose Technical Expert Group is chaired by Johan van Helleman?

Professor Tweedie: 'The endorsement mechanism is quite cumbersome; we would have much preferred to have kept the politicians out of the process. The EFRAG looks at our standard and makes a recommendation to the Commission, which does not have to accept it but makes a recommendation to a "political" committee consisting of representatives of member states. I am delighted that the members of EFRAG are internationalists, that Johan is in the Chair and that the Commission has indicated that rejection of an IASB standard will be a rare event. The issue is going to be that any committee can come up with a different view from ours. The question is what happens when this occurs. It is very important that there are no surprises and so we have suggested to the EFRAG that one of our board members could attend part of their meetings to provide some early warning. The EFRAG is designed to be proactive which is very important. It is essential to get in at the beginning of the debate; it's no use coming in at the end and saying that things have gone in the wrong direction. In this respect, the exposure draft stage is much too late. We want to have constant contact with the EFRAG in order to provide and receive feedback. Of course, we receive views from the standard-setters, the SEC, IOSCO, etc. – as well as the EFRAG. After we have heard all the arguments we have to make a decision in order to produce one set of standards. It is certainly possible that we will have to tell any one of the above-mentioned parties that we do not agree with them, but we can guarantee that if the standard we propose doesn't work after three years of operation, we will put it back on the agenda again. However, if the EFRAG or one of the other groups won't accept our proposal then there will be no unified global standards.'

Will the IASB be producing a lot of new standards or merely 'repairing' old ones?

Professor Tweedie: 'The first thing we have to do is to fix the existing standards. We know that if Europe is going to change by 2005, we really have to finish all the improvements this year (2003). We are very aware that since the funding costs will be about EUR 20 million per annum if we don't produce signs of convergence within three years, companies will start to question the expense and ask why they don't use US GAAP instead. We have to prove ourselves in three years.

'Secondly, we have to make improvements (probably new standards) that will lead to convergence. Some of these improvements can, quite frankly, never be made by any individual standard-setter because of the political reaction. For example, it is essential that eventually we introduce a new financial instruments standard since the existing one is flawed. We must produce a new leasing standard – we could converge right away on leasing since none of the existing standards in this field are working. The leasing industry is up in arms about this. They are very worried about what is going to happen because more assets and liabilities may be included on the balance sheet. As for share based payments we have now already started looking at the situation with respect to hi-tech companies. We now have a situation where companies are paying suppliers and employees in share options and some dot.com companies could almost go straight from revenue to profit because there is nothing in between. It is very difficult to justify the existing rules. Looking at the US, for example, if companies charged employee share options as remuneration (using the FASB measurement) the profits of US hi-tech companies last year would have been down by 33%, the profits of telecom companies would have been down by 17% and overall profits would have been down by 9%. This would not be a popular standard therefore. Denmark considered the issue. Germany has produced an exposure draft that advocates charging share options as an expense, but they are a bit nervous of being on their own. The UK has also issued a proposal for charging share options, but there is a lot of opposition, as this would represent a big minus in the income statement. The issue is complex – measuring non-traded options will not be easy.'

Should international accounting standards apply to all companies or just to public, listed companies?

Professor Tweedie: 'We focus on large international listed companies, but the standards should apply to all companies because ultimately as companies grow they will be moving into the listed ranks. However, it is quite hard for small businesses to get to grips with something quite complicated like the leasing standard. In the UK, small companies are able to use a simplified set of standards so that, broadly speaking, the income measurement is the same as with large companies, but disclosures are much less. This system has been quite popular in the UK and over half our small companies use the system. Obviously, if the banks are lending money they will require a full set of statements from companies, but then the market decides. In cost/benefit terms, I believe it is unrealistic for all companies to apply the full set of standards. We therefore do need a simpler set for small and medium-sized enterprises – especially when you consider that there are only 3,000 listed companies in the UK but almost a million companies in total.'

Do you think there should be an enforcement body like the SEC for the European countries?

Professor Tweedie: 'It depends how you set up such an enforcement body. There are two choices. You can either be proactive, with pre-clearance, which is how the American SEC operates, or you can do things in the same way as in the UK. In the UK we don't have the resources to employ 100 people to check accounts before they are issued. What we have instead is quite a cheap but effective organisation, the Financial Reporting Review Panel, that acts on complaints and also automatically receives any qualified accounts going through the stock exchange. The complaints could have come from me as Chairman of the Standards Board, but, for example, could also come from disgruntled employees or be picked up on the basis of critical comments in the *Financial Times*.

'The organisation consists of a panel of long-standing professionals. For a particular case, normally five or six in number would be drawn from a group of about 25 standing members, including finance directors, experienced auditors, lawyers and businessmen. The chairman of the group is a lawyer and the vice-chairman always a very senior accountant, usually a former technical partner. If they think that the accounts do not show a true and fair view or that the accounting standards are not properly applied, they call in the company and its auditors and ask them to explain the financial statements. If they are not satisfied with the explanation, they will invite the company to withdraw the accounts and reissue them. If this is refused, the company can be taken to court and, if the review panel wins in court, the cost of the court action and the cost of the republication fall on the individual directors rather than the company. This involves huge amounts of money and, up until now, no-one has ever been taken to court. There have been two or three cases where court action was close, but the parties involved backed off at the last minute when they realised what it would entail.

'We had a very interesting case in the UK early in the 1990s involving Trafalgar House. After the company showed profits of about £120 million, the *Financial Times* described their accounting as "British financial engineering at its finest" and the review panel examined its accounts, reducing its profits to a mere £20 million. The company chairman, the finance director and the auditors left the company and from then on everyone was terrified of the review panel. The result of this, and I have confirmation from my former partners in KPMG, is that auditors have become more confident because they can tell clients that they will be unlikely to get away with inaccurate reporting. Furthermore, lawyers have warned companies that they have little chance of winning a court case against the review panel and that even if they do win a case on a legal technicality, they would still be torn apart by the financial press and there would be pressure for the law to be changed.'

Do you think that the concept of the true and fair view should be retained in the new accounting standards?

Professor Tweedie: 'Within the G4, the UK was the only country to argue in favour of the retention of the true and fair view. The reason we did so was because we believe that there should be an overriding philosophy of accounting. Whether you call this fair presentation or faithful representation doesn't matter; ultimately I don't think standard-setters are smart enough to think of everything. The concept of the true and fair view could possibly be saved by means of enforcement, by forcing the company and the auditors to obtain pre-clearance from some other body such as a review panel or an SEC if an override were proposed.'

When preparing standards, how do you maintain objectivity in the face of pressure from the countries contributing financially to the IASB?

Professor Tweedie: 'There's only one way to deal with the pressure, and that is to ignore it. Fortunately, I am not responsible for obtaining the money, that is the trustees' job and they are not allowed to comment on technical issues. I think the trustees might not be happy if (say) the USA or Germany pulled out of the funding of IASB, but I think their view would be that if we felt that the answer was right, we couldn't possibly allow the paymaster to tell us what the standard should be. The contributors could wreck us, of course, but I believe it is better to be wrecked and then try to find a better way out.

'A better way of funding the IASB would be to put a levy on the stock exchange listing fee for each company. If this were automatic, this issue would disappear. It is possible that this will come in time. In the UK, the contribution to fund the ASB is partly funded by a levy on the stock exchange listing fees and about one third of ASB's income comes from this source. If a levy were to be imposed, however, this would probably have to be done worldwide because stock exchanges are also competitive and would consider it unfair if the levy were to be imposed by one exchange and not by the other.'

Chapter 5

EFRAG: a new force to be reckoned with in the reporting field

An interview with Johan van Helleman

Johan van Helleman

Professor Johan van Helleman RA (1944) is Professor of Accounting at the University of Tilburg (formerly at the Free University of Amsterdam) and partner at KPMG. Since 1 July 2001 he has been Chairman of EFRAG. Until 15 October 2001 he was Chairman of the Council for Annual Reporting (the Dutch standard-setter).

Before the IAS are actually introduced by the European Union in 2005, various procedures must be completed to give these international accounting standards the required legal force. A new advisory body, called EFRAG, has been created partly to help streamline this process. EFRAG stands for *European Financial Reporting Advisory Group*. Its Chairman, since 1 July 2001, is Professor Johan van Helleman RA.

What will EFRAG do and in what context?

Professor Van Helleman: 'The regulation that led to the creation of EFRAG was proposed by European Commissioner Bolkestein. The ultimate aim is to arrive at a single European capital market that uses a single financial language and is governed by a uniform set of rules. The IAS have been selected as the "standards" for this purpose, at least in so far as "Europe" has endorsed them. In this connection a new procedure, known as the "comitology procedure", has been introduced. The new procedure shifts powers from the European Parliament and the Council of Ministers to the European Commission which will consequently play an important role in the acceptance of existing and new IAS.

In addition, a new body is to be set up: the *Accounting Regulatory Committee (ARC)* comprising representatives of all member states. That body is to be given a key position in the procedure for approving the application of IAS by European companies. The European Commission makes proposals to the ARC concerning the acceptance of the IAS. The role now assigned to EFRAG is to advise the European Commission on whether to adopt the IAS or not and also to make a proactive contribution to the IASB in its efforts to bring the IAS to completion.'

What does the co-operation with the IASB amount to? Will they listen to you?

Professor Van Helleman: 'There is of course contact with the IASB and we have a "Memorandum of Understanding" outlining our mutual relationship. Apart from contacts between the members of the IASB and EFRAG at official level, there will also be contacts at work level. That's important to ensure Europe makes a contribution right from the start of the development process. On the other hand, it also means that EFRAG must initiate a process in Europe so that the European contribution, that is, the opinions formed on the standards, is properly channelled and presented. Two bodies have been created for this purpose. First of all, there's a forum of "Standard setters" from the member states. These 15 representatives meet at least twice a year in Brussels to talk with us about the developments in the IASB and in Europe. Secondly, a network is being set up with European organisations that are involved in some way or other in the financial reporting process, such as accountants, businesses, financial institutions and so on. Contacts are also maintained through observers with the stock exchange supervisors and with the European Commission. Professor Karel van Hulle is one of the observers in EFRAG.'

Can EFRAG develop into a European 'standard-setter'?

Professor Van Helleman: 'We have no intention of introducing European standards. The standards must be genuinely international. There is always the possibility, incidentally, that a certain IAS standard is not accepted in Europe. If that weren't the case, ratification by means of a formal approval would not be required. We currently have the EU "accounting directives". The Fourth and the Seventh Directive are particularly important. These form part of European law and have been incorporated into the national legislation of the various member states. Following their adoption, these Directives determined the content of the financial reports. Many member states now see a kind of foreign element being brought in, an externally developed set of reporting standards, and they are obviously not intending to blindly accept the newcomer. This explains why there's a ratification mechanism to make sure that the standards imposed on listed companies actually meet the demands of the European capital markets and interested parties in Europe. I should also point out that accounting covers a wider field than the financial statements alone. So far, the IAS have exclusively focused on the financial statements as we know them: in other words the balance sheet, the profit and loss account, the cash flow statement and the notes. But the European Directives also contain rules for the management report. We in Europe attach a lot of importance to this, so I can imagine that at some point in the future the IAS will also say something about the management report. Otherwise, we would be left with an undesirable gap. If that were to happen, the EFRAG might well make an issue of this. Its task, after all, is to make sure that the content of the standards is adequate for financial reporting in Europe.'

What is the composition of EFRAG?

Professor Van Helleman: 'In our governance structure we have a *Supervisory Board* consisting of representatives of the "Founding Fathers", as they are known. These are organisations from the private sector which have created this body on the initiative of the European Commission and also provide it with financial support. These organisations represent accounting firms, industrial companies, analysts, banks, insurance companies, stock exchanges and the small and medium-sized enterprises sector: in short, a spectrum of European organisations that jointly make up a supervisory board. This *Supervisory Board* appoints the members of the *Technical Expert Group* (TEG) who are required to act independently. They are expected to represent European interests in general and not just the individual interests of a particular country or sector. I should add that they are all part-timers. So there is in principle the risk that "he who pays the piper calls the tune". To avoid this, explicit arrangements have been made to ensure they act as independent experts when doing this work.

'The members of the TEG come from the widest possible diversity of backgrounds. With a composition numbering about 10 people, a balance has been found in terms of experience, background and perspective and 10 member states are represented. Greece, Sweden, Luxembourg, Ireland and Italy are currently not represented in the TEG but they do have representatives in the group of "standard-setters" which meets at least twice a year. In addition, a point was made of including people with standard-setting experience in the group. Some, such as the penultimate chairman Stig Enevoldsen, have sat on the IASC, others had or have a seat on their national standard-setter. Overly prominent contacts are not permitted however. So I am not allowed to be chairman of the Dutch standard-setter and of the EFRAG at the same time. The freedom to form an independent standpoint must be guaranteed as far as possible.'

How is the relationship between EFRAG and the Council for Annual Reporting?

Professor Van Helleman: 'My colleague Hans Leeuwerik is the second Dutch member of EFRAG and he maintains the relationship with the Council for Annual Reporting now that I have left them. The role of the Council for Annual Reporting will change in the future incidentally because the emphasis is to be placed on unlisted companies, including non-profit organisations. This means that the Council will no longer have a direct task in relation to stock exchange companies and other companies that are entitled or required to report according to the IAS from 2005 onwards. The same applies *mutatis mutandis* to all European countries.

'This raises the question as to what the relationship should be between the reporting of non-listed companies and that of listed companies. The current consensus is that *grosso modo* the method used to calculate the profits and determine the financial position should be identical for all organisations, regardless of whether they are listed on the stock exchange or not, but that differences should be allowed in terms of the information and notes to take account of the different groups of users at which the reports are targeted. At a listed company the interested parties will be mainly investors and analysts. As these companies use public funds, it may be justified to ask for additional information. But the situation may be different for family-owned companies and other non-listed companies. So a certain degree of divergence can be justified in principle. Even so, the tendency almost everywhere is not to permit too many differences and some member states are even considering making IAS obligatory for non-listed companies as well. That decision would probably be made easier if a special IAS were formulated for small and medium-sized enterprises.'

So EFRAG is not a 'standard-setter' that is insisting on imposing its own rules while Europe is actually opting for international standards. But does the European voice carry sufficient weight at the IASB and isn't it the Americans who have the dominating voice?

Professor Van Helleman: 'It is true that Europe has opted for international standards. Europe is very clearly committing itself to the IASB in the expectation that European insights and interests will be adequately taken on board in the IAS. So EFRAG has a very thankful task there, particularly considering the frequent doubts about whether the European voice is heard sufficiently in the IASB and whether the American's aren't drowning the others out.'

What will the accountancy profession look like in the new situation in the year 2005 if the IAS are actually adopted?

Professor Van Helleman: 'A certain cultural turnaround will be necessary. We are moving towards a reporting structure and environment with lots of American traits. The SEC is adamant that there must be clear and detailed reporting rules before IAS financial statements are accepted. Accountants will also have to make sure that the rules are complied with. In addition, there must be a regulator who monitors the entire process and takes alert action if there are any snags. At the present moment there is a number of European countries where the quality and content of reports are not subject to any supervision other than the annual audit. That includes the Netherlands and Germany. But this is about to change. Because a European supervisory system was recently created where a national regulator will be set up in each member state and co-ordinated at European level by the Committee of European Securities Regulators (CESR). What this means in a nutshell is that a new playing field and new rules are being introduced for companies, accountants and regulators, although the sport will essentially remain the same.'

Will we be getting something like the SEC?

Professor Van Helleman: 'You don't build a body like that overnight. Remember that the SEC already has almost 70 years' experience under its belt and has worked hard on the reputation it has today. Perhaps we shouldn't aspire towards that either; at least not in the same degree and depth. Even so, we will have to investigate more actively than before whether companies have embraced the new rules and are applying them properly. That is in the interests of investors and other participants in the capital market. No organisation in Europe has that "clout" yet. A lot is still possible within the limits of the law, but not everything is equally desirable. If the bar is raised higher and companies are required to comply with more stringent rules, the accountants and supervisors will take these higher norms as their starting point. In other words: a great deal will change, and that goes for the accountant too.'

Won't this make accountancy a less attractive and varied profession? Won't the accountant's role soon be reduced to ticking off procedures on a checklist? It may be a good thing to have a guarantee that the standard rules for reporting are complied with, but it may also make people less inclined to think independently about the essence of good reporting.

Professor Van Helleman: 'The latter strikes me as a rather idealistic presentation of the current situation. As if each and every controller or financial director goes to great pains to devise a wonderful reporting regime for his or her company and then engages some fantastically erudite auditor who puts tremendous reporting expertise at the company's disposal just to add the finishing touches. That hardly seems a realistic portrayal of affairs to me. Similarly the notion that companies will soon be handed a simple recipe for the straightforward production of financial statements that are then formally audited is also greatly exaggerated. No, in my opinion the profession will actually be presented with an additional challenge because it will soon be required to give a "to the point" opinion about the financial reports within an evermore stringent framework and in increasingly complex situations.'

Goodwill must be amortised in the Netherlands, while the opposite is the case in the US. What tensions does this create?

Professor Van Helleman: 'In the Netherlands we traditionally charge goodwill paid on acquisitions against the shareholders' equity. In response to international standards the Council for Annual Reporting has issued guidelines stipulating that goodwill must be capitalised and then amortised. The latter obligation, incidentally, is also provided for in the European directives: fixed assets must be depreciated. This Guideline of the Council for Annual Reporting came into force in 2001. Meanwhile there has been a debate in America about the question whether "pooling of interests accounting" – which is an alternative reporting method in the case of mergers – should be abolished because it was practised on far too wide a scale. The "pooling of interests" method basically entails that no goodwill is capitalised on the balance sheet. This debate ended with a compromise: "pooling of interests" is indeed to be banned, but goodwill arising on acquisitions that has been capitalised need no longer be amortised. Every year, however, a test must show whether the goodwill has retained its value; if not, the value is written down against income. That is the true substance of the compromise, which is sometimes explained too briefly as "goodwill need not be amortised". That, however, is only a half-truth because the value has to be repeatedly reviewed to establish whether it is still intact or not.

'If it is found that the acquired goodwill has clearly lost value, it must be written down against income. Often this will happen in situations when the company is going through a bad spell so that, on top of its existing hardships, it is hit by the additional blow of having to apply a kind of backlog amortisation in recognition of the perceived reduction in the value of the goodwill. It's also fair to wonder whether the prudence we normally exercise when calculating the financial results isn't put in jeopardy by this method. After all, the "impairment test" is carried out at a fairly high level; at the level of a division or a sub-segment in the organisation. When a company is taken over and incorporated into a division, you must determine for that division as a whole whether the profitability is still sufficient to maintain the acquired goodwill. In certain situations the acquired company may not be performing well at all and even go bankrupt, while the goodwill paid remains capitalised on the balance sheet because the division as a whole is making a healthy profit. This is basically tantamount to capitalising home-grown goodwill which, though at odds with normal accounting practices, would in this case be sanctioned. It is still too early to say how the new method will work out in practice but to see this as some great improvement that we must immediately introduce in the Netherlands or in international standards is taking things too far in my view. You can also wonder whether it's wise to entirely abolish "pooling of interests" accounting. Aren't we throwing the baby out with the bath water? Because I can certainly think of some situations where "pooling of interests" is a perfectly adequate solution.'

Basically the need for good and proper accounting is a notion that has only recently started to come to fruition. Surely this should also apply to unlisted companies?

Professor Van Helleman: 'Reporting also plays an important role in such sectors as healthcare, which is a 60 billion guilder industry, or housing associations, fund-raising institutions and the entire medium-sized enterprise sector. In the context of "corporate governance", people concerned with these organisations also need to know how these have acquitted themselves of their entrusted tasks. In other words: Have the targets been achieved? What about the financial management? In this sense the financial reporting is also very important in these sectors. Moreover, the financiers of these operations need to know the financial position of the organisation and whether the management is functioning properly.

'Also, when a company making an acquisition is required to pay a price for operations that are not listed on the stock exchange, the buyer will often use the financial statements as a basis for setting the price. In short, the unlisted sector constitutes an important part of society and reporting plays such a central role there that it must be of good quality. If a number of member states extend the scope of the IAS to unlisted companies, the applied principles will be the same as those used by listed companies, naturally with certain adjustments in view of the absence of the public dimension.'

Does responding to the new situation also mean further training?

Professor Van Helleman: 'Definitely, quite a few accountants believe they know all they need to know, while their knowledge is actually fairly superficial. So it is necessary for accountants to follow further training. Companies too must adapt themselves to the IAS and prepare for the transition well in advance. Systems and business practices have to be adjusted. We already see that new reporting practices are prompting many companies to hold their pension arrangements up against the light. I think we will see a growing appreciation of the economic consequences of the reporting rules and this will automatically stimulate an interactive process. This does entail however that companies must ready themselves for the forthcoming changes before the new reporting rules are actually introduced.'

Reporting practices are steadily drifting away from historical cost to fair value; is this a trend to be welcomed?

Professor Van Helleman: 'Apart from the application of replacement value, our model was traditionally a mix consisting largely of historical cost, based on facts and transactions, and elements where there was a compelling case to use current market value, particularly if that had fallen below the historical cost. This valuation rule is applied to stocks, and the "impairment-test" for fixed assets is also consistent with this principle: if the economic value has sunk below the book value the latter must be adjusted.

Now we see a more general trend towards valuation based on fair value, particularly for financial instruments but also for investments and real estate. Switching over to this valuation method means that one has to determine the current prevailing value in each reporting period. This value can no longer be derived from the books, so there is a task here for the controller and the accountant to determine what the value is. However, the services of valuators will also often be required and procedures will have to be developed to ensure a reliable valuation process. In many cases there will be huge margins in the estimations, unless of course there is a direct market value ready to hand. If you want to know what a company's shares fetch on the stock exchange, you can simply take the market price of that day. But a different approach is required for unlisted securities. And as for real estate, different valuators can still come up with totally different amounts, despite the existence of clear valuation procedures. So quite a few actions need to be undertaken in order to draw up the balance sheet; and the numbers will become increasingly difficult to verify.

'But will all this lead to greater relevance? In general, the right balance must be struck between relevance and reliability. This is important for users. In addition, it must be clear what the underlying transactions and events were and how the figures are to be interpreted. With a system based on "fair values", the controller, the valuator and the accountant will play an important role in determining the figures. That can have a negative effect on the reliability while increasing the complexity. Analysts are also struggling with that dilemma at the moment. They prefer information that is as factual as possible so that they can then work out for themselves how the company or its shares are to be valued.'

Is it wise to move towards a completely new model? Have the disadvantages, particularly in terms of objectivity and reliability, been sufficiently recognised? And aren't we going too fast? A moment ago we were speaking about further training, learning new rules and forming an idea of what the new environment will look like. How quickly do the legislators and regulators need to respond to this?

Professor Van Helleman: 'I think we need to take a step-by-step approach to this subject matter and look at each item individually. But with one clear criterion in mind, such as insight into the size of the company's financial results in a given period. One important question in this connection is when these results were achieved. If the company was set up with the object of selling products and services to customers, then this process is not completed until the other party has kept its side of the agreement, that is, when the reward has been reaped. When the product or service is sold, the costs are set off against the revenues. This leads to a margin, a result that is booked as profit for that period. A problem arises when the value of the actual means of production changes in the course of that process. If the company intends to sell the factory building, it will be necessary to determine the market value. But is that also necessary if there are no plans to relocate or sell the building? Some say that you are better off with an asset that was bought cheap and has subsequently appreciated in value than with an asset whose value has remained unchanged. I agree, but the question is: How do you express this in the financial statements. One possible route is to state the assets at their respective fair values and calculate an operational margin on the basis of these values. But analysts evidently prefer information based on historical cost because that is more transparent.

'As a "standard-setter" or as an entrepreneur perhaps, you may think you have conceived some wonderful concept, but if nobody wants it, why force it upon them? So I'm against saying categorically at this stage that valuation should take place on the basis of historical cost or replacement value. The territory simply isn't suitable for that. It is much better to ask whether the means is relevant to achieving the end you have in mind and whether it is sufficiently reliable, which brings us back to the basic principles of financial reporting.'

Chapter 6

Not partial, but full application of IAS

An interview with Leo G. van der Tas

Leo G. van der Tas

Professor Leo van der Tas RA (1960) is partner at Ernst & Young Accountants (responsible for Ernst & Young's policy in the field of International Accounting Standards) and is attached as Professor of Financial Reporting to the Business Administration Faculty of the Erasmus University of Rotterdam. He is Chairman of the VERA Steering Committee on Financial Reporting. Professor Van der Tas was a member of the Standing Interpretations Committee (SIC) and is currently a member of the International Financial Reporting Interpretations Committee (IFRIC) of the IASB.

Count Tolstoy (*War and Peace*) once observed that it's easier to make rules than to rule. Making rules is a beginning – but formulating them in such a way that they can be put into practice, achieve their objective and be recognisable and unambiguously comprehensible to everyone is a different matter altogether. In most societies the courts interpret the law, but what happens when a supranational non-public body produces the rules, as is the case with the IASB and IAS? Well, a committee is set up to literally explain chapter and verse. This task has been entrusted to the SIC, a committee in which Professor Leo G. van der Tas RA also has a seat.

So what exactly does the SIC do?

Professor Van der Tas: 'The SIC answers questions about the application and interpretation of IAS, because it is clearly not only extremely important that everyone understands the rules in the same way, but also that they apply them in the same way. You can compare the SIC to an interpretative body like the "Emerging Issues Task Force" in the United States. The British, Canadians, French and Australians also have a similar institution whose task is to issue interpretations quickly and effectively to avoid standards having to be adjusted. Avoiding standards is a time-consuming process, while an official interpretation can fill a gap within a matter of months.

'Interpretations of the SIC have the same status as IAS. If a standard remains silent about a particular subject, the SIC cannot make additional rules on its own initiative. It can only interpret existing standards. At the present moment slightly more than 30 interpretations have been published. They are not all equally incisive. Some interpretations concern details, others such as the SIC 12 ("Consolidation of Special Purpose Entities") go very far.

'The SIC ceased to exist at the end of 2001. The new IASB decided to continue with an "Interpretative Body" and this resulted in the creation of the current "International Financial Reporting Interpretations Committee" (IFRIC) of which I am also a member. The composition of the IFRIC is not all that different from the SIC incidentally. This committee also consists of 12 voting members, only now there is an independent chairman who has no vote and can therefore concentrate on running the meetings in a purely technical sense. He is the Australian, Kevin Stevenson (director designate of technical activities). In addition, the IFRIC will enjoy expanded powers. We will now also issue interpretations on subjects that have not yet been laid down in standards. The powers of this body have thus been brought more into line with its US, British and Australian counterparts. The composition of the IFRIC will be as diverse as possible. So it will not only consist of accountants but above all of preparers and users, with as many countries as possible being represented.'

What is the relationship between the IFRIC and the IASB?

Professor Van der Tas: 'Under the old structure all interpretations had to be approved by the IASB first. That will remain the case. The SIC and now the IFRIC are not authorised to issue interpretations independently without the approval of the IASB. Members of the IASB also attend the meetings of the IFRIC as observers. This is to prevent interpretations that are in conflict with what the IASB had in mind.'

How do you see the role of the EFRAG in Europe in relation to the IASB?

Professor Van der Tas: 'The current task of the EFRAG is to analyse the existing standards of the IASB and to find out whether there are any obstacles to introducing them in Europe. This will result in a recommendation to the European Commission. The interpretations are of course also taken on board in this connection. So there must be a really close relationship between the IASB and the EFRAG. In fact, that is precisely what the EFRAG was created for. Let's hope that this body is taken sufficiently seriously by the IASB and that European standpoints are taken into account wherever justified. The EFRAG has a fair amount of clout, and also has its own supervisory board and a few top experts, all of whom are authorities in their field.

'One thing I applaud in particular is that a special insurances sub-committee has been set up in the EFRAG to exert pressure on the IASB to have the insurance contract standard ready for 2005 when European insurers will also start applying the IAS. The EFRAG can help to guide this process.'

Is it really feasible for a company to apply IAS partially?

Professor Van der Tas: 'No, if you refer to IAS, they have to be applied in full; not as the entrepreneur sees fit. IAS 1 has been amended, so that "IAS lite" (partial application of IAS but still qualifying for "IAS compliant" status) is no longer permitted. Many companies incidentally have abandoned that policy since IAS 1 was amended. And wherever entrepreneurs still want to enjoy the best of both worlds, the accountants and supervisors will just have to make sure everyone follows the same line. This is also receiving a lot of attention from us at the moment. Wherever the applicable IAS are not applied in full and this has a material effect, the audit opinion must be adapted because there is no point in striving for international comparability if everybody does as they like and interprets the rules according to their own insights and convenience. As far as that's concerned I am also pleased that the European Union is intending to set up supervisory bodies to monitor compliance with the IAS more stringently.'

How must the accountant handle this?

Professor Van der Tas: 'IAS 1 forbids the company to apply IAS only partially. If the IAS have not been fully applied while the company claims IAS compliance and there is a material effect, then the accountant cannot give an unqualified audit opinion. And if the financial report completely fails to give a true and fair view due to divergences from the IAS, then the accountant is even required to give an adverse audit opinion. We are actually seeing instances of this at the moment.'

Are the rules of the IASB stricter than the Dutch rules?

Professor Van der Tas: 'Yes, the Dutch rules leave certain options open which the IAS no longer accept. The IAS also have a higher status: you either apply them, or you don't. There are no two ways about it. While there is room for discussion with the Guidelines of the Council for Annual Reporting, in practice we see that not everyone applies the Guidelines in full. Well, that is at least one problem that the IAS get rid of because the IAS are completely clear. But a Dutch company that follows the Guidelines of the Council for Annual Reporting in full will find that the differences are not that great. It's worth noting incidentally that as from 2002 companies will in all likelihood be required to report whether their financial statements are based on the Guidelines of the Council for Annual Reporting or not.'

Wouldn't it be better if Dutch GAAP disappeared altogether to make the transition to the IAS easier?

Professor Van der Tas: 'I don't think it's wise to oblige all Dutch companies to apply the IAS. The Netherlands has an extremely large and diverse group of companies that are required to prepare and publish financial statements. If the bakery "on the corner" has a BV (private limited company), it must prepare and file financial statements. But to oblige all these companies to meet the IAS requirements simply doesn't bear thinking about. I think a separate standard should be introduced for small companies, preferably by the IASB to ensure these are in line with the rules for larger companies and are also internationally comparable. However, the IASB has no intention of doing anything about this in the short term. But Dutch rules would also be adequate and in that case the Council for Annual Reporting could do the job. The British have something similar, namely the "financial reporting standards for small and medium-sized enterprises". These spell out exactly what requirements a small company must satisfy and the available exemptions. You could have something similar in the Netherlands.

'There are also companies that could fall within the scope of the IAS but for which no rules have been made at present. You can find various examples of this in the Guidelines. But it would be overdoing things to force this group into the IAS regime. Separate rules could also be made for them. So I wouldn't go so far as to say that we should abandon all Dutch rules and embrace the IAS wholesale. That would be rather hasty and ill-considered.'

Don't you think the rules of the Council for Annual Reporting should be made identical to the IAS?

Professor Van der Tas: 'The IASB is working hard to minimise the number of alternatives. The Guidelines of the Council for Annual Reporting offer more options. So as soon as we decide to follow the IAS here, these options will also disappear. And consequently so will the differences between Dutch and international practice. The international comparability will thus be greatly improved and that was precisely the motivation for this operation.'

Suppose the EFRAG doesn't support a standard, what then?

Professor Van der Tas: 'The EFRAG gives advice to the European Union, and the member states ultimately decide for themselves what they will do. There is a difference between the technical process and the political process. Suppose that the EFRAG gives a negative recommendation, then the European companies have a big problem. If the standard in question concerns a subject for which no arrangements have been made yet, then a company could opt to apply the standard voluntarily, provided there is no conflict with other rules. Problems arise if such a conflict does exist. I don't think exceptions are a good idea. Europe shouldn't become an island in a world ocean. So if there are differences in opinion, we'll just have to accept that the world evidently wants A and not B, even though that may be Europe's preferred option. It is up to the EFRAG and the EU to convince the IASB of the merits of their standpoints. If the IASB decides to follow a different course after a "due process", then it's important for the EU not to be obstructive. That would be pointless and it would also cause severe problems for companies in the EU.

'If we all apply IAS, the role of national regulators will be minimised. The smaller their contribution, the smaller the investments in maintaining and developing accountancy know-how will become. That would not be healthy because it entails that only a single centre, namely the IASB, would be responsible for thinking through the implications of new developments. I think the EFRAG has a responsibility here to maintain a positive-critical stance with the minimal resources at its disposal and for instance to take up projects so that proposals can be made to the IASB or the EU on the basis of its own research.'

Should the EFRAG also issue interpretations of IAS?

Professor Van der Tas: 'If interpretations were published at European level about how European companies are to apply the IAS, then we would completely fail in our objective, namely to achieve comparability of financial statements. In that case, every country would start interpreting the IAS according to its own insights. In addition, an interpretation of the European EFRAG could conflict with that of a European supervisor or body outside the EU. Interpretation shouldn't take place in the EFRAG but should be handed over to the IASB or the IFRIC which, after all, gives interpretations that are applicable all over the world and not just in Europe.'

And should the supervisor interpret?

Professor Van der Tas: 'You see that the SEC gives interpretations of the IAS that are not always in line with the ideas of other supervisors. These interpretations could even conflict with one another. That would obviously confuse companies. The accountant cannot possibly tell them that the financial statements meet the IAS but not the SEC's interpretation of the IAS. So everything points in the direction of interpreting the IAS uniformly and unambiguously. Perhaps we need to set up a type of SEC in Europe which can take this task upon itself. But it would be better for everything to be channelled through the IASB and the IFRIC.'

Who is really the 'owner' of the IAS? Who is responsible for the interpretations?

Professor Van der Tas: 'Though the IASB formulates the standards and issues the interpretations, the enforcement of the rules does not rest with them. That's the job of the accountants, the supervisor and ultimately, in the case of conflict, the courts. In 2005 every listed company will be obliged to apply the IAS. Suppose that a conflict arises in the Netherlands about financial statements based on the IAS. Then that will go to the Enterprise and Companies Court. They will then interpret the IAS which, under the European Regulation, have legal force in the Netherlands. The Enterprise and Companies Court may refer particular cases to the European Court in Luxembourg. But it may also put the matter to the IASB as that, after all, is where the rules came from in the first place. This raises the question as to who is authorised, in the highest instance, to pass judgement.

'These are interesting questions which I think lawyers need to look at. And then: What happens if the IAS financial statements are drawn up in conformity with Dutch legislation? The IAS are applied to listed companies on the grounds of the European Regulation. If the Netherlands decides to extend their scope to other types of companies, will these then come under Dutch legislation and not under the European Regulation? Will that have legal consequences or implications for the legal procedure to be followed? Will it have consequences for the question as to who is ultimately authorised to decide in the case of a concrete dispute about a particular company's financial statements?

'I do not know whether the IAS financial statements have ever been put to a Dutch court yet, but that's obviously bound to happen some time. Who, in that case, will be the authority in the last instance? So here too internationalisation has led to such far-reaching intertwining that we can no longer map out our own course.'

Full 'fair value accounting'. Does that mean stating all balance sheet items except shareholders' equity at fair value and recognising all resulting value differences in the profit and loss account?

Professor Van der Tas: 'That is a trend that can no longer be stopped. The IASB has embarked on this road and cannot in all decency abort the process now. The question is whether that is such a bad thing. We must also try to keep things as practical as possible. Nobody will deny that "fair values" are relevant to the user of the financial statements. But the current form in which the profit and loss account is presented makes it difficult to apply the "full fair value model" as users of the financial statements may draw the wrong conclusions because all the results are lumped together. So something needs to be done about that first. It must be completely clear that the future profit and loss accounts – if that's what they are still called – need to make a distinction between different kinds of results. Otherwise the user will not be given adequate insight into the company's actual results or in external influences, such as changes in market interest rates, share prices, markets and so on. Another aspect that I find very important is that fair value is not in itself the best yardstick for a user. He or she wants to know where the company is most vulnerable. Fair value is at best an estimated points score and that is usually not much use if you don't know what it's an average of and how the risks are distributed. Users tend to prefer sensitivity analyses, answers to questions about what risks are run and where and when these may occur. They want to know what happens if market interest rates fall or rise by 1%, or if share prices fluctuate, or if oil prices start to go up. Things are more likely to go in that direction, I think, though such information can also be provided in the notes.'

Chapter 7

IAS and the European Union

An interview with Karel Van Hulle

Karel Van Hulle

Professor Karel Van Hulle (1952) joined the Company Law and Annual Accounts Law sectors of the Internal Market Directorate General of the European Commission in Brussels in 1984. In 1990 he was appointed head of the newly set up Financial Reporting Department and in 1998 of the Company Law Department, so that he is now in charge of both departments.

The EFRAG, as Professor Johan van Helleman explained earlier (see Chapter 5), has an advisory task in the IAS decision-making and implementation process. The recommendations subsequently go through the Company Law and Annual Accounts Law sectors of the Internal Market Directorate General before finally reaching the European Commission in Brussels. Top civil servant Professor Karel van Hulle 'guides' the EFRAG recommendations to the Council of Ministers which must ultimately decide what shape the IAS are to take in the opinion of the European Union. The IAS decision-making process is gathering momentum in the European Union. On 12 March 2002, the European Parliament approved the proposed regulation for the application of IAS (in 2005) by a large majority. This regulation has in the meantime been ratified by the Council and Parliament.

Isn't that decision-making process rather complicated and elaborate?

Professor Van Hulle: 'A great deal is at stake so we need to proceed with all due care. Moreover, each member state that is going to introduce the rules must be given an opportunity to put forward their views. They, after all, are the ones who will have to incorporate the rules into their own legislation and see to their correct application. That calls for a meticulous and careful approach.

'The strategy of the European Commission (EC) must be seen in the light of the financial services programme that the EC presented in 1999. That programme places emphasis on some 40 measures that are ultimately to lead to an effective, integrated market for financial services in Europe. This is a core project because it is aimed at integrating the markets in Europe. Quite a lot of resistance remains to be overcome, however.

'The programme also devotes attention to annual reporting and accounting. Once the capital market has been integrated and is operating efficiently, companies will be able to attract capital at the lowest costs. To this end, the information underlying the decision-making processes must be complete and reliable. As soon as the capital costs are no higher than strictly necessary, European companies can become more competitive, particularly in comparison with the United States.

'The attainment of such an efficient capital market hinges on two crucial elements. First of all, the financial reports need to be made more comparable. The second concerns improved enforcement of the standards that the companies apply. As far as comparability is concerned, the Commission has set its sights on a single framework of accounting standards. We do not want to leave the market a choice in this connection. The European Commission has deliberately opted for IAS, but wants to retain influence over these standards at technical and political level. The technical adjustments come from the EFRAG. Let me emphasise here that the private sector has expressed a willingness to make substantial investments in this.

'The technical component really serves a double purpose. First of all, proactive intervention must take place in relation to the IASB for all annual reporting and accounting projects that are planned in the international context. This is unique, considering that Europe has so far contributed little towards the international standard-setting procedure. So the EFRAG should eventually be able to give voice to Europe's views. Only one important standard-setter has been active in Europe so far: the UK ASB. The other standard-setters are less important and work less efficiently than the British organisation and certainly don't have the same kind of resources. So it will be interesting to see whether the UK ASB will seek co-operation with the EFRAG, because that is basically the intention.

'Secondly, the EFRAG must advise the European Commission. Once a standard has been approved, its practical feasibility must also be tested. The Commission assesses the EFRAG recommendations and as a rule will also endorse them. Next it will put the recommendation to the Accounting Regulatory Committee (ARC), which is the political body in which the member states are represented. The ARC is presided over by the EC and is responsible for issuing regulations. Ultimately the decision will be taken by the EC which will then officially announce the regulation in all the languages of the European Union. That's how the ratification mechanism works.

'The next step is to ensure that the standards are complied with. Companies have a tendency to apply rules creatively. This is worrying, particularly considering that there are no real systematic controls to monitor compliance with the standards. To remedy this situation we approached the Securities Commissions which are responsible for supervising the securities markets. These supervisors all have different characters, structures and statutes. They are united in the CESR, the Committee of European Securities Regulators, which used to be called FESCO. We are currently consulting with that Committee in an effort to improve our supervision over compliance with the standards.

'All this entails that we must have good standards and that interpretations must be communicated adequately and on time. The EFRAG should also be given a certain responsibility in this connection. Sound and reliable auditing is important too. Which is why the Committee on Auditing is taking part; a body is required to supervise compliance. Finally, effective sanctions must be put in place to counter any breaches of the rules.'

Are sanctions actually possible? How do you propose to impose them?

Professor Van Hulle: 'Until now the sanctions policy has been left to the individual member states themselves. Which is natural, as they are in a position to impose and implement sanctions effectively. What the EC is doing now, is to encourage the member states to pursue the same sanctions policy. This will help to create uniformity and prevent companies from seeking stock exchange listings in those countries that have the weakest sanctions or the most lenient enforcement policy. Because that's what often happens in practice.

'The ultimate sanction – delisting – cannot be ruled out, and that can have severe consequences for investors. Publicity, too, is an important sanction and so is timely auditing of the information in the financial statements. Disciplinary sanctions can be imposed on the accountant. Numerous gradations and variants are of course conceivable. All that matters to the EC is that the sanctions are applied throughout the EU and in the same consistent manner.'

European culture is threatened with take over by what is already commonplace in the Anglo-American world. In the United States, for instance, it is customary to go to the courts and arrange everything in great detail. Will that also become normal practice in Europe?

Professor Van Hulle: 'No, certainly not. The Americans have their own specific approach to rules and regulations. They like to spell out the small print. That has to do with their liability-driven litigation culture. Accountants there need to protect themselves against liability claims as best they can. Which explains the plethora of formalistic rules: conditions, provisos, exclusions and so on. We in Europe have a very different approach, which you can call European in the broadest sense of the word because it's equally common in the UK and in Germany. What we do is lay down the principles and leave the rest to the accountant's professional opinion. In my view the Americans will just have to learn to live with these cultural differences. In fact, it may offer them a good opportunity to get rid of that paralysing claims culture. But bridging the gap is not easy. The Americans point out that the US GAAP make up an entire library, while the IAS are merely a fat tome. The thing is: we don't want the IAS to become a library.'

What influence do the US GAAP have?

Professor Van Hulle: 'They have a huge influence. Which is understandable: large European corporations that are listed on American stock exchanges are subject to US GAAP. The SEC calls the shots. These listed companies are naturally not keen to prepare two sets of financial statements: one according to US GAAP and one according to IAS. They are also worried that the IAS may turn out to be stricter than the US GAAP. If that is the case and they are required to apply the IAS, they will be at a disadvantage compared to their US competitors who will continue to be governed by US GAAP for the time being. Goodwill is one specific example that springs to mind in this connection.

'The IASB must pay particularly close attention to what is happening in America. In the coming years convergence will be one of the top priorities for both the IASB and the European Union. And that does not mean taking over the US standards. It does mean that the Americans will have to bid farewell to their US GAAP and start working with us on the IAS. This is a joint project, so it must contain elements of both the Anglo-American and the European-Continental culture. As soon as either of the two becomes too dominant, the other will be unable or unwilling to accept the end result. Convergence leads to more broadly based acceptance and gives the rules the stamp of authority they require.

'The question of course is whether the United States are prepared to go along with this. As a rule, Americans are generally unwilling to live with the smallest common multiple. They insist on quality, and rightly so. Unfortunately, that is precisely a term that cannot be mathematically, scientifically and objectively defined. It is often used as a political device to impose a veto. In view of their long-standing tradition and authority, US GAAP will certainly exercise a lot of influence on the IAS that are still to be formulated, but I think that Professor Strauss [see Chapter 3] will have a lot more to say on this subject in his contribution.'

So is Europe really fighting a losing battle?

Professor Van Hulle: 'Europe has done far too little to promote the standardisation of annual reporting and accounting. We are now paying the price for that. If we want a single regulatory framework for our capital market in Europe, we have left ourselves no option other than to accept something that isn't from our own drawing boards: that is, US GAAP or IAS. Ever since 1995 the European Commission has made it perfectly clear that it wants IAS. These standards can be given worldwide force provided they are meticulously worked out and every country is able to make its own contribution. That way you can build widespread acceptance and support. I expect a lot of the EFRAG in this connection: creativity, alertness and quality. Europe cannot afford to drag its feet and leave the initiative to other countries; and certainly not to Anglo-American countries who have already built up a considerable lead in this field. But I am optimistic, because I have seen that there is a lot of enthusiasm inside and around the EFRAG. What's more, the participants include many excellent and highly motivated experts.

'The American influence will of course remain undiminished, for the simple reason that the US capital market is the biggest of its kind in the world. But nothing is certain in this world. Major changes can take place. Who knows, the EU may soon have the strongest cards in its hands. As things stand, the idea is to create a capital market that is at least as big as its American counterpart. We have the potential, we have the resources. It is only a question of willpower. Success will serve to bolster the EU's position in the international arena. But to achieve this, Europe must build on EFRAG's work to play a more active role through the IASB.'

Aren't you worried about corporate lobbying? The IASB is funded by the business community and the large accountancy firms.

Professor Van Hulle: 'That comment is made quite regularly: how can business and industry subject itself to the rules imposed by an organisation that is actually working on its behalf. This is definitely a problem because one of the thunderclouds hanging over us concerns the royalties that must be paid for IAS. The IASB charges royalties for printing the standards. And also for the translations. That obviously doesn't go down well. It is inconceivable that European citizens must pay for the law that they are required to apply. The financing system of the IASB would be in jeopardy as soon as the users refuse to pay the royalties. That's why the IASB itself is looking at ways of revamping the financing system which they actually copied from the American FASB system and which is mainly based on publication fees and contributions from business and industry. This should lead to a financing system that does not rely on royalties for publications and contributions from companies. That's the way forward in my opinion.'

What is being done to facilitate the introduction of the IAS in Europe?

Professor Van Hulle: 'Quite a lot of pressure has been brought to bear on the Commission to work out its own European transition arrangement, outlining the rules that are to be applied when a company changes over to IAS for the first time. The problem is that according to the interpretation of the old IASC (SIC 8), a company is obliged to go a long way back into the past. More specifically, a company that has made a number of important acquisitions over the past 10 years must recalculate all of them back in time. That of course hardly makes sense. Which is why companies are putting so much pressure on the Commission to include a transition arrangement in its proposed regulation. That is an extremely hot potato. We are against this, because the Commission does not wish to develop a euro-IAS. We don't want to redo everything that has already been worked out in great detail at international level. This is also why we are resisting the adoption of a transition arrangement for Europe alone. We have asked the IASB to put this high on the agenda. So an attempt is now being made to solve the problem by devising an acceptable arrangement for the first application of IAS all over the world and therefore also in Europe.'

Are the Fourth and Seventh Directives in their amended form obstructing the adoption of fair value?

Professor Van Hulle: 'At the end of May 2001 the Council and the Parliament approved a Directive which amended the Fourth and Seventh Directives, thereby permitting the application of IAS 39 (fair value for certain financial instruments). This has eliminated the conflict between the annual reporting guidelines and IAS 39. But it does not imply permission to apply fair value to all financial instruments. An intensive exchange of ideas is still taking place in this connection. The Joint Working Group of Standard Setters has published a discussion paper and the Commission gave its reply to this in the autumn of 2001. This is to be distinguished from our amendment that took effect in May 2001.'

Shouldn't the 'true and fair view' be removed from the Fourth EC Directive?

Professor Van Hulle: 'Certainly not. The true and fair view is and remains the basic principle of financial accounting. What we mean by this is that financial statements must provide insight into the financial position of the company. The financial statements must present the actual situation within the company as truly and fairly as possible. If the standards do not lead to a true and fair view, then divergence from these standards is permitted, naturally provided this is extensively explained and justified in the notes.

'At the end of 2001 we presented a proposal aimed at modernising the accounting and reporting guidelines and removing other conflicts with IAS. We are doing everything in our power to provide practitioners with manageable rules. It is important for the Dutch accountancy profession to realise that the adoption of IAS means that Dutch companies whose current accounting methods are in step with US GAAP must prepare themselves for a transition to IAS. I'm afraid that anyone who believes that some last-minute transition regime will be conjured up for US GAAP compliant companies is in for a disappointment. We are firmly resolved – and the same applies to the Council of Ministers – to carry out the IAS transition in 2005. For accountants this means that, even though there are reportedly only 7,000 European listed companies, the number of companies to be confronted with this reform in Europe will actually exceed 100,000. So they need to start retraining and readjusting themselves to the IAS mind-set very quickly. That will probably be slightly easier for a Dutch accountant than for his European colleagues, because financial reporting in the Netherlands has traditionally tended to be more economics-driven than tax-driven. Even so, as things stand the IAS still constitute a hefty tome of more than 1,500 pages, so the accountants have a lot of reading to catch up on. Those who complete the task first can of course look forward to rich pickings. So the VERA certainly has its work cut out for it.'

Chapter 8

IAS and legislation
An interview with Jan Klaassen

Jan Klaassen

Professor Jan Klaassen RA (1943) is Dean of the Faculty of Economics and Business Administration at the Free University of Amsterdam. Prior to this he was a partner at KPMG, special- ising in technical matters, and a member of the Dutch delegation to the IASC. He is a consultant to the Ministry of Justice on legislative issues in the area of annual reporting. He is also a member of the Enterprise and Companies Court of the Amsterdam Court of Appeal. Professor Klaassen has lectured at VERA seminars since the organisation's establishment in 1974.

Legislation in the area of financial reporting has been developed for many years on the drawing boards of the ministries of Justice and Finance. The latter ministry has traditionally been involved with reporting in con- nection with supervision of financial markets. The Ministry of Finance is actively concerned with a variety of corporate governance questions and has taken the view that information on directors' remuneration should be included in company reports. Furthermore, the Traas Committee has been set up and has already made recommendations for the improvement of annual reporting by insurance companies. We asked Professor Jan Klaassen a number of questions on this subject.

How do you, as an official consultant to the Ministry of Justice, regard the attention that the ministries are paying to the quality of reporting?

Professor Klaassen: 'Annual reporting will have to be regulated intensively in order to positively influence the financial markets. Participants in the financial markets must have greater confidence in the quality of the information. Companies must be transparent in their reporting. By definition, the Ministry of Justice is involved in all draft legislation, including, therefore, the bill on directors' remuneration and the involvement of the general meeting of shareholders in directors' remuneration. This explains the ministry's interest in the subject. The Ministry of Justice also plays an important part in discussions in Brussels on future legislation concerning reporting. And the regulations from "Brussels" undeniably have considerable influence on the Netherlands. IAS is not "just" being decreed from Brussels, but being brought about in consultation with all member states of the EU.'

The Ministry of Justice has drafted a bill under which Dutch companies may apply international standards (IAS or US GAAP). Will companies actually do this? Or will it have virtually no effect?

Professor Klaassen: 'There is a report from VNO-NCW (the Dutch employers' association) which suggests that the commercial sector is very interested in this. I wonder if this really is the case. Up to now, it has struck me that Dutch industry only chooses those elements of foreign regulation which suit it. This is euphemistically called "arbitrage". This practice will, to a certain extent, be hindered by this bill, which takes the position that you must either adopt international rules entirely or not at all. And also make the decision clear and defend it.

'The requirement to clearly state which set of standards have been used also applies to RJ (Raad voor de Jaarverslaggeving – Council for Annual Reporting) guidelines. In short, there will be greater clarity. Until now, the Ministry of Justice worked on the basis that IAS, insofar as the Fourth and Seventh Directives do not conflict with them, were already permitted and that they would therefore offer relatively little new room for manoeuvre. The text of the legislation will explicitly state that IAS are permitted. But there is not yet much interest in this in the

Netherlands. Within three years IAS may be compulsory and perhaps companies will push ahead in the meantime.'

One of the changes which the Ministry of Justice has included in the bill is the compulsory capitalisation of goodwill with effect from 2002. The RJ wants this to take effect from 2001. This has become a point of debate. Will this cause confusion in practice?

Professor Klaassen: 'Up to now, there have always been RJ directives which have been entirely absent from the legislation. No-one lost any sleep over this. The problems clearly arise because some companies will see this as their chance to defer their goodwill reporting for a year. But those companies would not have been concerned with the RJ guidelines under the previous system, so why should we now worry because they fail to comply for the 2001 financial year? The real reason for the legislators setting 2002 as the first year is that legislation cannot be adopted retrospectively in 2002 which has a bearing on 2001's financial statements. This would give problems for some companies in their interim reporting. Legislation takes time, and in any case the RJ had not raised this issue with the Ministry of Justice.

'I consider the FASB's new point of view that goodwill should not be amortised as somewhat risky. The Netherlands and Europe should resist the view that goodwill should not be systematically amortised. I do not know whether this actually will happen at a European level, but current European guidelines require amortisation of all assets which do not have a clearly indefinite lifespan. No single asset on earth other than land has an indefinite life, and so goodwill should not either, although this is not to deny that the choice of a particular lifespan is arbitrary.

'The "do not amortise" rule is also arbitrary and no less risky. You will see that companies which get into difficulties will avoid writing down goodwill as much as possible. Indeed, capitalisation already leads to that risk. The more you have already amortised, the less you have to write off. The American rules implicitly assume a "fair-weather scenario", but in a "bad-weather scenario" these rules result in inadequate reporting due to write-downs which are made either too late or much too early. It is the case that many subjective elements (such as future expectations) play a role in valuation, and that major interests are at stake. For auditors there is also an enormous audit gauge in this area, in the sense that write-down of goodwill cannot be verified accurately.'

Soon only the IAS will be valid, and all quoted and unquoted financial institutions will have to comply with them. Will there still be a job for the legislator?

Professor Klaassen: 'We are now also doing without the guilder, but that is clearly not unacceptable, at least if we believe the statements by Mr. Zalm, the Dutch Minister of Finance, and Mr. Wellink, President of the Dutch Central Bank, that the Dutch do not have a strong bond with their national currency. We in the Netherlands cannot make a unilateral decision on introducing summer time. Reporting for quoted companies, world players that they are, is international. It would be wrong if a national legislator formulated regulations in this area, since then they may differ from those which apply elsewhere. Certainly with a single European financial market and a single European currency, and in a situation where banks lend and raise money internationally, where the mortgage market is globalising and stock markets no longer recognise borders, it is essential that international rules apply. And, after all, shareholders come from all over the world, don't they?'

But Dutch legislation will remain important for all unquoted companies in so far as they are non-financial institutions. Does this mean that the legal regulations will no longer have any significance for most quoted companies? Or will there be interesting and meaningful additions?

Professor Klaassen: 'That depends on how the supervision of quoted companies is organised. International rules require international supervision. If such a supervisory body was properly constituted, I do not think there would be any major problems. Of course, there are also matters which will still have to be organised differently at a national level, such as capital protection, but they can be properly organised separately from financial reporting. Certain legislation will therefore continue to apply, but it will no longer cover the provision of financial information. I don't have any problem with that.'

In the Netherlands, directors' remuneration has to be disclosed, soon for each individual director. Such regulations do not exist in the IAS. Should the legislator stick to its guns here?

Professor Klaassen: 'International co-ordination is increasing in the area of information beyond that contained in annual reports, which must be provided to financial markets. The Americans already have fairly extensive disclosure requirements concerning remuneration. If various initiatives on this should come about at a European level, then obviously we will line up with them. Sometimes, though, there are political reasons in a particular country for requiring information from companies. The legislator often sees no other way to do this than via annual reporting. In fact the annual report has developed inappropriately into an instrument for collecting information about the company in question. But if a country has no other means to come by the information, it is of course just a tool like any other.'

There has already been a debate on the question of whether information about a single managing director should be included in the annual report. Under the proposed legislation, it will be possible to identify the level of the director's remuneration. In the meantime, the complaints about excessive management remuneration have not gone away, certainly now that calls for wage restraint are becoming ever louder.

Professor Klaassen: 'Yes, directors and supervisory directors must be able to justify why they pay a senior manager EUR 900,000 per year. In practice they manage to do this by quoting market forces, thus starting a debate as to whether the remuneration really is in line with the market. A bill is being drafted which will give shareholders a say in directors' remuneration. The nature of the problem is that remuneration is partly a question of negotiation, and you cannot negotiate with a shareholders' meeting.'

Political opinion is that shareholders should have an input into directors' salaries.

Professor Klaassen: 'On the one hand there is a debate on transparency, and on the other hand the question of giving shareholders the right to have a say in remuneration. The discussion on transparency is over: it is clear that everyone must know how much is paid in salaries and who receives what. A completely different problem is that someone must decide, on behalf of the company, whether a particular salary demand will or will not be met. Investment decisions cannot, in general, be left to the shareholders. This is precisely the role of management, or perhaps the supervisory directors. The question of transparency is a different matter from the question of who decides salary levels.'

Can the legislator be satisfied with the observance of the law? Or are companies being a bit lax?

Professor Klaassen: 'There is a need for more supervision and so the government is considering giving the Authority for the Financial Markets (formerly the Securities Transactions Supervisory Board) the duty of supervising quoted companies' compliance with reporting guidelines (see the interview with Paul Koster, Chapter 11). We should not be thinking so much in terms of complying with every little detail, as answering the question of whether, in general, sufficient (that is, quantity) and adequate (that is, quality) information is provided *and* that the information is not misleading. The United Kingdom has a well-functioning supervisory body. The Netherlands is the only other country in the EU which has anything similar in the form of the Enterprise and Companies Court of the Court of Appeal which can hear cases on financial reporting. The financial interest is only significant enough to bring a case before the Enterprise and Companies Court in exceptional cases as this always costs money, time, energy and thought. Nevertheless, it is thought that attention is being paid to compliance with the rules, and that gives a certain feeling of confidence.'

This could, of course, also be achieved via the Disciplinary Committee; and less expensively as well.

Professor Klaassen: 'Perhaps less expensively, but this is not the right way. Because who is responsible for the financial reporting? It is the enterprise, not the auditor. An auditor can only be accused of having issued a report improperly. He or she will argue that in his or her opinion all the generally accepted rules have been complied with and that in the worst case certain rules were so unclear that there was good reason to believe that they had been satisfied. But, of course, you cannot drag in companies' books.

'It is said that disciplinary cases are brought to obtain a verdict which could be used in subsequent civil proceedings. But how does that save time? If the company goes bankrupt, you can bring a case before the Enterprise and Companies Court, although it will not get you very far. Then you can always try to get compensation from the auditor. In other words: the sanctions of the Enterprise and Companies Court are not financial. If you win and wish to apply sanctions against the auditor, you still have to go to the disciplinary committee. If you want to go after the company, you must go to the civil courts. You will only stand any chance of success before the disciplinary committee in fairly clear instances where the financial statements are defective. But not in "grey" situations. You must in fact first demonstrate that the financial statements were wrong, because otherwise you cannot prove that the auditor's report was improperly issued.'

As a consultant you are following the debate on legislation surrounding auditors. This includes the question of whether there should be 'certifying auditors'. Should the legislator clarify this if the profession does not?

Professor Klaassen: 'Certainly. I am a strong supporter of the introduction of the certifying auditor, particularly where it concerns the strict demands of experience and training imposed on that profession. The accounting consultants' (AAs) reaction is understandable. If the certifying auditor is introduced, it will soon be forbidden for the same accountant to both prepare and audit financial statements. A company will therefore have to hire one accountant to prepare the financial statements and another to audit them. Furthermore, these accountants will have to come from different firms.'

Is the training and education that the accountant can follow on financial reporting adequate?

Professor Klaassen: 'That differs between universities. I am in favour of making a distinction between accountants who work for large companies and those working for small and medium-sized enterprises. The new reporting technology is now very complicated, as large internationally-oriented companies in particular have experienced. People leaving university nowadays generally have some knowledge of this, but probably not enough. Current higher vocational education graduates have far too little, if any, knowledge of this subject. There is, therefore, a need for a lot of training and follow-up education. In a way this means a strengthening of the profession, particularly for accountants who go to work at the larger enterprises. In my opinion this applies to both controllers and auditors. I think that a divisional controller of a large company who has never worked at a central level is also relatively remote and knows relatively little. What this means is that it is a specialism needing considerable investment.'

And in which areas then exactly?

Professor Klaassen: 'In America, SEC-related companies may only be audited by specialised audit partners. These individuals receive considerable education and follow-up training, specifically directed towards auditing that kind of company. We are also moving in that direction. You can already see that separate departments exist in accountancy firms specialising in "assurance" for multinational clients. Furthermore the emphasis is placed upon training in IAS and all kinds of other subjects. We are moving towards a situation where auditors who have not followed such courses cannot and may not have responsibility for this kind of work. The auditor's training will become a basic training.

'Financial analysis will play a far greater role in training on reporting than is currently the case. This training places great emphasis on the skills for preparing a set of financial statements according to the rules. There is therefore considerable focus on techniques, but not on practice. More attention will be given to the question of what the various figures actually mean and what can and cannot be done with them. There are not many textbooks on financial analysis, and this deficiency needs to be made up. Accountants should also drastically improve their knowledge in this area and be more concerned about essential information missing from financial statements. In practice they only check compliance with the rules, and are often not very critical of significant notes.'

Should the auditor not be required to warn management much earlier if he or she notices that certain matters will not go down well with the stock market?

Professor Klaassen: 'The markets also want that. But it will be very difficult to give auditors more responsibilities if the rest of the world is doing nothing. The more alert the outside world becomes, the greater the incentive for the auditor also to be alert. Otherwise you will reach the situation I experienced about 15 years ago, when a client was refused a clean audit report unless he presented certain information in a certain way. We insisted. The newspaper *Het financieele Dagblad* later reported on this in a way which we felt made us appear foolish. That does not encourage the accountant to be strict the next time. *Het financieele Dagblad* is nowadays much better on this point. If the outside world is taking this kind of thing seriously, that will certainly have a positive result.'

Chapter 9

Shifting towards an Anglo-Saxon perspective on rules

An interview with Egbert Eeftink

Egbert Eeftink

Professor Egbert Eeftink (1962) began his career as an auditor in the Dutch audit practice of KPMG and, subsequently, in the UK. He is presently partner at KPMG and a member of the Auditors' Delegation in the Council for Annual Reporting. He is also a part-time Professor in Financial Reporting at the Free University Amsterdam, teaching at the post-academic controllers' programme. He was a member of the former IASC Steering Committee on Reporting Financial Performance and has been lecturing at VERA seminars for many years.

Quality, as a concept, occupies a central position in accountancy. Its exact meaning is open to interpretation, however. What is certain, though, is that quality remains the endeavour of every auditor from the very first day that he or she enters the field. It is the credo of a respectable professional organisation interested in 'upholding its image'. Yet, according to Professor Egbert Eeftink, the auditor is not the primary but rather the secondary party responsible for the quality of financial reporting.

What kind of influence does the auditor have on the quality of financial reporting?

Professor Eeftink: 'Although the company itself is responsible for the quality of financial reporting, the auditor can certainly leave his or her mark on it. The auditor can and will play a stimulating and guiding role. In environments subject to great change, clients particularly appreciate the advice and perspective of an auditor. On the other hand, a client aiming for a "six out of ten" cannot be forced to include information that would help it achieve a mark of eight for financial reporting. Mind you, not every company is competing for the Sijthoff Award[1]. Nevertheless, auditors still need to explain to their clients that some information is more illustrative than the information which the client already considers good enough. Controllers and managers may naturally prefer a different kind of financial reporting method than what the auditor has in mind. The auditor, for his or her part, need not avoid this discussion. But if there are valid reasons for the chosen reporting method and this falls within the applicable rules, their choice is acceptable. On the other hand, the auditor must take a strong stance and insist that the financial statements be altered should they contain material shortcomings. Where necessary, this will also be the time to start talking about the consequences for the auditor's report.'

How should the auditor interact with an audit committee or supervisory board?

Professor Eeftink: 'In such a discussion or in a written report, the auditor must present his or her findings and key discussion points – also in terms of financial reporting – to give the supervisory board a good impression of the state of affairs. That is also the place to bring up any key differences with management, which certainly does not mean that the supervisory board will not draw its own conclusions. Yet it is always good to view matters from different perspectives, and information which can give the supervisory board a sharper picture is important. The key issues in particular need to be raised in this setting. The auditor will also need to indicate whether he or she was able to be candid with management. If certain issues could not be discussed or could not be properly investigated, the supervisory body will certainly want – and expect – to be notified.

'Nor is financial reporting ever 100% objective. The same economic event can sometimes be reported on in different ways – each with their own valid arguments and reasons. As such, the audit opinion can never be completely 100% objective if it concerns something which in itself is not

---

[1] The Sijthoff Award is presented each year to two listed companies in recognition for the quality of their financial reporting.

100% objective. These are of course related. If an auditor renders an opinion on a report with figures deemed important by management, to a certain degree he or she also gives an opinion on management judgement.'

But if management makes a subjective choice – and every choice is subjective by definition – in respect of financial reporting issues, shouldn't the auditor take that into consideration if he or she finds their decision faulty and suggests their own variation as apparently better than that of the management? Should the auditor discuss this with the audit committee or the supervisory board?

Professor Eeftink: 'Of course. Just because financial reporting is primarily the responsibility of management does not imply that the auditor should indiscriminately approve of all subjective choices! Incidentally, I would also like to posit that not everything is subjective. There are now many more reporting rules and regulations than in the past, which considerably limit the freedom of which financial reporting method to elect. Where material financial reporting decisions arise, the auditor will need to make a careful analysis by taking into consideration those factors which influence a decision. Ideally, arriving at a decision means letting oneself be guided by certain arguments, certain considerations, a certain strategy or tactics – perhaps even certain emotions. These are all decision-making factors; and there are indubitably more factors that could be mentioned. By analysing this decision-making process and the related arguments and considerations – are they valid or not? – the auditor comes to a conclusion on the acceptability of the judgements made by management. If the auditor is unable to accept management's decision, he or she will have a serious problem to deal with, which will need to be discussed, first of all, with management itself. Should that fail to produce a melting of minds, a meeting with the audit committee will need to be convened without delay to establish common ground. Even if such an analysis ends up confirming management's judgement, an audit committee will often appreciate such an expert opinion. Although such a result is not as highly charged, it would still make sense to share it with the audit committee.'

In the past it appears that accounting firms issued unqualified auditor's reports to companies claiming to satisfy IAS but that were not fully up to scratch in that department. Don't we need more supervision in this area?

Professor Eeftink: 'We certainly do. Yet here we can discern a cultural difference between the United States and Europe in general and the Netherlands in particular. Over the past decades, we in the Netherlands have started taking quite a lax attitude towards rules and regulations. We are positively keen on negotiation and tolerance, giving and taking: in short, what has come to be known as the famous "polder model". In practice, this means that the rules may be seen as recommendations or guidelines rather than dos and don'ts. Take, for instance, cycling through red, which has become the norm in the large cities. We've grown accustomed to thinking that most rules can somehow be bent, certainly if these have no legal status such as the Guidelines of the Council for Annual Reporting. And no rule has to be complied with for the whole 100% as long as one sticks to the "main provisions".

'This culture has had a huge impact on financial reporting practices in the Netherlands. Compared to the rules in the United States, we pride ourselves on our financial reporting system, which is largely based on substance and principles and not on form and detailed rules. I, too, am an advocate of reporting on the basis of substance and principles. Yet substance is no reason to ignore the rules if you do not like them. The flexibility and substance, which has always served as our guiding light in the interpretation and application of financial reporting rules, is not an international institution. This is something that we really must get used to. So if we are soon to adopt international standards, we will truly need to mend our ways as to their application before an international enforcement body gives us a good chastising. Compliance is compliance.

'I do not find it a particularly strong basis for companies to claim that they conform to IAS to a "significant" or "reasonable" degree. After all, people who read their financial statements want to know whether or not the accounting principles are in conformity with IAS. That is the aim – and the reference point. And in certain cases that will mean a shift from our culture and Dutch views to an Anglo-Saxon perspective on rules – yet hopefully without bidding farewell to the positive Dutch elements.'

What does this mean for accountancy as a profession?

Professor Eeftink: 'There will be less room for forming an individual professional opinion. The job of the auditor will shift more towards "auditing according to a checklist" and away from interpreting general principles and rules according to the specific situation. On the one hand, I find that an erosion for the profession and a great pity. At the same time, though, we naturally need a guarantee for compliance with the more detailed international rules on financial reporting. The "quality of financial reporting" concept will take on a new meaning. This also implies a new exchange of ideas between auditors and company management about proper reporting. Clients will find it aggravating to have to comply with rules imposed by an organisation serving other interests than their own. They will attempt to scrape by with the bare minimum of compliance and will not be very willing to make any extra efforts.'

Will this change the audit process, since financial reporting will follow more of a cook-book approach?

Professor Eeftink: 'Of course, especially the last part of the audit, which focuses on presentation and disclosure in the financial statements, will change. If substantially more data require explaining in the reporting process, they will also need to be included in the audit process. Some companies will also have to modify their internal systems to capture the data required by external parties so that they can report on them. Financial instruments, in particular, presently fall into this category. Radical system modifications have proven necessary for recording the right financial instruments in the right section in order to get to the bottom of their fair value.'

How do you feel about the application of fair value?

Professor Eeftink: 'The established financial reporting model shows a strong shift towards fair value. In a number of cases, the use of fair value can lead to more relevant information. In that respect, I am certainly in favour of it. This is the most obvious with financial instruments, where accounting standards move towards full valuation at fair value. Full fair value still holds some challenging points of theory for discussion, which we shall leave aside for now. Yet the importance of fair value is also on the rise for the valuation of plant and equipment, intangible assets and goodwill – not to mention for the valuation of debt and provisions. In the past, one purchased a machine and charged depreciation in 20 years. Each year, a flat 5% of the acquisition price of the machine was recorded in the profit and loss account as a pure historical cost based expense. Nowadays, one must determine in the interim whether the asset is subject to impairment, and 'valuation' has become a part of the historical cost system. The impairment test is made in terms of 'realisable value'. In essence, this is a form of fair value, which is usually determined by the discounted cash flow method. Recently, there has been tremendous attention to the new US standard on goodwill (SFAS 142), which stipulates that impairment of goodwill, too, must be determined on the basis of fair value.'

The application of fair value primarily concerns the valuation of assets and liabilities in the balance sheet. What does fair value mean for the profit and loss account?

Professor Eeftink: 'There is still a lot of debate about whether to include all the changes in fair value of assets and liabilities in not just the balance sheet, but also in the profit and loss account. The key question concerns its timing: at the point of a change in value or upon realisation. The future form and content of the profit and loss account – or the performance statement – remains to be seen. The IASB are still discussing this matter, particularly in response to the importance of giving fair value information a true meaning in such a performance statement.

'As concerns content, the IASB will most likely propose including all changes in the fair value of assets and liabilities in such a performance statement. That goes beyond the traditional profit and loss account as known today and will lead to more bottom-line volatility. Such a proposal will not be popular with many companies in the light of this increased volatility.

The format of such a statement is still the subject of fundamental debate. I do, however, expect to see a subdivision into operating result and result from financing activities. I dare not predict how it will progress after that. Given the trend for measuring assets and liabilities at fair value, we are now in a situation in which some items might be shown at historical cost and others at fair value – all in the same balance sheet. Both accounting systems send out signals in a performance statement with different economic meanings. It would therefore make sense to me that fair value changes and historical cost effects are somehow separately visible in such a statement. It will take quite some doing to make these kinds of subdivisions workable in practice.'

So the advance of fair value is a positive development in financial reporting?

Professor Eeftink: 'Yes, in theory. It is, however, a pity that the ultimate consequence – a full fair value reporting model – has not been developed yet. In the further rollout of fair value applications, I believe that this is greatly missed. Although it troubles me, standard-setters such as the IASB do not seem to be particularly concerned about this lack of conceptual underpinning. In addition, they often assume the presence of a sufficiently mature market where fair values of financial instruments and some other assets are readily available. Reality is sometimes different. That goes for some financial instruments and even more so for non-financial assets for which no mature, liquid market exists. In such situations, valuation models or professional appraisals are used to determine fair value. Projections and assumptions used to forecast cash flows will then play a huge role. In the absence of a mature market, fair value is often highly sensitive to these assumptions. The fair value of certain items therefore runs the risk of being rather inaccurate, since it depends on the degree to which the forecasts are adjusted in time. In this respect, I expect that complex assets – such as business complexes and goodwill – will not be written down to a lower fair value until past prognoses no longer prove feasible. And I am afraid that this will often be recognised too late. To my mind, standard-setters such as the IASB are not paying enough attention to these disadvantages of fair value.

'In short, although fair value information will produce more relevant information in a number of cases, it does have its disadvantages. It is frequently less objective, less accurate and, accordingly, more difficult for the auditor to audit than information based on historical cost. The fair value discussion once again shows that the quality of financial reporting is a complex concept – one subject to opposing forces. When applying fair value, one should weigh the potentially greater relevance of information against the possibly greater reliability risk that arises in the face of diminished objectivity and accuracy.'

How should auditors approach fair value in this light?

Professor Eeftink: 'It will certainly not make life any easier for auditors. They often experience difficulty in testing the accuracy or reasonableness of prognoses and assumptions in a valuation model. This will make valuation at fair value even more difficult to audit; the only option for the auditor is to rely on the expectations of management. Auditors will thus often find themselves testing the reasonableness of these expectations, which implies having an understanding of the company's business plans. Small fluctuations in the discount rate can also have a large impact on the outcome of such an impairment test: how does one know whether the right discount rate was used? I imagine that in such situations the company – or perhaps the auditor – will increasingly rely on valuation experts to help in assessing such aspects. I have already seen the first signs of this in practice, where a growing number of valuation experts have begun delving into the fair value accounting rules, such as in the area of impairment of goodwill.'

The auditor is also someone who exercises supervision. Nevertheless, it has been suggested that a body such as the SEC should provide extra supervision – perhaps on auditors as well. Is such a regulatory body now a threat, and do we really need it? Wouldn't it be more effective to trust the auditor?

Professor Eeftink: 'I believe that the accountancy profession should actually be pleased with outside supervision. This will improve the financial reporting infrastructure and place the auditor on a sounder footing. It also means supervision on the compliance with financial reporting rules by companies, which will only make the position of the auditor more transparent. That is an improvement. And I do not see this as a vote of no confidence against the auditor.

'The auditor includes in his or her audit various factors which are unique to the company under review. He or she goes into depth with the audit process and considers whether or not certain changes in the company's individual circumstances necessitate a change in reporting. To my mind, the regulators will take a different approach. Incidentally, I cannot imagine that the regulators would repeat the work conducted by the auditor. That would be quite inefficient. Instead, I would expect a regulator to exercise more general supervision on the scope of financial reporting and on compliance with reporting standards.

'Nor do I believe that a regulator will aim to repeat the work conducted by the auditor or that it will review the substance of business-specific risks to determine whether they have been properly disclosed in the financial reports. I hope and expect that their oversight will be more supplemental, with the focus on compliance with the reporting standards in general, and with an emphasis on bolstering the reporting infrastructure. This will also strengthen the position of the auditor.'

Will auditors therefore need to be more vigilant when auditing for compliance?

Professor Eeftink: 'That will come about on its own accord, at least if a regulator makes it clear that it does not see compliance with the rules according to the polder model or tolerance concept. A regulator may have more say than an auditor, who actually has but one instrument: the auditor's report. That is an "all or nothing" instrument to be used only if absolutely necessary, otherwise it will lose its power and make the auditor look ridiculous. A regulator, on the other hand, can rectify things much more quickly and put the company on the spot, fine it or apply another sanction. Just look at the SEC. Companies don't mess around with them. And that gives the auditor an extra instrument, for he or she can warn the company about the regulator. In the Netherlands, some companies may now say, "I'm not going to comply with this rule and if you think you can make me, just let me see you try." And one must really go quite far before being dragged before the Enterprise and Companies Court of the Amsterdam Court of Appeal. The general interest in complying with the reporting standards is rather lax at present. Only the financial press and the world of finance are somewhat alert.'

Chapter 10

Uniform rules are important, but they must not block the view

An interview with Jean den Hoed

Jean den Hoed

Jean den Hoed RA (1937) worked as director of finance, corporate controller and finally Chief Financial Officer (CFO) at Akzo-Nobel. After his retirement in 1998 he accepted a position on the supervisory boards of Vendex/KBB, ASMI and Connexxion. He is a member of the Council for Annual Reporting, deputy justice in the Enterprise and Companies Court and Chairman of the Supervisory Council at St. Jansdal Hospital in Harderwijk.

One of the most important conditions for properly administering a country is a common language. The number of inhabitants who speak their own language at home or in small circles is irrelevant as long as they are capable of communicating on a broader level with the rest of the country in the common tongue. It is exactly the same with regulations that have been created to bridge gaps (cultural or otherwise). Uniform rules that are written in clear language – one which can be interpreted in one way only – are essential to international comings and goings. And that applies to annual reports as well according to Jean den Hoed, former auditor, ex financial director and presently supervisory director at several companies, who has recently been intensively engaged in the establishment of the EFRAG (see the interview with Professor Van Helleman in Chapter 5).

'The harmonisation of financial reporting is a key step forward – although I must add straightaway that companies will still never tell the whole story,' according to Den Hoed. 'If IAS are in place in 2005, that will significantly improve the quality of financial reporting. It is crucial to all parties involved that we should adopt one set of financial reporting regulations in Europe. Fortunately, the European Council for Annual Reporting does not indiscriminately accept whatever is on offer. Its members are keen to participate proactively in the IASB via EFRAG's technical committee. Those required to apply the rules must be properly trained. Europe is in need of a good supervisory authority that knows what it is doing. For the time being, the present chairman of the Authority for the Financial Markets will also be the one to head the similar co-operative bodies in the EU member states.

'Introducing a rule is a doddle; enforcing it is another story. Everyone is equally convinced of the necessity of applying IAS properly in every country. As soon as deviations are detected, people in the United States, in particular, will apply a brake. The Americans will only accept IAS in their own country if the standards are upheld with the same vigilance elsewhere in the world. That will be the big challenge.'

The Americans are sceptical?

Den Hoed: 'Quite so. I recently read that the SEC was in consultation with the US Senate, which had been rather "beleaguered" or "worked on" by the FASB. And "therefore", scores of senators – not exactly experts in this field – voiced their doubts. They fear that Europe will not be capable of organising itself by 2005 to make IAS mandatory. They are, of course, entitled to their opinion. But in the meantime, we need to leave no stone unturned in order to create a counterbalance. EFRAG needs to advise the European Commission to take those steps necessary for creating a climate in which IAS will be declared applicable.

'It is quite plain to everyone that, for the sake of the business community, we need to create transparency, provide clear information and see to the introduction of a single accounting system. Only then can one draw comparisons and take decisions on the strength of the same information. This has always been one of the conditions for the perfect equity market, in which everyone can access the same information at the same time. It is also important in terms of competition.

'Yet we still have a long way to go. The French understanding of "net income" is different from the Dutch concept of the term. The difference is so great that readers of financial information find it difficult to determine how one arrived at such a figure. So in this regard, it would be good for us to lump this together in a European context. The ultimate objective is to keep the SEC from causing trouble for European companies that apply IAS and are interested in a US stock exchange listing.

'We have now reached a point in our legislation here that Dutch companies may apply IAS together with the FASB rules up to 2005. Their last chance ends in 2005. But it would be disastrous if IAS were not yet accepted by the SEC for foreign companies seeking a listing in the US, while we in Europe place much less stringent requirements on US companies knocking on our stock exchange's door.'

What form should this supervision take?

Den Hoed: 'At any rate, it should not take the shape of a detailed analysis of every set of financial statements or publication ever released. That would take too much time and money and would probably not amount to much. It would be more effective to make a good review of certain companies on a random basis. The SEC takes a look at certain companies once every five years. These are gone over with a fine-tooth comb. Allow me to add in this respect that the SEC has 3,000 experts in its employ for this purpose. And that naturally carries a price tag.

'I believe that we do need to keep things in perspective. Supervision must, at any rate, take centre stage and be arranged at European level. If each country was allowed to exercise its own supervision, it would not be long before we had a whole range of different approaches, interpretations and such on our hands. In that case, there would be a good chance of the Americans turning completely away from IAS. So, I am in favour of supervision, as long as it does not turn into a real audit.'

Most of the doubts have been voiced by controllers: the rules must not be allowed to block the view. Is this a valid concern?

Den Hoed: 'It most certainly is! Rules and regulations are great, but one must not forget that the rules serve day-to-day practice and not vice versa. The point is, after all, the true and fair view that the financial reports must afford controllers and management. They need to be given the right tools for making a proper report on operations. The purpose of the regulations is to promote transparency and not to cloud things up with all manner of complicated procedures. Rather, the aim of management and the controllers is to make it clear to the public what the company wants, how it has performed and how the figures can be explained from a policy perspective. The rules are a means to an end.

'In the Netherlands, we have always said that content is more important than form. So content comes before the rules. And this has led to room for interpretation. Take for instance the creation of provisions – this is left completely up to management. It is now quite clearly stated that management can only include a provision if it can clearly demonstrate that there is a real obligation. Another area where we took a somewhat different approach than in other countries was in the treatment of goodwill. Yet not every change is an improvement. For instance, I find that which the Americans have been pushing via the FASB – the capitalisation of goodwill, no amortisation, impairment test – a definite step backwards. I prefer the system of capitalisation and systematic amortisation based on a timeline set by management. In the unlikely event that problems should arise which force us to take a different decision – but that also applies to all assets in the balance sheet – an impairment test will need to be performed. So in that respect, I am not at all pleased with what the FASB has produced. In the aim towards harmonisation, the political influence of the United States is apparently more important than the creation of workable financial reporting rules.'

Controllers and managers are having their hands tied?

Den Hoed: 'Indeed. It therefore depends on the relevant management and thus also on the controller as to whether they will succeed in giving their own view on the state of affairs. The role of the management report, the explanation of the figures, will be more important than the figures themselves. After all, management will have to base its decisions – and thus company policy – on the figures. The point is not only how others will view the figures and which conclusions they will draw from the comparisons (which will be easier to make thanks to IAS) but also – and above all – how management itself interprets the figures. And that brings me back to what I said earlier: the company will never tell the whole story – even if it were only to keep the competition from finding out too much.

'Incidentally, I am not pleading for the institution of specific guidelines to force management to be completely open about business. As they say, people who try to find out too much are often taken aback by what they discover. And panicky and hasty decisions on the basis of the wrong conclusions would be no help to anyone. Here, the old laws of prudence must prevail. Financial reporting needs to include the main items, but management needs to be given space to present its own interpretation of the results. Here I see a great challenge for the controller in particular.'

Will earnings management soon become virtually impossible? And is that good or bad?

Den Hoed: 'The term "earnings management" can be construed in various ways. It is still a topic of discussion. I am thinking of the Traas Committee and the role of the insurance companies. Growth in earnings can only be shown gradually as earnings are actually generated. With earnings management, one uses rules to show a figure that has little to do with profit. I do not advocate it, because it is misleading. And whether IAS will truly succeed in banishing earnings management – only time will tell.'

Is it commendable that fair value accounting is gaining ground rapidly?

Den Hoed: 'It has its advantages and disadvantages. Fair value represents a moment in time. Some people, even professors, believe that the balance sheet should be structured such that the value of the assets and liabilities fits in seamlessly with the stock market price. That would be the true value of the company – they say. So allow me to draw your attention to the recent fluctuations. The AEX fell from 720 to 400. That was largely the result of panicky decisions and the skyrocketing share prices from the year before. And those were primarily driven by ordinary greed, while the decisions to sell everything all of a sudden were dominated by fear. In my view, neither fear nor greed is a good counsellor or reliable indicator.

'It would go too far for my liking to claim that a company such as KPN has suddenly became worth exponentially less than a few months ago. As if all of the expertise and experience that the company has amassed is no longer worth a thing. I find fair value a capricious indicator, one that means little for the long term. Companies cannot be managed on that basis. I am, however, in favour of a statement based on historical cost. Fair value could then be given as a memorandum item – as nothing more than secondary information. If every company were to report solely on the basis of fair value, the people reading their financial reports would no longer see what is really at play in the company. Nor would they see the trends, since there would be too many factors playing a role that have nothing to do with the company's operations.'

If companies show volatile profit figures, isn't that bad for business in general? Or should the analysts just get used to it?

Den Hoed: 'That is the disadvantage of fair value. It produces a volatility that bears no direct relation to the real operations of the company. That makes people nervous. If a company has investments, these will have dropped 60% in value during the past months. But maybe they will increase again by 50% in a year. And that indeed produces a fluctuation in profits, which will certainly have an impact on the company's relationship with its stakeholders. One could naturally say that everything can be explained, but if we want to introduce a system that requires constant explanation, what is the point? And with fair value, one constantly speaks of unrealised profits that no-one really wants to realise either. But that just happens to be the value.'

You have had legion positions: director of finance at Akzo-Nobel, supervisory director, member of the Council for Annual Reporting, involvement with EFRAG. How do you, depending on your past or present positions, see financial reporting?

Den Hoed: 'That depends indeed on one's capacity at the moment that one is faced with financial reporting. People active in business as controllers or financial experts often experience the regulations as a hindrance. After all, it is not always opportune to report on certain things. No matter how realistic or desirable, information is not always useful. It is understandable that certain executives believe that it would be better to wait a bit before disclosing certain information to the public.

'In a supervisory position, one sees things differently. Then it is nice to have the same rules everywhere. On the other hand, one also has responsibilities in this capacity as well, such as convincing management that the big picture is greater than the sum of the rules. The people who make the rules, that is, the members of a body such as the Council for Annual Reporting, might see things differently depending on how closely they are involved in business. And indeed, I have seen it all. That makes me somewhat less black and white in my judgement and more cautious with rendering an opinion. For the stakes are much higher and extend much further than most people would suspect. But as long as that is borne in mind, one can form a relatively well-accounted-for judgement. And auditors know everything there is to know about taking account of things, isn't that right?'

Part III

Supervision and compliance

Chapter 11

Towards a new supervisory landscape
An interview with Paul M. Koster

Paul M. Koster

Paul Koster RA (1962) was head of the Audit Bureau of the Amsterdam Stock Exchange, merger and business specialist at the former Coopers & Lybrand (now PricewaterhouseCoopers) and Chief Auditor at Philips, among other things. Since 1 March 2001, he has been a member of the board of the Authority for the Financial Markets (previously Securities Transactions Supervisory Board).

'Due to Enron, financial reporting has come to the top of the political agenda. Enron is in fact the business community's 11 September.' These are the words of Paul Koster, member of the board of the Netherlands Authority for the Financial Markets (previously Securities Transactions Supervisory Board), a supervisory body that first saw the light of day in 1989 and which has developed rapidly during the past few years, partly on account of the 1995 Securities Transactions Supervision Act.

What are the statutory objectives of the Authority for the Financial Markets in the Netherlands?

Koster: 'The statutory objectives of the Authority for the Financial Markets are to strive for the efficient functioning of the stock markets and the protection of the investors. The Authority supervises the proper implementation and application of the rules and regulations to ensure fair market operations. This is also important in an international context. Without an active local supervisor, a local or regional market is unable to collaborate with the major parties. The Authority for the Financial Markets is charged with the supervision of the Dutch capital market. We have been commissioned to do this, as an independent governing body, by the former Dutch Minister of Finance.'

The government wants to structure the financial supervision in the Netherlands. Will the Authority for the Financial Markets exercise supervision over financial reporting?

Koster: 'We have been given many tasks and I think that we have been reasonably successful in tackling them up until now. If the government wishes us to supervise financial reporting as well, then we will take up the challenge. It is quite understandable for the Authority to be considered for this role because we are closely involved with listed companies and IAS relates to them in particular.

'How far the supervision of the financial reporting should go is quite a different question. This should be seen in an international perspective. We will have to wait and see if and when the SEC will approve IAS. A lot of work is being done in this field with, among others, IOSCO. In 2000, the SEC in principle committed itself to accept IAS for foreign companies, but the implementation of this resolution is a long time coming. When this happens, however, there will be little to stop the IAS from being adopted worldwide. I want the responsibility of the Authority for the Financial Markets to emulate that of the SEC. That supervisory authority interprets its responsibility in such a way that the space created within the rules – and this is certainly present in the IAS, as it is in our current financial reporting rules – is filled when there is a lack of clarity. Its role is also to ensure that the limits of acceptability are not transgressed in order to prevent stakeholders from receiving misleading or too little information.

'It is vitally important that the Netherlands continues to follow international developments because it is essential that Europe avoids creating 15 different national interpretations of IAS. The Authority for the Financial Markets is also participating in this field and is represented in various international networks, such as IOSCO, but also CESR (Committee of European Securities Regulators – the umbrella organisation of European stock exchange supervisors) and, of course, within the context of Euronext. Only then can Dutch financial reporting secure international confidence. IAS is coming and it is important to quickly prepare ourselves for this. The Authority for the Financial Markets can assist companies in this respect.'

How far is the decision-making with respect to the introduction of IAS in Europe?

Koster: 'It has almost been completed. We expect the compulsory introduction of IAS for listed companies in 2005. Until 2007, there will still be exemptions for companies that are listed on a non-European exchange and for companies that only issue bonds, but these will also report on the basis of IAS after 2007. Euronext will already make IAS compulsory for two segments, NextPrime and NextEconomy, with effect from 2004. This means that the comparable figures for the year 2003 will already have to be calculated on the basis of IAS, and that the initial capital for 2003 will also have to be recalculated. In fact, companies must now already start with the preparations for IAS. People underestimate the effects of the introduction of IAS. Many companies will have to rigorously reorganise their accounts.'

Will the supervision of financial reporting have a lot of depth? Is this, for example, based on company publications or on the basis of random sampling?

Koster: 'There are a number of lines of approach. First of all, you have the annual report that you must pick up on as a supervisory body. This in any case involves an examination. If the supervision comes to lie with the Authority for the Financial Markets, then we consider testing on the basis of risk analysis and thematic examinations. These thematic examinations are determined on the basis of global trends and the agenda of the IASB. We would then want to establish a forum within the Authority for the Financial Markets in which all parties are represented – thus the business community, the accountants' world, the university world, investment analysts and others. We want a sounding board and want to hear which subjects are of interest to the various parties. We will deal with a few of these in the forum. Subjects include, for example, goodwill, consolidation and stock options, or the international trend of publishing all kinds of profit figures, such as EBITDA, which do not stem from our reporting rules. Such thematic examinations may lead to additional guidelines, as long as they are in keeping with IAS. As a result, the business community is provided with instruments to improve their financial reporting. Naturally, we will also respond to signals that we receive via the media, for example, or other channels.'

How do you find enough qualified people to exercise the supervision?

Koster: 'Up until now, we've had no problem attracting motivated and expert people. We also offer people an excellent opportunity to learn all the ropes in this sector. That's what you also see at the SEC. People work there for a number of years to gain valuable experience before they return to the business sector to work for an accountancy firm. They have worked in the "kitchen" and really know what's going on.'

Is it a good idea to already structure supervisory tasks in the Netherlands, while everything is still developing in the European context?

Koster: 'It is not yet clear what the supervision will look like in a European context. The Netherlands appears to be running ahead of developments in this respect, but there is a specific policy behind this. If there must be a form of supervision in the future, it is unwise not to have developed any ideas or moves for this. I believe this to be an entirely defensible point of view. It will still take some time before IAS is mandatory. The supervision of financial reporting is in preparation, however. In the securities industry, we have seen that a particular form of supervision does not take shape from one day to the next. It takes quite some time.

'We have various co-ordinating bodies of supervisors in which the discussion takes place. And the Euronext supervisory authorities are increasingly working together. Naturally, we want to pursue unequivocal policy within Europe. However, from a political point of view, the function of national supervisor is still maintained, this being necessary to guarantee decisiveness. Member states will not be willing to rapidly abandon their powers or sovereignty, but you can still see a move towards harmonisation in supervision. These developments are still continuing and it is therefore better to have sufficient expertise available.'

In co-operation with the Dutch Ministries of Economic Affairs and Justice, the Ministry of Finance has produced a policy document on supervision that interested parties could respond to. The Council for Annual Reporting, the Confederation of Netherlands Industry and Employers and Royal NIVRA have responded to this. Is there wide support for the notion of an umbrella supervisory body?

Koster: 'Yes. And the Authority for the Financial Markets is considered to be suitable in this respect. There is still some discussion about the supervision of accountants themselves. This is a sensitive issue. The reason is that you must take care that the supervisor not only plays a strong role in the financial reporting field, but also in the area of supervision of accountants. This supervision must be designed in such a way that conflicts of interest do not arise. The Dutch Second Chamber recently adopted a motion explicitly requesting that the supervision of accountants be lodged with an existing supervisor. The Authority for the Financial Markets was one of the bodies considered suitable. The possibilities for this are now being examined. It is clear that there is synergy between the supervision of financial reporting and the supervision of accountants.

'We have indicated that an important aspect is the possibility of imposing a particular sanction if an accountant has reprehensibly given a wrong opinion. In our opinion, he or she should not be permitted to sign financial statements for a period of time. Others consider that this task should be reserved for a "review panel". Whatever the case, it should be possible to call to account anyone with such a responsible task, if it appears that they are seriously in default.'

The Dutch Second Chamber has now decided to divide the financial supervision into prudential supervision and conduct supervision. What does this entail exactly?

Koster: 'The new supervisory structure ensues from the investigations of the Minister of Finance in response to national and international developments on the financial markets. In the case of both institutions and products there is considerable overlap between saving, investment and insurance. This development is at odds with the sectoral classification of supervision that existed in the past, which has now been abandoned.

'A functional model has now been chosen without any distinction being made between supervision by sector (securities, insurance or banks). Instead, the basis is functional objective: supervision of conduct and prudential supervision. Conduct supervision focuses on the conduct of parties on the financial markets and prudential supervision on the business and economic aspects. This functional system has already existed for some time in Australia. It is based on observations of and discussions with the relevant authorities. It appears that supervisory bodies and financial institutions are, in practice, easily able to get to grips with the demarcation between prudential supervision and the supervision of conduct. No complaints have been received about overlap or unclear tasks.

'Now this system has been introduced in the Netherlands, the prudential supervision is in the hands of the Pension and Insurance Supervisory Board and the Dutch central bank. The Authority for the Financial Markets is responsible for the supervision of conduct. This means that there has been a reorganisation of tasks. The supervision by virtue of the Act on the Supervision of Investment Institutions has, for example, shifted from the Dutch central bank to the Authority for the Financial Markets. When the supervision of financial reporting is covered by the Authority for the Financial Markets, there will, of course, be co-operation where the tasks of the financial supervisory bodies meet.'

The 'Financial Integrity' memorandum dating from 1997 was a consequence of the three-year Stock Exchange insider trading scandal (known as 'Operation Clickfonds'). Do such memoranda give an extra impulse to the supervision of financial institutions?

Koster: 'Certainly, when I think of all the major issues that have been dealt with since then. Apart from the results of Operation Clickfonds, it became clear that supervision is indispensable and certainly not gratuitous. This has also been recognised by politicians. The attacks on 11 September 2001 have also once again emphasised the importance of proper supervision of the financial markets and the combating of financial criminality, such as fraud and money laundering. Supervision must have substance and thus co-operation as well; the exchange of information with international supervisory bodies is therefore vitally important.

'I would like to mention here that you must watch out that you do not supervise everything and you must not "over-regulate" trade in a free market. At the end of the day, we must be able to continue competing. I keep hammering away on this point: the competitive game must be played. The Authority for the Financial Markets must not be a referee that takes the pace out of the game by blowing the whistle every time. It must remain functional, however.'

What do you think about the quality of the content of annual reports during the past few years?

Koster: 'Clear improvements can be seen on a number of points. I think that the report of the executive board must become part of the financial statements. At the moment, the accountant – I exaggerate a little here – only has to read them through and search for contradictions. I believe that they should do more. If the supervision of financial reporting becomes the responsibility of the Authority for the Financial Markets, I certainly see a role reserved for us there as well. Secondly, I believe that the cash flow statement must be compulsory for all companies, to include not only large, but also small and medium-sized companies. I would say here that the cash flow statement should be given more of a prospective character, because information is far too often withheld from investors, while they are jointly responsible for financing. The bank as financier does, however, receive the information that is withheld from shareholders. I do understand that sensitive information cannot be made public, but this must be "hedged". Recently, we have all too often seen that companies which suddenly appear to be in trouble have never issued warning signals. Their annual reports appeared to be rather more like doctored reports from disaster zones. Doomsday scenarios are excluded, while it does seem that they could certainly become reality.

'I therefore believe it would be a good thing if the accountants – and here I point to the major shortcoming in the annual report – could produce an opinion about cash flows. They will have to evaluate and elaborate upon particular scenarios so that we are not surprised by continuity problems. As things are at present, accountants offer too little added value for the user of financial statements. The legislator must come to their assistance here by compelling executive boards to also make connections with the cash flow statement. A clear indication must be given of the commitments, the redemption schedules for example. I am therefore in favour of a broadening of the accountant's professional outlook.'

Will the discussion about 'comprehensive income' intensify?

Koster: 'Even though the results in the Netherlands are not so fantastic, "comprehensive income" does give a better idea of a company's actual performance. I am therefore all in favour of this. It is virtually impossible to manipulate cash flows. Income is easily a target for creative accounting, but "comprehensive income" does in any case provide greater clarity.'

Should profit warnings be issued at the right moment, however? And should there be guidelines in this direction?

Koster: 'The Herkströter Committee is currently studying the reports to the stock exchanges. It is unpleasant if a company receives a reprimand, but it is not really as bad as all that. It is important that the company management is aware that shareholders depend upon information. This information concerns the probability, the expectations with respect to profit, turnover, income and the like. And then as seen from the point of view of the company's management. In our opinion, investors should receive reliable information on the basis of which they can make an economic decision so that they can understand exactly what the management is expecting. Incidentally, I expect that the Securities Transactions Supervision Act will be amended on this point so that the Authority for the Financial Markets will also have an additional task. I think that a profit warning is a typical example of postponing the misery and then hoping that everything will turn out better than expected. Accountants should have the possibility of forcing companies to make statements about realistic expectations. That's why the supervision of annual reporting is so important, since the accountant also needs support from the supervisory body.

'We should not underestimate the pressure that is sometimes put on accountants to present the annual figures in a particular manner. The accountant is then fairly powerless, because everything is permissible as long as the rules say nothing or do not forbid anything. But if you have a supervisor in the future who is very diligent, the situation changes. The accountant can then turn to the supervisor. The accountant is not in a very enviable position: on the one hand, he or she must not lose sight of the client's interests, but on the other hand, the public wants the accountant to be rigorous and if necessary provide unpleasant information or opinions that are contrary to the company's interests. This may imply enormous tension and the accountant can then certainly use some help from a supervisor with authority.'

To what extent is the Authority for the Financial Markets faced with matters in which insider trading leads to fraud?

Koster: 'Such matters receive a lot of attention, but if you look at what the Authority for the Financial Markets does, they only represent a very small element of the work. There are many, more significant, aspects that are much more important for the investor than inside knowledge. I don't want to trivialise matters, but in our opinion it is certainly not as important as the media sometimes makes out. It is a sensational subject. If you look at the heart of where our supervision lies, thus the work that in practice requires the most manpower and man-hours, then the focus is on the audits of the institutions that are under our supervision. We have recently developed a new audit strategy that forms the basis for the exercise of our supervision. This is expressly based on the responsibility assumed by the institution itself.

'We have a model in which we place the responsibility for an evaluation of the internal systems with the management of the institution, the bank or the broker. Based on this analysis of their contribution – and this is the contribution to the objective of the legislation – we have developed a questionnaire together with the market participants. The questionnaire is presented to the companies and we then select subjects that the management itself indicate as problematic.

'We also hold discussions with the management based on the plans for the future and the influence that these are expected to have. In this way we try to identify risk areas. If a company wishes to grow by 15%, which measures will it take? How will it recruit personnel? What kind of training does it provide? Has it got its administrative organisation sorted out? Has it taken any measures in the IT field? This audit strategy should lead to a situation whereby we focus far more on the problem areas, thus on risk management. And that is a totally different facet of supervision.'

Chapter 12

The Enterprise and Companies Court as supervisory body
An interview with J. (Huub) H. M. Willems

J. (Huub) H. M. Willems

Huub Willems (1944) has been attached to the District Court of Amsterdam as a judge for more than twenty years, the past few years as Vice-President and Chairman of the Enterprise and Companies Court. In addition, he is Chairman of the Disciplinary Council for Registeraccountants.

Even though a judge will perhaps never endorse such an idea, in a sense he or she is a supervisor. After all, the judge, as an independent link in the enforcement chain, does supervise the judicial process and also sees to it that justice prevails. This also applies to very worldly and material matters, such as company law for example. The Enterprise and Companies Court, the companies' division court of appeal, was established for this purpose. The chairman of this special court is Huub Willems.

What is the Enterprise and Companies Court and what does it do?

Willems: 'The Enterprise and Companies Court is a court with a number of special characteristics. First of all, there is only one such body. It therefore has national jurisdiction. Secondly, the Enterprise and Companies Court as part of the Court of Appeal, as a special court, has an equally special composition. Two of the five judges are lay judges and thus not members of the judicature. They are called "lay appeal judges". The others, however, are members of the judicature. The lay judges are appointed on the basis of their specific expertise in all kinds of fields; accountancy is one of them, general strategic policy issues relating to doing business is another. There is thus a group of about 15 lay judges available. The Enterprise and Companies Court sessions include five members, two of whom are lay judges in rotation.

'The Enterprise and Companies Court is a specialised court with powers in particular fields. Disputes that may occur in a company are brought before us. The issues dealt with not only concern financial statement legislation, but also those pertaining to employee participation, the discharge of supervisory directors, the law of inquiry – examples include Rodamco North America, HBG, Gucci, Vie d'Or – where a case is brought before the court at the request of particular interested parties, such as shareholders, trade unions, company councils and the like. These kinds of cases come in all shapes, sizes and gravities: company buy-outs, minority shareholders who can be bought out, placement under the supervision of pension funds that don't do their work properly. Examples are rules on the settlement of disputes between shareholders. To put it briefly, a multitude of cases with one thing in common: the legislator considers it necessary for them to be brought before a specialised court. More and more cases are brought before us, such as those which will emerge in the future when the legislative proposal concerning the lifting of anti-takeover measures is adopted.'

Should it be made easy to go to court?

Willems: 'That is not for judges, but for the legislator to decide. The Enterprise and Companies Court was not created because it was believed that we should be a supervisor. On the contrary, that is not our duty. We settle disputes that parties submit to us. We do not act because we believe that there should be intervention. When the Annual Accounts (Business Concerns) Act came into force in 1991, it was decided that a special court should be created that had expertise specifically in that field; the other fields at that time being the law of inquiry and employee participation. Incidentally, the proceedings pertaining to financial statements are commenced by a writ of summons and the latter are dealt with on the basis of proceedings commenced by a petition.

'It has been quiet for some time in the field of accounting and reporting legislation, but this situation has suddenly changed. In the last few years we dealt with six accounting cases. This sudden interest perhaps ensues from the discussion among accounting experts about the future direction that accounting and reporting should take in the Netherlands. In addition, the public, political discussion about whether the Authority for the Financial Markets should be responsible for supervision and how the Public Prosecutor should act in this respect, draws attention to this subject. Maybe that is the reason for all these cases.

'The law prescribes that the proceedings go quickly and that only written arguments can be put forward about the role and that any other procedural pleadings can be brought in only with the permission of the chairman of the Enterprise and Companies Court. The idea at the moment is not to give this permission too quickly in order to keep things moving. Where it is within our power to make the procedure more accessible and quicker, we will do this. What is beyond our power is the complexity of the subject matter. Difficult issues require meticulous procedures in which the assistance of expert lawyers and accountants is indispensable. And the engagement of expertise costs money. This makes litigation an expensive affair.

'Seeking justice and getting justice also involves cost/benefit analysis. If a shareholder has objections to particular decisions of the company or to the reserves or the profit, he or she will think twice before turning to the Enterprise and Companies Court. It costs a lot of money and what will be achieved if the shareholder wins the case? There is always a risk that he or she will come away empty-handed. At the very most, the company will have to do its work over again. You can talk about this for as long as you want, but the reality is that it is debatable what a claimant who wins the case actually achieves. Period. That doesn't alter the fact that it is in everyone's interest that accounting and reporting suits can be judged. And this is the reason why the Public Prosecutor has been given the jurisdiction to act as litigant.

'If a judicial examination of the financial statements is required and if legal precedents are wanted so that everyone knows what the rules they should conform with are, then a mechanism could be created that makes all this possible. It is then, for example, the Authority for the Financial Markets that is responsible for supervision and is able to turn to the courts when there are discussions.'

Many consider that six accounting cases is very few. Does this mean that financial statements in the Netherlands are generally pretty good?

Willems: 'That is not a conclusion I would dare to make. I think rather that the most important reason for not taking legal action is that litigation is thought to be too expensive and too long. Therefore, I don't know whether or not financial statements are in general good or bad. What I do know is that there are fierce and passionate debates among accountants about whether financial reporting in the Netherlands does satisfy the highest standards. I regularly read that leading and expert accountants also consider that things could be improved.'

In the magazine Tijdschrift voor Management Accounting, *Professor L. Traas wrote that the quality of reporting is poor.*

Willems: 'Apart from the fact that Professor Traas is a member of the Enterprise and Companies Court, it already says enough when a professor, who is also chairman of the jury for the Sijthoff annual reporting prize, considers that there is something wrong with financial statements and that there should be more litigation. In these kinds of cases, we judges rely heavily on the expertise of the lay judges, who are members of our court for good reason. As a professional lawyer who has not studied the subject – and I find myself in the same position as chairman of the Disciplinary Council for *Registeraccountants* – I will have to rely on the opinion of experts.'

If a shareholder has a problem with financial statements and is reluctant to turn to the Enterprise and Companies Court, can he or she not just as well submit a grievance against the accountant to the Disciplinary Council? If this latter council judges against the accountant, does the shareholder possess fairly strong arguments for the civil division of a court?

Willems: 'In 1999, I delivered the N. J. Polak lecture entitled "Accounting and reporting rules in a broader perspective". This was included in *FMA-*

Kroniek 1999. In this, I covered cases in which judges, also those from the Disciplinary Council, made decisions about financial statement issues. These included criminal court judges, civil court judges, disciplinary court judges, accounting judges, committee of inquiry judges and so on. All kinds of people can speak out on the subject, but when all is said and done the Enterprise and Companies Court determines whether financial statements are in conformity with the law or not. The Disciplinary Council may come to the conclusion that an accountant has made a mistake with respect to accounting and reporting legislation (and thus expresses an opinion about how something should be shown on the balance sheet), but this is not to say that the court which has jurisdiction also finds that this is the case. In answer to the question whether a particular kind of provision can be shown as a liability or not, the disciplinary court judge may say: "I believe that what you have done is not in conformity with the law; you, the accountant, have done this and in my opinion you made a mistake." The Enterprise and Companies Court may say: "In our opinion what you have done is entirely in conformity with the law. End of story." The point therefore is that the competency of the various judges relates to a particular subject matter. If opinions diverge, the verdict of the Enterprise and Companies Court prevails because its authority is binding within the scope of accounting and reporting legislation.

'The former practice of Royal NIVRA was that the accountant was officially "summoned" for disciplinary proceedings by a shareholder for the financial statements if the Enterprise and Companies Court considered the annual reports not in conformity with the law. This has happily been done away with because you cannot make a direct connection between an accountant and misleading financial statements. I still owe *de Accountant* magazine an article on this subject. I would like to say the following about this subject here. You go before the Disciplinary Tribunal and say: "The auditor has completely misjudged the financial statements that show a particular profit; according to accounting and reporting rules, it should be entirely different." And the Disciplinary Tribunal could say: "Complainant, you are quite right about that; it should have been much different, the profit should not have been 10 but 100 according to the interpretation about the presentation of financial statements, and the fact that it has become 10 is merely a blunder by the auditor." On the basis of this verdict, someone with an interest in the matter can go before the civil court and say: "Look here, the financial statements are completely wrong, the auditor has made a mistake; as a result of these misrepresented financial statements I have suffered a loss of 1,000, I call upon the auditor before the civil court to pay me damages of 1,000." In a defended action, the auditor may say to the court: "The complainant is wrong; the Disciplinary Tribunal has decided that I have made mistakes in the preparation of the financial statements, but that is not the case; I will now come and explain to you that what is stated in the financial statements is as it should be." The civil court then has a problem, because it has its own responsibility to decide whether the financial statements have been correctly prepared or not. Suppose that the civil court would say to the complainant: "You are quite right, the financial statements are no good and, furthermore, the auditor has blundered, so much so that he is liable for damages under civil law." Suppose the same question was put before the Enterprise and Companies Court. The Enterprise and Companies Court could decide that the financial statements have been prepared entirely in accordance with the law. If the question under discussion is which verdict is binding from the point of view of the content of accounting and reporting legislation, then it is only that of the Enterprise and Companies Court. But the Enterprise and Companies Court doesn't have to get involved in the entire proceedings at all. The civil court will then be confronted with a civil claim for damages. In this case, the auditor can plead in defence: "If you were to ask the competent court, it would probably come to a completely different decision." The civil court then subsequently has a problem. But it must produce a verdict, however. The dilemma therefore is that the judges state an opinion that also has (disciplinary or civil) consequences, while you think that if it was dealt with in the Enterprise and Companies Court, both the courts have actually assumed an incorrect point of view, at least according to the Enterprise and Companies Court. Incidentally, this problem cannot be solved, unless you plan things in such a way that you go first before the Enterprise and Companies Court for a preliminary hearing in which a verdict should be given about financial statements in a particular case that is not strictly concerned with financial statements. The problem would not then occur. But that's not how it works.

'The Supreme Court of the Netherlands has now determined that the mere circumstance that the Disciplinary Tribunal has judged unfavourably about the work of an auditor does not automatically imply that the auditor is liable according to the law of Tort or for breach of contract.

'The point is that society has an interest in honest financial reporting. I want to avoid moralising about this. The discussion must remain *ad rem*. There are simply some differences of opinion of an intellectual legal nature and there is a body that is able to pronounce decisions on the subject. I do not like the American "claim culture". And it certainly won't improve matters if that is where the emphasis comes to lie.'

How will the Enterprise and Companies Court specialise in the field of IAS in the future?

Willems: 'We have the best experts available for this. If I run through the list of lay appeal judges, I see a number of famous names: Traas, Van Hoepen, Mees (Nationale Nederlanden; has now left), Appelo (Philips; has now left), Wortel (Ernst & Young), Timmermans (DSM), Lemstra (former mayor of Hengelo, now chairman of the Netherlands Hospitals Association), Klaassen, Izeboud (PricewaterhouseCoopers; has now left), Den Hoed (AKZO), Rongen (DSM) and Glasz. Not a bad selection I think, with some having more expertise in the field of accounting and reporting legislation than others.'

How do the standards of a body governed by private law, like the IASB, fit within Part 9, Book 2 of the Netherlands Civil Code?

Willems: 'Accounting and reporting legislation in the Netherlands is still Dutch legislation. It is partly dependent upon judicial interpretation. In addition, international law has precedence over national law. But that is only the case if a special treaty has been ratified in this respect. International rules will only apply if a financial statements treaty to decide that question exists. In deciding whether or not goodwill must be charged directly to shareholders' equity, Dutch legislation still always applies. If this leaves room to deviate from what is internationally generally adopted, then it is possible. But the question is whether this is wise. It is conceivable that a court could choose to interpret Dutch law with the aid of "internationally harmonising methods of interpretation" in such a way that it is also regarded internationally as being complete. That is a consideration. Nevertheless, the outcome is still a decision about Dutch law with the court retaining freedom of choice.'

On the Netherlands Antilles, 8,000 reports of unusual transactions are received every year. The three people who are responsible for taking these to court naturally do not have enough time to do this. How does the Enterprise and Companies Court ensure it has sufficient capacity?

Willems: 'Our controller asked me what the developments in the coming six years will be with respect to the workload, the number of cases and the backlogs. I was then given a thick report full of management jargon which I immediately threw in the wastepaper basket. I don't like that kind of thing. As long as we are faced with an annual 10% increase and this percentage does not increase any further, I have no wishes with respect to facilities, personnel and suchlike. I do not want to be pinned down by any figures or agreements or promises. We do not have any backlogs at the Enterprise and Companies Court. An example: one afternoon we were called by the shareholders of Rodamco North-America. They wanted to take legal action. The case was down for a hearing at 10.00 a.m. the following morning and the verdict was delivered a week later.'

What is your opinion of an independent body that conducts research into the quality of annual reporting, such as the 'Review Panel' in the United Kingdom and the SEC in the United States?

Willems: 'There are both advantages and disadvantages. If you have a conflict, you can always go to court. If it concerns a serious problem in society, with poor financial reporting leading to enormous and social calamities, then a kind of "Review Panel" may be able to exercise a preventative influence. But the problem remains how this should be situated in terms of authority towards companies. Incidentally, I have a strong view about this. I don't think it is acceptable for an executive body to impose a penalty or other kinds of sanctions. And this is happening in the Netherlands. We have already seen this with the new Road Traffic Act. If you drive too fast, you must first pay the penalty and then you can go to court. This is still acceptable in the general public interest, but you can see a shift into the idea penetrating into supervision legislation. I believe that sanctions should be a matter for the courts, because that is consistent with a democracy based on the rule of law. I can accept the situation if the measures are confined to discussions, warnings, comments and suchlike. But not otherwise.'

So there is no role for the exchange authorities here?

Willems: 'Financial statements should be reliable. That is in the public interest. This applies to creditors, foreign investors, small investors, to name but a few. There should be a mechanism in place to look after this interest. I have to admit that a lawsuit before the Enterprise and Companies Court is an expensive and time-consuming business such that the public interest is inadequately served. That is why a mechanism to monitor the public interest can be defended in all respects. From a legal point of view, this is the responsibility of the Public Prosecution Service in Amsterdam. You must acknowledge, however, that the Public Prosecution Service has not assumed this responsibility. You are then faced with a situation whereby others who do want to take up this responsibility, such as Mr. Lakeman from SOBI, are jumping onto a moving train that has been set in motion by others. I doubt that this is the solution, because if something is in the public interest – and the legislator has let it be known that this is the case – then this should be protected by a public body, and not by a private corporation. The question is whether another institute should be established if the Public Prosecution Service doesn't pick up on this? Perhaps something like the Authority for the Financial Markets, with representatives from the field of investors, banks and stock exchange specialists? However, if you see that there is a problem, you have got to make a choice and the Authority for the Financial Markets is not a bad idea. Just give that body the public supervision function.'

How is 'corporate governance' progressing in the Netherlands?

Willems: 'A company represents a collection of interests. Not all interests run parallel and you see that different interests are given priority at different times. There is nothing wrong with this as long as there is transparency, and other interested parties can see and understand what is going on. The accountability requirement has been sharpened on all kinds of fronts. We also notice that in the Enterprise and Companies Court. The company council is a special body. The management cannot just do what it wants; nor can the director-major shareholder. Where there are important decisions to be taken, the company council must be consulted. If a dispute arises, the company has to "more or less" account for its actions before the court. "More or less" of course, because the Enterprise and Companies Court only examines the situation and formulates limits, but the final decision lies with the responsible management.

'This process, of accounting for one's decisions or plans, has become increasingly important during the past few years, certainly now that shareholders are more and more often becoming involved in the discussion. Those in charge – and this not only applies to companies – are increasingly being called to account for sound management. The Enterprise and Companies Court has developed the principles of proper management. And so everyone makes their own contribution to the concept of responsible business practice and sound management.'

Does the system of statutory two-tier rules that we have in the Netherlands function properly?

Willems: 'The system you refer to is often called the "Wonder of The Hague". The general opinion is that company councils and shareholders are too often sidelined and this is also endorsed by public debate and politicians. In a system in which shareholders and company councils are disappearing from sight and in which power is concentrated in supervisory boards and boards of management, it is easier to seek one another out than when there are rather more checks and balances in this entire system. The circumstance that a proposal has been made for company councils to nominate people and for the general meeting of shareholders to appoint supervisory directors implies that the system is less dominated by nepotism. For the rest, I believe that these discussions should be conducted in a businesslike fashion.'

But the Netherlands is becoming more international and it is quite likely that we will move towards an Anglo-American system.

Willems: 'There's no denying that this is the case. This is evidently what people want. I have been teaching English law in Tilburg and Leiden for the past 15 years and have studied and followed two totally different legal systems, the English and the Dutch. I wouldn't dare suggest that one is better than the other. Most systems have a social, historical and cultural background and have grown the way they have for a good reason. Every society chooses the system that fits it best. From a legal point of view, the British have for a long time found it hard to accept the legal personality of companies. They weren't acquainted with it and didn't want it at all. They believe that people, and not vague entities like a company, should be liable for debts. We have dogmatically accepted this earlier on. For a long time, the British have recognised a different, stronger position for the shareholder than us, even though this situation is now changing here as well. This can be compared with a clock pendulum. In the Netherlands, attention for the position of employees and their opportunities for participation in organisations has developed strongly. Supervisory directors and shareholders are now more in the picture again. Why is that? Ask a sociologist with an economic/historical background, not a lawyer, let alone a judge. What else can you say except that all these interests must be checked and that there must be debates about particular choices from time to time. Continuous consultation will be required in order to preserve the shaky balance between all these interests. This means reaching compromises, moderating demands.

'As a court, we do however see what it means if yet another new regulation is introduced. But we are not the first party designated to create all kinds of models for society or to dictate matters. We do not direct our attention towards the making of choices from various possibilities that are all more or less defensible. That is not the reserve of a court. But we are not beyond the scope of this process either. We observe and play a certain role in this, but only after the political discussion has finished.

Incidentally, the dispensation of justice also evolves without political decisions being taken. After all, case law is also a product of social developments; but then in a different manner. It is inconceivable that a court would abolish rules applicable to statutory two-tier entities. The legislator could do this, but not just "willy-nilly". As long as the trade unions, Crown-appointed members and the legislature believe that the system must remain in existence, it will continue to exist. But if you ask whether the dispensation of justice is partly influenced by the changed opinions about how you should treat employees or shareholders, the answer is yes. This public discussion is not without its effect on judicial decisions.'

Appendix

Enterprise and Companies Court 1996–2001

	1996	1997	1998	1999	2000	2001
sessions	31	40	71	88	92	93
new cases	68	99	142	152	158	178
judgements	38	65	91	127	182	202

developments in percentages bases on 1996 = 100%

	1996	1997	1998	1999	2000	2001
sessions	100	129	229	284	297	300
new cases	100	146	209	224	233	262
judgements	100	171	239	334	479	531

Chapter 13

Globalisation is OK, as long as it takes account of Dutch culture

An interview with M. (Rien) A. van Hoepen

M. (Rien) A. van Hoepen

Professor Rien van Hoepen RA (1948) is Professor of Economics and Accountancy at Erasmus University, Rotterdam. As chairman of the auditors' delegation, he is also a member of the Council for Annual Reporting. Further, he is a lay appeal judge in the Enterprise and Companies Court of the Amsterdam Court of Appeal and partner at Deloitte & Touche. Professor Van Hoepen has been an instructor for VERA courses, such as on participating interests and IAS, for about two decades.

In times when cultural differences grow dim through globalisation, one's own identity – and everything that has been cultivated and acquired through the ages – is also at risk of fading: standards, values, opinions, mindsets, cultural heritage. This is not necessarily a direct loss or a negative development. Sometimes it is good for a forest fire to clear away the dead wood so new life has a chance to grow. On the other hand, not all change automatically implies an improvement, of course. At any rate, the influence of Anglo-American culture on continental European, in general, and Dutch culture, in particular, is undeniable. That goes for financial reporting as well. National regulations are being influenced by international (read: Anglo-American) rules. The guidelines of the Council for Annual Reporting are being 'converted' by stealth into international accounting standards. Someone who has been following it all from close by is Professor Rien van Hoepen, Professor of Business Economics and Accountancy at Erasmus University, Rotterdam.

Does the Council for Annual Reporting seek to emulate IAS?

Professor Van Hoepen: 'The developments in Dutch financial reporting have accelerated on the road to IOSCO endorsement. The Council for Annual Reporting seeks to adapt its guidelines to IAS, given the Dutch situation. A striking example of this can presently be seen in their adaptation to the standard on Employee Benefits (IAS 19). That will take some doing. Further, we still do have to adapt to the developments, such as those in FAS 87 and IAS 19. Nonetheless, some specifically Dutch circumstances, such as those created in the Pension and Savings Funds Guarantee Act [*Pensioen- en Spaarfondsenwet*], will not be so easy to incorporate into the framework of IAS 19.

'After 2005, the Council for Annual Reporting will need to guide the application of IAS in Dutch GAAP – or maybe even translate them one to one. Interpretations of certain points – given the unique Dutch situation – will always be necessary for application in the Netherlands. Even if there already is a Standing Interpretation Committee (SIC) within IAS, there is simply no way it can foresee all possible aberrations in all legal precedents. So in that sense, the Council for Annual Reporting still has a task *vis-à-vis* listed companies even after 2005. By the same token, however, one must prevent all manner of national/opposing interpretations from arising on the, in principle, clear IAS.

'Something else that has recently started to weigh upon us more heavily – which we have certainly noticed in response to IAS 32 (the disclosure and presentation of financial instruments) – is the feeling that many of the disclosure requirements have been intensified so much that one starts wondering whether it is not too much of a good thing for many small and medium-sized enterprises and non-listed companies. Companies subject to US GAAP and which fall under the jurisdiction of the SEC cannot exactly be compared to the tobacconist "down the street" who has chosen to cast his or her business in the form of a private limited company. This is something that the Council for Annual Reporting might be able to influence, just as with the development of "small GAAP". In addition, we also need rules for special lines of business for which there are yet no IAS; for example, the healthcare industry, housing corporations and such. In principle, I commend our move towards IAS, but I am still keen to find a place for our unique Dutch circumstances therein.'

What is the role of case law?

Professor Van Hoepen: 'To my mind, case law from the Enterprise and Companies Court will, apart from developments in the field of supervision, adapt accordingly. In the past, some people implicitly reproached the Enterprise and Companies Court for paying little attention to the guidelines of the Council for Annual Reporting. I was never able to subscribe to that view. It is indeed so that the Enterprise and Companies Court – certainly in the past – never explicitly mentioned the specifics of the guidelines in the legal precedents on financial statements. But that is not to say that the Enterprise and Companies Court ignored the guidelines. On the contrary, I believe that the provisions of those guidelines have always played a key role in the decision-making process in the Enterprise and Companies Court. As of recent, we are seeing the Enterprise and Companies Court refer explicitly to the guidelines where necessary. This is also evident in an increasingly common phenomenon: the rise of all manner of legal precedents in respect of financial statements outside court actions in this field. Financial statements are often handled during inquiries; the latter also clearly take account of the guidelines and often make special mention of derogations from them.

'Apart from the tendencies in the relevant laws on supervision, I believe that such developments will automatically lead the Enterprise and Companies Court to rely more often on IAS in this respect. That makes perfect sense, since the article on professional judgement is leading. The principles for the valuation of assets and liabilities and the determination of profit/loss (not to mention presentation and disclosure) must reflect what is generally accepted. That is where the Council for Annual Reporting comes in with its authoritative interpretations.

'If the tendencies towards IAS continue to play a more important role, this means that the generally accepted standards are also shifting. Then it will be impossible for the Enterprise and Companies Court to disregard those developments in financial statements proceedings when ruling on financial statements in the context of inquiries or dispute settlements. A common example is the trend in respect of goodwill. We can now say that the law still gives us the option of charging goodwill to shareholders' equity – at least in a share-deal merger. The Council for Annual Reporting has expressly stated that goodwill may no longer be charged to shareholders' equity in share deals. Alas, in spite of the fact that the law still allows this, I can imagine that it will become a dead letter. Just remember section 362: the generally accepted standards beg to differ. We always speak of derogation from the law in the name of professional judgement, but here one could also say: options in the law can sometimes become a dead letter in connection with the development of professional judgement and its rationale.'

Many of the legal precedents from the Enterprise and Companies Court arose in a time that the Council for Annual Reporting played much less of a role. Are these old legal precedents from the Enterprise and Companies Court still relevant in the year 2002? Should students still study them in their programmes or should they learn IAS by heart instead?

Professor Van Hoepen: 'There are not many recent legal precedents relating to financial statements any longer, even though there are still some cases on financial statements up before the Enterprise and Companies Court. Mind you, not all of these will lead to rulings nowadays. A great many legal precedents on financial statements have also arisen outside formal proceedings: in disciplinary rulings and inquiries. In my accountancy lectures, I sometimes cover an inquiry where certain aspects of financial statements played a role. The Council for Annual Reporting has always endeavoured to incorporate legal precedents on financial statements of a general nature into its guidelines. Yet it no longer makes much sense to cover the Witteveen or the Van Gelder Papier judgement, since the portent of the legal precedents – in so far as it was of a general nature – has already been incorporated into the guidelines (just like IAS). IAS and the guidelines of the Council for Annual Reporting are all on my list of required readings, with more emphasis destined for IAS. Now, however, the main course in treating the guidelines of the Council for Annual Reporting is in relation to IAS and US GAAP. Yet I believe that IAS will form more of the basis in the future, in addition to exceptions for 'small GAAP' in connection with special Dutch company situations and deviations from US GAAP.'

How do you see the role of the Enterprise and Companies Court in terms of compliance with the financial reporting rules in the Netherlands? It has recently been suggested that not enough cases are brought to the fore via the Enterprise and Companies Court. Do you share this view?

Professor Van Hoepen: 'Yes, I do. There are not enough legal precedents pertaining to financial statements. The reasons for this are various. Financial statements proceedings are commenced by a costly writ of summons.

Moreover, these proceedings take a lot of time. We have, incidentally, shown that there are definitely ways of speeding up the process and that such proceedings certainly do not need to run on for years. Other obstacles are the "interested parties" issue – the double circle doctrine of the Supreme Court – and exceeding the term. These play no role in disciplinary actions or inquiries. An inquiry is commenced by a petition. There is no need to demonstrate one's interest in the case, as long as one is authorised pursuant to article 2:346 or 347 of the Netherlands Civil Code to file a petition. Nor is there a risk of exceeding the term. One can simply have one's say – as they put it.

'The same goes for disciplinary actions. Anyone can commence proceedings at the Disciplinary Tribunal. That is therefore where the cases against financial statements show up. It is cheaper and quicker, there is no risk of exceeding the term and no problems regarding the interested parties issue. But matters are, however, more touch and go. An inquiry places the state of affairs at a legal entity in the spotlight, but the auditor was formerly prohibited from having his or her say. I once said something about that in an annotation to the first judgement handed down by the Trade and Industry Appeal Tribunal in disciplinary cases. It would be useful to hear the auditor, too, in inquiries involving financial statements. So now, auditors can also be called to give testimony as an interested party.

'I still always consider it a pity that company management is not heard in disciplinary actions, in principle. If financial statements come into play in such actions, the auditor is heard by the Disciplinary Tribunal. The auditor is the person who conducted the audit and his or her actions are therefore under scrutiny in disciplinary proceedings. Yet it would also be good to hear the company management for a change – simply to obtain a proper understanding of exactly what happened and what factors played a role.

'Proceedings on financial statements are becoming rarer. But in general, parties to financial statements proceedings are not primarily out to obtain a proper set of financial statements. Financial statements proceedings, disciplinary actions and inquiries are almost always conducted with other interests in mind, such as civil damages and the like. Nor do I find the small number of financial statements proceedings so surprising. Such cases focus on whether the financial statements are acceptable or whether they ought to be redone. It could be that someone has a direct interest in seeing the financial statements revised, perhaps because of profit-sharing, etc. Yet such proceedings are often conducted to demonstrate that the company management has failed. And some proceedings are brought as the first step towards a civil action to win damages. Yet that also applies to disciplinary actions and inquiries. I therefore consider it quite logical for people to avoid expensive financial statements proceedings in favour of cheaper alternatives.'

In your opinion, is supervision on financial statements desirable?

Professor Van Hoepen: 'It most certainly is. For the fact that few proceedings are conducted on financial statements does not necessarily mean that financial reporting in the Netherlands is so brilliant. That is not to say that it is bad, but we are certainly not top of the list. It would therefore be good to have some clear legislation on supervision along with a corresponding supervisory body – or actually a kind of second line of supervision. The auditor remains in the first line of supervision. I have the impression that many auditors were traditionally more likely to render an opinion based on technical matters such as – to phrase it the old way – the completeness of income and compliance with regard to the legitimacy of expenditure and such, than that their opinion on the financial statements was primarily dictated by the laws on financial statements. Not so long ago, the technical auditing aspects of the auditor's report were more prominent than the external reporting aspects. Now this has certainly changed, although it did take a long time to reach this point. I do not want to call the financial reporting rules a lucky dip, but they do offer a number of options and possibilities for interpretation which do afford the company management a certain degree of liberty to leave their auditor tongue-tied now and again. If the law provides an option which makes us wonder whether it would really be generally accepted given the circumstances, the auditor does not have many possibilities for blowing the whistle on management. In that respect, a second line of supervision would make perfect sense.'

Should such a second line of supervision move in the direction of the SEC?

Professor Van Hoepen: 'No, that would not fit in particularly well with the Dutch model. In fact, it would imply repeating the work of the auditor. That would not make much sense, would it now? To my mind, we should look instead towards a kind of review panel such as the one in the UK. An umbrella organisation, such as the Authority for the Financial Markets, could take the initiative in that respect.'

Or involve the Advocate General, who is legally competent to initiate financial statements proceedings in the public interest?

Professor Van Hoepen: 'What is the public interest? It is not by definition a public interest that the financial statements of this or that company should be in order. If you are cycling through the countryside in the dark, it is in the public interest that your rear light should function properly, that is, in the name of road safety. But the fact that a company's financial statements are not what they should be is not necessarily a public menace. No, I see more in the review panel approach. This could be achieved by boosting the power of the office of Advocate General in such manner that he or she no longer has to derive competency from the public interest and by allocating sufficient staff. For there is not much the Advocate General can achieve alone.

'Another way would be to rig up the Authority for the Financial Markets as a kind of review panel. The advantage of such a body is that it would eliminate the pillory effect of financial statements proceedings. That was definitely the case in the past. The panel could bring up certain subjects; not necessarily the financial statements of company A or B, but rather the financial statements of a number of companies in general that have a clean record otherwise. I am thinking of the treatment of goodwill or of certain financial instruments. Various topics could be raised throughout the years. This would enable us to create somewhat more systematic "legal precedents" in respect of financial statements than what the Enterprise and Companies Court has been producing via its financial statements proceedings. The Enterprise and Companies Court is dependent on the "supply". A review panel could take certain topics by the horns on its own accord, thereby building up a systematic body of legal precedents. Nevertheless, I would still like to see the "directive" of such a review panel ultimately tested by the Enterprise and Companies Court, in terms of both legal certainty (appeals) and enforceability.'

When the Financial Statements Act [Wet op de Jaarrekening] *was being given shape, three options were considered: a company chamber, an Enterprise and Companies Court and a penal sanction. They ultimately opted for the Enterprise and Companies Court. Are you now pleading for a review panel?*

Professor Van Hoepen: 'Well, we never had a company chamber in the sense of an SEC. Nor would I want one today. The Enterprise and Companies Court is what we ultimately achieved. Yet it is not perfect, as we just demonstrated. A review panel would occupy a sort of middle position and would be able to review financial statements systematically; in the UK, that body has a high standing. When it talks, people listen. That puts an end to the necessity of taking a company's financial statements to court. And in my view, as already mentioned, it would be highly desirable to have the Enterprise and Companies Court available to handle appeals.

'As concerns the penal imbedding, I am particularly pleased that this was not our primary choice in 1970. The rules on financial statements were so vague and general then that penal sanctions would have been impossible. Moreover, since the law on financial statements is part of civil law, penal sanctions would not really be appropriate. Nevertheless, I believe that the time is finally ripe to ask ourselves whether it would be desirable to bring penal sanctions – as the ultimate remedy for patently incorrect financial statements – more to the fore than the opportunities afforded by the laws on balance sheet fraud, fraudulent bankruptcy and forgery.'

What kind of sanction-imposing powers should the review panel be given?

Professor Van Hoepen: 'Whenever the review panel raps the knuckles of a company's management by way of a directive, I find, as already mentioned, that the company should have recourse to the Enterprise and Companies Court. I would not find it just for an administrative body to be given both power of review and the authority to impose sanctions. That would go against the principles. A division of powers is of the essence. The law on financial statements – as part of company law – falls under the judiciary, just like any penal sanction possibilities. That must never be given administrative law standing. That is why we have an independent judiciary. The Netherlands boasts the unique situation in which the Enterprise and Companies Court combines legal expertise with expertise in the field of financial statements and prudential matters. Yes, I must admit, I am one of its members and the Enterprise and Companies Court simply fits in better, in my view, with our polder model than an administrative law body would. So in that sense, you are preaching to the converted. It would be a pity to get rid of such an utterly legal body of expertise for no particular reason.'

The Netherlands is seen as the country with the most liberal financial reporting culture. This view is confirmed by a comparative study by Nobes and Parker. The Netherlands is in a category of its own. Its distinguishing feature is professional judgement, that is, the combination of individual discretion with relatively few rules. We have broad laws with general standards. Legal precedents, in so far as they exist, have little impact. The guidelines of the Council for Annual Reporting have no legal status. Is this image still valid?

Professor Van Hoepen: 'No, not at all. To my mind, the Netherlands is in line with IAS, relatively speaking. We are no longer the exception to the rule. Mind you, our special position had more to do with the prudential imbedding of financial reporting in the Netherlands and less with being some kind of arbiter of liberalism. After all, people in the United States were familiar with more kinds of cookbook accounting than here. If we look at the first Financial Statements Act, we see that the only valuation rule was that intangible assets may not be valued above the amount paid to a third party. And that was it. Of course it did develop quite a bit in the course of time (partly under the influence of IAS), but it was certainly not spurred on by any liberal agenda. In the 1920s, large Dutch multinational companies such as Shell, Philips and Unilever were pioneers of proper financial reporting. They often went further than what US GAAP prescribed in those times. Elsewhere, one sees an increase in the influence of regulations. We must therefore ensure that we keep thinking about financial reporting and that we do not unwittingly annex the "international" rules, apart from the need for harmonisation. Nevertheless, I believe that the Netherlands has fallen somewhat behind because of the development of regulations elsewhere. To my mind, the Netherlands is no longer seen internationally as top of the list.

'Whether the guidelines should be given a legal framework? They already have a high status. The auditor is required to conduct his or her audit on the basis of the guidelines of the Council for Annual Reporting. The Disciplinary Tribunal has been saying that for years now. So whether that justifies giving them a legal status...

'The Explanatory Memorandum to the Financial Statements Act stated that the point was to take stock of and test what was generally accepted. That does not mean that we should try to lead the band, which is incidentally a typically Dutch piece of rudeness. What we are left with is a type of semi-legislation in the field of financial reporting without parliamentary control. With all due respect to the other members of the Council for Annual Reporting, we are not democratically elected. That is why I have been somewhat hesitant to give the guidelines true legal standing. That still needs to develop. If we have reached the point towards 2005 – or preferably even earlier – that the law requires listed companies to apply IAS in their consolidated financial statements, that will most likely be imposed by Europe yet consciously chosen at the same time. That will certainly hold true if we carry IAS through to non-listed companies and/or company financial statements. But I also think that we need a controlling authority. If new IAS emerge, someone needs to pay attention to whether they are still acceptable. That is the background of the EFRAG, which advises the European Commission on what is acceptable or not for Europe. If the guidelines are given legal standing without further ado, we will be left without such a safety mechanism.

'The law could be made to refer to the guidelines, but then we would still need to create a body to flag possible developments which might be good to evaluate in a democratic manner. The financial reporting standards are, in my view, too important to entrust to interested parties only. For no matter how one looks at it, in spite of the tripartite composition of the Council for Annual Reporting, its members include providers, users and auditors. Those are, in essence, the interested parties where financial reporting is concerned. The evaluation of financial reporting standards cannot be left solely to them. We at least require a final democratic judgement.'

What do you think of the derogatory effect of the true and fair view?

Professor Van Hoepen: 'There are many misunderstandings about this in the Netherlands. There is a lot of openness for invoking the derogatory effect of the true and fair view. If read carefully, the law states that one must provide supplementary information if compliance with the law would fail to give a true and fair view. If that does not suffice, it is not as if one has the option of derogating from the law: it is required. Then that should be expressly indicated. Another matter is that we have always been somewhat under the impression that we were unique in respect of that catchall section. But that is not true. The derogatory effect of the true and fair view features in IAS 1. That expressly states that one must derogate from IAS where necessary. Yet such situations are described as extremely rare circumstances, which puts it quite a bit stronger than in Dutch law. And we did not invent the derogatory effect of the true and fair view in the Netherlands either. This can be found in the fourth guideline. So it is not so unique after all.'

What is your general impression of the framework of standards in the Netherlands?

Professor Van Hoepen: 'Standards are there to be obeyed. It would be quite useful to have more supervision on compliance with the standards in the future. That should certainly not be taken as a disqualification of the first line of supervision, that is, the auditor. Rather, I see it more as a fortification for the auditing profession. After all, the auditor is in the front line and is often left – given the lack of a second line of supervision – without enough cover to do his or her job. The auditor does not have enough clarity in the guidelines since – as a matter of necessity – a great many financial reporting rules are phrased in general terms and a clear translation is not always at hand. These are often tools that crumble in his or her hands. So, in my opinion, this should not be seen as a disqualification. Instead, it gives the auditor a weapon for making his or her standpoint clearer.'

The law states that listed securities must be carried at the lower of cost and fair value. The Council for Annual Reporting maintains that one should derogate from the letter of the law for the sake of clarity. What do you think?

Professor Van Hoepen: 'I have a problem with it as a generalisation. I think there are situations in which transparency dictates that one indeed state listed securities – if they are recorded under current assets and are thus truly an investment with a liquid market – at higher fair value (read: market value). That is what the Council for Annual Reporting says, too. The Council certainly does not say that listed securities must always be stated at fair value. It mentions situations in which that is inevitable.

I can find peace with that – yet not with a generalisation. One must ascertain on a case-by-case basis whether complying with the law would produce a clear picture. There will naturally be situations in which one must carry them in the balance sheet at market value, but one cannot generalise and say that we should derogate from the law for the sake of clarity. For that would place the Council for Annual Reporting on an equal footing with the legislature – which is not possible. Incidentally, I see that in the framework of IAS 39 reliance upon this derogation provision has been made irrelevant now that IAS 39 makes the valuation of these securities at fair value inevitable, as long as they are not classified as held-to-maturity.

Are people taking the application of the standards seriously in practice?

Professor Van Hoepen: 'They are, but since there is still too much of "something for everybody", people are still too free to do as they please. There are, for example, enough prudential arguments available for charging goodwill to shareholders' equity. I do not find these arguments so strong, but others may think differently. At any rate, we cannot continue allowing ourselves to be the only country in the world that charges goodwill to shareholders' equity. As far as I am concerned, it would not hurt to limit the choices. We need to take greater efforts to toe the line via harmonisation and such.

On the other hand, we must not forget that standards are set on the basis of political choices. Standard-setting is policy-making. There was a heavy battle between the United States and other Anglo-Saxon countries about the rules on the pooling of interests. US GAAP seemed rather stringent, but actually gave the user quite a lot of freedom in that area. Too bad for the companies in countries where pooling was practically impossible and which were fishing in the same acquisitions stream. To soften the blow of the abolishment of pooling, this was coupled with the possibility of subjecting capitalised goodwill to an impairment test instead of amortising it. Now that is what I call politics and decision-making which is not based on healthy prudential arguments. I would not rule out that in a number of years – once people forget that it was used to soften the blow – it will become mandatory again in the US to capitalise and amortise goodwill. Perhaps a number of huge, unexpected, impairment charges will make many people think back longingly to capitalisation and amortisation.'

If IAS are soon in place, how will the framework of standards develop? Will compliance be different? What role will the auditor play?

Professor Van Hoepen: 'Compliance with IAS is being paid a lot of lip-service at present – there is no denying it – while the reality of the matter will be hammered out differently and, above all, regionally. If IAS are embraced at European level, they will still be interpreted differently in the course of time. As concerns the role of the auditor, it is quite obvious that he or she will have to say something about the application of IAS in the report. The auditor does not have to find fault with everything, but if he or she discovers that the company has been doing things differently than promised, then it will have to be disclosed and the auditor will not simply be able to issue an unqualified auditor's report.'

Enforcement of IAS is crucial for the realisation of a global standard for financial reporting

An interview with Ruud G. A. Vergoossen

Ruud G. A. Vergoossen

Professor Ruud Vergoossen RA (1961) is Director of Assurance and Accounting at Ernst & Young in Rotterdam and Professor of International Financial Accounting at the University of Maastricht. His inaugural lecture (1999) was entitled 'International Accounting Standards: Esperanto or a Tower of Babel?'. Until April 2001, he was 'technical adviser' to the Dutch delegation in the Board of the IASC (now called the IASB).

Two interesting articles were published by Professor Ruud Vergoossen, director of Assurance and Accounting at Ernst & Young in Rotterdam and professor of International Financial Accounting at the University of Maastricht. Until 1 October 2002, he was deputy director at Royal NIVRA. In the October 2001 issue of *Maandblad voor Accountancy en Bedrijfseconomie*, an article appeared about the supervision of the financial reporting of listed companies; this will be discussed in more detail later. In a contribution in the July/August 2001 issue of *Tijdschrift Financieel Management*, the former 'technical adviser' to the Dutch delegation on the Board of the International Accounting Standards Committee (IASC – changed to the IASB in April 2001) outlined a number of subjects that the IASB will deal with in the coming years.

What is the reason for the new state of affairs?

Professor Vergoossen: 'The IASB is the new regulatory body of the IASC Foundation. The Board comprises 12 full-time and two part-time members. Each member is appointed on the basis of his or her expertise and functional background. The Board includes national standard-setters, issuers, users and auditors. The old IASC Board comprised country delegations. A NIVRA delegation, for example, represented the Netherlands. In addition, there were delegations of interest groups from companies and financial analysts. The IASB members are currently employed by the IASC Foundation and receive a substantial remuneration for this. In the old situation, it was a labour of love.

'In principle, the nationality of the IASB members is not important, although I cannot avoid the impression that this has nevertheless played an important role in certain cases. First and foremost, it is their expertise that is important. They must certainly be independent and must not be swayed by the interests of a particular country, a particular body or a particular interest. Totally independent, therefore. The IASB members are appointed by a board of 19 Trustees who must ensure that their independence is assured and that the composition of the IASB is well balanced. To put it briefly, the changes have been quite sweeping and are intended to work faster and more effectively in order to produce sufficient support for the IASB standards.

'And this support is growing. The European Commission wants all companies listed at EU stock exchanges to prepare their consolidated financial statements in accordance with these standards with effect from 2005. In addition, the EU member states may decide for themselves whether they make the IAS compulsory or optional for the company financial statements of listed companies and for the consolidated and/ or company financial statements of unlisted companies. Now that is going quite a long way and it is therefore more than likely that financial reporting practice in the EU will be determined to a great extent by the IAS.'

Which projects are high on the agenda of the IASB?

Professor Vergoossen: 'One of the topics is business combinations, for example. The question is whether the pooling-of-interests method is still possible if equal parties merge. If so, it must be clear which conditions apply. But it is also possible to apply the so-called purchase accounting method for mergers as well as acquisitions. In that case one of the merger partners must be designated as the acquiring party. Well now, if the pooling-of-interests method is applied, there is no goodwill and so the question doesn't arise how it should be incorporated in the financial statements. This is because the book value of the assets and liabilities of the merger partners are simply combined in the financial statements of the new entity. In the United States, the pooling-of-interests method was recently prohibited. At the same time, it is no longer permitted to systematically write-down the goodwill paid on the acquisitions; write-downs to the debit of the profit and loss account are only necessary when the fair value of the goodwill falls below the book value. A major disadvantage of the purchase accounting method is thus removed. It is vitally important that there is international uniformity in this area. Where goodwill is concerned, it appeared until recently that the world was converging towards the capitalisation and systematic amortisation of the goodwill amount. This is different now, therefore. The question is what the IASB will do: Will it follow the Americans? At the moment, there are fierce discussions within the IASB about these subjects, but in my estimation this will be the case in the end.

'I should also mention a subject that extends to several international accounting standards: the presentation of financial performance. When the international standards with respect to financial instruments and investment property were being drafted, it appeared that the traditional profit and loss account had shortcomings. How should you account for movements on the basis of fair value? If you adhere to a model that is based on fair value, it is not an obvious step to incorporate these movements directly in shareholders' equity. You should actually have a total summary of the results, a summary that provides insight into the quality of the profit. This can be achieved by means of a breakdown according to category, such as operating results, results from financing activities, from treasury activities and other profits and losses.

'A controversial issue that the IASB is tackling is the incorporation in the financial statements of share-based payments. This mode of payment is popular in the technology sector, particularly in the case of new companies. As a result, scarce liquid assets are spared, while for the recipients of shares or options it can lead to high future income.

'Intangible assets are still occupying many minds. The standard on the subject dates from 1998, which is still fairly recent. Nevertheless, the IASB wants to get to grips with this subject again. This is because there are still considerable differences with national standards and the importance of intangibles is constantly increasing. The subject must therefore be tackled with a wider scope than it has been until recently. Besides the traditional financial statements, it may perhaps be necessary to report separately on the intangible aspects of the business operations.

'Furthermore, the reporting on financial instruments will undoubtedly remain high on the agenda in the coming years, both in view of the criticism of the existing standards and the goal – particularly in the Anglo-Saxon world – of producing a full fair value model.

'This is only a small selection from the large number of projects that will be undertaken by the IASB. Incidentally, the IASB wishes to stick to the conceptual approach and not switch to a "cookery book" approach with every detail being prescribed how particular items should be incorporated in the financial statements. No, there must be room for flexibility. After all, the world is constantly on the move.'

Do you have a positive feeling about 'IAS 2005'?

Professor Vergoossen: 'Yes, I consider the fact that all listed companies in the European Union will apply IAS with effect from 2005 to be a desirable development. This is important for the harmonisation of financial reporting in Europe. In order to realise a liquid and efficient European capital market, we must speak the same language and apply the same accounting standards. The stock exchanges are integrating more and more; Amsterdam, Brussels, Lisbon and Paris have now been incorporated within Euronext, while other European stock exchanges want to link up with Euronext or are talking about other forms of co-operation. I expect that this will lead to a single pan-European stock exchange in the time to come. This is no longer a utopia.

'The European-wide introduction of IAS is insufficient, however. It is crucial that these standards are enforced throughout Europe as well. This therefore entails adequate supervision and this is not provided for at present.'

Does this supervision also determine the quality of the external financial reporting?

Professor Vergoossen: 'Yes, this is initially determined by the quality of the standards, which should be comprehensive, clear and unambiguous. Secondly, the standards must be compulsory. Thirdly, there must be enforcement. This is necessary to guarantee a consistent interpretation and application of the IAS. The enforcement of IAS is in fact the cornerstone for producing high-quality financial reporting. Well now, the completion of the set of core standards, the restructuring of the IASC and "IAS 2005" mean that the first two criteria are complied with. Only the supervision has not yet been adequately provided for, but a lot of hard work is being done in this direction because everyone recognises how important this is.

'For the rest, properly functioning supervision in Europe is not only of overriding importance for the harmonisation at the European level, but will also be decisive for the worldwide harmonisation of financial reporting. You need the Americans behind you for this, and they will only be prepared to move towards recognition of the IAS if there is strict enforcement of the standards in Europe.'

What will be the relationship between Europe and the USA, which is by far the largest capital market in the world and also the most liquid and efficient?

Professor Vergoossen: 'Let me take up the final words of this question. How has the US capital market become so liquid and efficient? The reason is that the Americans have a very good stock exchange supervisor: the SEC. That is why they keep reiterating the importance of supervision in order to produce global rules. It is also quite understandable that they do not want to throw overboard what they have achieved. I sympathise with their point of view and can imagine that the Americans wish to hold on to their own standards for as long as possible. For the time being, they have more to lose than to gain.

'Of course, the Americans do show some goodwill. They have also taken some steps and have provided assistance. They have helped with the restructuring of the IASC. The previous SEC chairman, Arthur Levitt, had a seat on the Nominating Committee whose duty was to appoint the Trustees of the IASC. The Board of Trustees – that appoints the IASB members and oversees their independence – also includes quite a few Americans. The same applies to the IASB, which has two members who originally had a seat on the FASB, the US standard-setter. In other words, they do take such matters seriously.

'The influence of the Americans is quite considerable. The IAS are generally consistent with US GAAP, although the former are less detailed. The current structure of the IASC is almost identical to that in the United States. Incidentally, that is a precondition for them to throw in their lot with the IASC.'

*The international regulators' representative organisation
IOSCO recognised IAS. The SEC is a member of this body.
You could say that the Americans would accept IAS as a
result of this.*

Professor Vergoossen: 'In May 2000, IOSCO produced a resolution in
which it recommended its members to allow IAS for so-called cross-
border offerings and listings, that is, enterprises that issue shares or are
listed in several countries. This was a recommendation and not an instruction, therefore. Furthermore, the recommendation explicitly allows
members of IOSCO to impose extra requirements with respect to the
financial information. As a matter of fact, the latter was required to win
over the SEC.

'The practical significance of the IOSCO recommendation for the
international harmonisation of financial reporting is very limited in my
opinion, also in view of the limited number of companies to which this
relates. In order to achieve proper international harmonisation, all listed
companies and not only the cross-border listings must apply internationally accepted rules. After all, not only the demand but also the supply of
capital is internationalising, which means that investors are also finding
their way to foreign exchanges.'

*So the United States will not recognise IAS for the time
being?*

Professor Vergoossen: 'Yes, that's correct. And if they do decide to do so,
the standards will be confined to the financial reporting of non-US companies with a listing in the United States. However, I would like to reiterate that this will very much depend upon the success with which IAS are
enforced elsewhere in the world, and then particularly in Europe.

'So, for the time being, Dutch companies that are listed in the US will
have to provide profit and shareholder equity figures on the basis of US
GAAP. What we are seeing, however, is that US GAAP and IAS are growing
closer and closer together. The number of differences between them is
thus becoming smaller. Incidentally, the treatment of goodwill already
discussed by me is an exception to this, although the chances are that
this is a temporary situation.

'What the SEC will in any case not do is impose IAS on its own US
companies. For this, we still have a long way to go. IAS as a world standard
is therefore not in sight at the moment.'

What shape should the supervision of financial reporting in Europe take?

Professor Vergoossen: 'In the first place, supervision must be confined to companies that borrow on the capital market, shall we say listed companies. The inclusion of unlisted companies goes too far in my opinion; the costs far outweigh the benefits.

'Stock exchange supervision in Europe is a national affair. The manner, intensity and effectiveness of the supervision differs considerably between the member states of the European Union. In order to make "IAS 2005" a success, the supervision of financial reporting will have to be reconciled and co-ordinated Europe-wide. The Committee of European Securities Regulators (CESR) was recently established and will fulfil a role in this. In my view, this will all eventually have to result in a single pan-European stock exchange supervisory body.

'The supervision itself will have to be active, that is, companies must file their financial reports with the supervisory body. The filed documents will then be evaluated at random or thematically. The supervision must therefore not be passive whereby the supervisory body waits until a complaint is submitted. Actually, what I have in mind is the SEC model. Nevertheless, I believe that the European stock exchange supervisors – in contrast with what the SEC does – must refrain from drafting financial reporting rules. Instead of this, they should inform the IASB of any problem areas. We must try to prevent the creation of a European version of the IAS.

'In the Netherlands, the government wants to charge the Authority for the Financial Markets with the supervision of financial reporting. The thinking in this respect is in the direction of active enforcement.'

How does this active stock exchange supervision of financial reporting relate to the audit?

Professor Vergoossen: 'The audit is more like first-line supervision: have the rules been complied with? Do the financial statements give a true and fair view of the financial position and of the results achieved by the company? That is the auditor's responsibility. Obviously, the financial reporting itself is the responsibility of the company.

'I see stock exchange supervision as second-line supervision. This should concentrate in particular on the consistent interpretation and application of IAS. Stock exchange supervision should not focus on determining whether the financial statements provide a true and fair view.

That is the job of the auditor. We should try to avoid a duplication of activities. Furthermore, stock exchange supervision of financial reporting has its limitations. It is a desktop review by the supervisory body that is based on the financial reports filed by companies. Stock exchange supervision is a matter for the company and the stock exchange supervisor; the auditor is in principle excluded. This does not preclude the possibility that the auditor can be consulted by the company management or brought in when the supervisory body has questions.'

What do you think about the fact that many companies do not appear to satisfy IAS on many important points, while their financial statements state that they do, or that the auditor's report states that IAS are complied with?

Professor Vergoossen: 'Yes, international research does indicate that this is the case. In the Netherlands, however, there cannot be many companies to which this situation applies; only three Dutch companies say that they apply IAS in their financial statements.

'It is, of course, an undesirable situation. The internationalisation of the business community and the globalisation of the capital markets require an audit that takes place all over the world in the same way. This is also recognised. Within IFAD, the International Forum on Accountancy Development, the Forum of Firms is being developed in order to bring the quality of the audit up to the same level worldwide, among other things by issuing a global quality standard for firms conducting transnational audits.

'The European Union is also active in this field. The European Commission is considering prescribing the International Standards on Auditing. In addition, I should mention the recommendations of the European Commission with respect to independence and quality assurance. This is all in line with the compulsory use of IAS. In fact, it is one total package directed towards the amalgamation of the capital markets in Europe.'

And what is Royal NIVRA doing about all this?

Professor Vergoossen: 'Royal NIVRA will ensure that the European recommendations are complied with as much as possible. Where independence is concerned, we have already prepared a draft standard. This is based on the recommendations of the European Commission. We will include the recommendations concerning quality assurance in the evaluation of our peer review system. This year we will complete the first four-year testing cycle. During this period, all accounting firms will be reviewed. Time for evaluation therefore. An important recommendation of the European Commission is, for example, that accounting firms with listed clients should be reviewed annually. There should also be external supervision similar to the peer reviews. We will certainly act upon these recommendations. Where the International Standards on Auditing are concerned, I can say that virtually all the standards have been included without modification in the Richtlijnen voor de Accountantscontrole, the auditing standards applicable in the Netherlands. In this respect, we are therefore ahead of the developments.'

Most auditors here are 'brought up' with Dutch legislation and standards. But how many auditors know the IAS so well that they are correctly applied?

Professor Vergoossen: 'If the auditors have kept up to date with their knowledge in the field of external financial reporting and have confined themselves in this respect to the Dutch Guidelines for Annual Reporting, they are in fact already familiar with the content of the IAS. That is because these guidelines have been adjusted at full speed to the IAS during the past five years, with only a few important guidelines still remaining in the draft phase. Therefore, Dutch auditors that take their continuing professional education seriously should already be pretty well acquainted with the IAS. I can imagine that continuing professional education is quite often pushed to the background due to the day-to-day pressure of work. Nevertheless, the auditor must pay attention to the IAS developments and be aware of the fact that they not only concern listed companies. The current developments have repercussions on the financial reporting of unlisted companies, and then not only the large companies in this category, but also small and medium-sized companies. The ultimate aim must be one system of principles for valuation and determination of results. In my opinion, there must not be any differences in this respect between listed and unlisted companies. On the other hand, I believe that differences in the field of disclosure are justified. Small and medium-sized companies will not have to provide such detailed notes, but the principles for the valuation of assets and liabilities and the determination of the results remain the same. And these are derived from the IAS. It is therefore really important for all auditors to acquaint themselves with the developments in the field of the IAS.'

Part IV

IAS and the users of financial statements

Chapter 15

Unambiguous rules, timely reports and close supervision

An interview with Peter-Paul F. de Vries

Peter-Paul F. de Vries

Peter-Paul F. de Vries (1967) has worked for the VEB (Nether-lands Association of Securities Holders) since 1989, since 1995 as deputy director and later as director. He is a member of various shareholder committees and is also Vice-Chairman of Euroshar-eholders, the confederation of European shareholders associa-tions including the VEB and its European sister organisations.

The Dutch phrase of 'a louse under one's skin' is a rather unflattering (or so it would seem) reference to someone or something that actually deserves praise for its critical and persevering attitude – naturally from others rather than its target subject. Something of this nature is also the aim of VEB, the Netherlands Association of Securities Holders [*Vereniging van Effectenbezitters*]. As its website tells us, VEB is 'an independent association that stands up for the interests of securities holders and which promotes securities holdings. VEB plays an active role in social discussions and undertakes, if necessary, group action on behalf of conned investors. The most well-known legal action taken by VEB was against World Online.'

When it became clear that KPN – the pride of the Netherlands – was having problems, VEB opened up its web page to everyone who had any plans or suggestions for saving the communications giant. This resulted in a hundred more or less serious proposals from the public, which were compiled in a report entitled 'Save KPN'. This telecom had found itself in turbulent waters (shipwrecked?) thanks to its purchase of German mobile provider E-Plus (for EUR 10.6 billion) and its investment in UMTS licenses (EUR 8.7 billion). Peter-Paul de Vries is the director of VEB.

What does VEB do?

De Vries: 'VEB is an independent association that stands up for the interests of securities holders. 'VEB attends – via its team of nearly 20 meeting attendants – about 160 annual general meetings of shareholders a year where we attempt to promote the interests of our members. We focus, above all, on the interest of the shareholder, with extra emphasis on topics such as dividends policy, acquisitions, financial position and corporate governance. Further, we publish *Effect*, a journal in which we provide background information to mergers and acquisitions, interviews with chiefs of industry, sector analyses, investment advice from experts and technical analyses. VEB is fully independent. Anyone with complaints or enquiries about their bank or equity management fund is welcome. Each year, VEB holds its "Share Day" investors convention in co-operation with NCVB. Together with Bank Labouchere, we have set up the "VEB Bottom Line", a stock market order line for placing orders at cost, which is often 70–80% less than what the traditional providers charge.'

What do you think of financial reporting among listed companies in the Netherlands?

De Vries: 'It leaves much to be desired. It affords much too much room for interpretation. Investors and analysts are thus frequently left in the dark. The financial reports leave too much room for influencing the figures. In our experience, therefore, the figures themselves do not tell us very much. In order to interpret the figures, one must rely on the accounting principles, the relation between the key indicators and industry-level comparisons. The view provided by the figures became even cloudier from the point that companies were allowed to adopt the large-scale capitalisation of goodwill. That really made things worse.

'The main objection is that goodwill is such an extremely ephemeral balance sheet item. Its valuation is highly arbitrary. If a company has EUR 2 billion in shareholders' equity and is bought for EUR 10 billion, goodwill is EUR 8 billion. Now, if I were a megalomaniac company chief who only thought about growing for the sake of growth, and if I wanted to ensure that I could steal a march on my rival, I would pay more than what the company was worth, for example, EUR 15 billion, and my megalomania would be recorded in the balance sheet as an asset. Indeed, there is something quite amiss here.

'Another disadvantage is that the asset's value will not develop over 20 years on a straight-line basis to nil. Even more so, if the acquired business has a strong brand name and that brand is properly groomed, it might even increase in value. This is therefore no way to achieve a clear reflection of reality, which is our objective after all.

'My greatest objection – and I had actually expected and hoped to receive more support from auditors in this respect – is that the capitalisation of goodwill is not in conformity with the prudence principle. If companies find themselves in trouble, they see a rapid decline in the value of their goodwill and intangible assets. This worsens their balance sheet position. In other words, if a company starts sliding down towards the abyss, it gets a severe beating on the way. That cannot possibly have been the intention of capitalisation. This was introduced in the past to give Dutch companies more purchasing power than would be justified on the basis of their shareholders' equity. Now, however, the facts of the matter have caught up with us.'

So if KPN had to make a downward value adjustment tomorrow, it would be technically insolvent?

De Vries: 'That was the case at year-end 2000, when the company had EUR 28.5 billion in goodwill and only EUR 13 billion in shareholders' equity. The old accounting principles would have placed it at a negative EUR 15 billion, which would make it technically insolvent. That is positively horrifying. At the end of 2001 some of the air was released from the balance sheet by recognising an impairment charge for E-Plus, but the UMTS licenses are still shown in the balance sheet at the (much too high) purchase price. There are some who maintain that an intangible asset, in percentages of the shareholders' equity, should never be more than 100%. But even then, that leaves nothing over. We could ask ourselves how the banks and other credit institutions could ever have swallowed this. My only explanation is that they were able to see through it and apparently decided to start financing more on the basis of interest cover. Yet if a company's profitability is impaired, the bank no longer has any guarantee of a positive balance upon the sale of its tangible assets.'

Carrying balance sheet items at fair value is in vogue. Is this a positive development?

De Vries: 'The intention of fair value is to arrive at a realistic balance sheet and profit and loss account on the basis of actual value. But it does not stop there for this means that intangible assets are also determined at fair value. Market value is computed in a rather arbitrary manner. If I look at goodwill, the timing and degree of the adjustment to fair value are connected to the wishes of management. KPN did not recognise the impairment charge until the issue of EUR 5 billion. Further, the impairment test was based on cash flow forecasts for the distant future. Of course, those can be influenced.

In 2001, a White Paper was published on financial statement supervision, which proposed bringing supervision in line with what the SEC does in the United States. Is that a good idea? Closer supervision with possible sanctions?

De Vries: 'Yes, we are in complete agreement. In the Netherlands, one can do as one pleases without any retribution. A supervisory body created to monitor compliance with the rules needs the power of issuing sanctions. And once it has that power, it should not be afraid of using it; otherwise we are back where we started. At present, if someone has complaints about a company's financial statements and wishes to take legal action, he or she must go to the Enterprise and Companies Court. That is a great hurdle. Moreover, private parties are always at a great disadvantage, since they have not seen the underlying figures. Pieter Lakeman (see Chapter 19) truly persevered in that respect. He demanded an explanation from KPN and certainly was successful.

'We have opted for a different approach. During KPN's annual general meeting on 1 May 2001 we announced our opposition to the valuation of goodwill, since we believed that it should be adjusted downward on that basis. That is also why we did not vote in favour of the financial statements. Supervision is important to everyone – including the company itself. But those who make use of financial statements are solely analysts and financial institutions. They need to be able to rely on them; but that is not always possible. That is why we need strict rules. The SEC seems to be an extremely well-oiled organisation. Projected income is not accepted. An SEC sanction serves as a red flag for the financial markets. A company that is placed in the penalty box is stuck with a bad image for years. Another sanction is that a company which has been in violation must disclose in its annual report or in a prospectus the fact that it once overstepped the rules. That is an effective sanction. It ensures that investors are forewarned.'

There is much work to be done to explain share options and other variable remuneration in the annual report. Is that really important to the people who rely on these reports?

De Vries: 'I am not sure whether I would be serving the interests of the investor in the short term by saying that I think such remunerations should be stated at real cost. If one gives away share options, one should make it clear that these value elements should be recorded under costs. As soon as profit is presented and the share options are kept apart and only allowed to play a role in shareholders' equity, one gives too optimistic a view of business. The company apparently feels that its managers would no longer work there without their share options. Or perhaps these managers could demand a higher salary at another company. In principle, this is clearly a matter for the profit and loss account.

'We occupy a place somewhere between Rhine country and the Anglo-Saxon model. An unfortunate by-product is that while we have elected the Anglo-Saxon form of remuneration, we have not accepted the Anglo-Saxon style of reporting, that is, complete openness. Nor have we embraced the Anglo-Saxon corporate governance of shareholder approval. This is kept at a distance, because we are afraid that shareholders will withhold their approval for excessive share option schemes. So if we elect the Anglo-Saxon remuneration model, we should also accept the Anglo-Saxon approval model.'

Should IAS also be introduced in the Netherlands, as the EU wishes?

De Vries: 'I am no expert on reporting systems, but to my mind the advantage to IAS is that they will limit companies' room to present their figures according to their own beliefs. In essence, that seems like a positive development to me, but it does not mean that we should think that this will do away with the room for interpreting and influencing the figures. That would still be there, albeit to a diminished extent. The aim for uniformity is, unto itself, a wise move, since we no longer see our share market as local but rather as European or global. We live in a world in which the figures from a company's financial statements are considered absolute rather than relative – in the sense of the applicable accounting principles.

'I would like to see a limitation of the elbow room for valuing goodwill according to one's own beliefs. KPN's most recent response to the issue of capitalising goodwill is not very encouraging. They insist that the plans and forecasts on future income from E-plus and UMTS licenses justify their optimism. They see the auditor's signature as a guarantee that the future cash flows from their acquisitions will exceed the amount recorded for them in the balance sheet. This is certainly starting to smell like Fokker. For what is happening now? They have forecast the number of mobile telephone users, the income per mobile telephone user and its growth and, if necessary, these forecasts will (or can) be adjusted. This notwithstanding, they still justify this figure's place in the balance sheet. And what about the discount rate: KPN's credit rating saw a sharp decline, which means that the discount rate must have skyrocketed. During the general meeting of shareholders on 5 October 2001 we therefore enquired whether any changes had been made to any of these factors – income per user, growth in the number of users, discount rate and the point at which UMTS services could be offered. The board refused to give us an answer. Since then, the share prospectus has raised a new humiliating fact. The relevant cash flows are undiscounted and therefore not stated at their present value.

'If I hear analysts saying that KPN cannot sell any part of E-plus because that would turn its shareholders' equity negative, then this is quite an extraordinary way of treating the figures. Their balance sheet has therefore placed them in a commercial bind. As far as I am concerned, KPN could have made these investments as long as it had secured proper financing. There is nothing wrong with a Mercedes, but if one has no income and no equity, it remains a bad buy. And their story that "We were just doing the same as our European rivals", is not a valid argument. The other telecommunication companies (French Telecom, Deutsche Telekom and Telefonica) had a much stronger balance sheet. And moreover, KPN is not one of the herd. It is its own enterprise!'

So the balance sheet is not 'sanctifying'. Would financial reporting according to IAS be better?

De Vries: 'We are now in the unfortunate situation where we in the Netherlands receive most of our information from the USA. The bottom fell out of Lernout & Hauspie, for instance, in the United States. The information content of Ahold's Dutch annual report is vastly different from its US report. That is a pity, because it makes us dependent on information which people in the USA have at their disposal. This just shows how far we are lagging behind in that respect. So I am always pleased whenever a Dutch company obtains a US listing. Not because I believe that it will help to generate more trade or that it will help to curb the cost of capital or boost its share price, but simply because more information will be disclosed. What a brilliant reason to commend a US stock exchange listing – wouldn't you agree? All in all, I cannot predict whether IAS will lead to dramatic improvements. But the informational value of US financial reporting and figures is indubitably higher than here.'

What else needs to be changed?

De Vries: 'The elbow room that the Dutch regulations give companies to play with figures. I have always been staunchly opposed to the situation in which a company acquires a business in August but consolidates it with effect from 1 January of the same year. I also have great objections to writing down the shareholders' equity of the acquisition target. This makes the goodwill turn out higher and all manner of provisions are created which can be used later to pep up the proceeds. These are all established possibilities, which are used in full. There are even some companies that do not consolidate the activities of wholly-owned subsidiaries, because they have announced their intention to hive them off. They repeat this each year. Schuttersveld (now Kendrion) is one such company, but if one holds 100% of something, it simply must be consolidated. The financial statements need to reflect the whole truth. The figures should not be manipulated. Yet companies that make a lot of acquisitions do not give much insight into their figures. Nor is organic growth properly elucidated. And I do not have much trust in the figures that are presented. If a company claims to have achieved 7%, 10% or 13% organic growth, there is no way for me to check that. It could be true, but I do not know how they came up with those figures. In this respect, we have become very suspicious.

'I was originally an advocate of the old system where goodwill and its valuation were disclosed – but without incorporating it into the figures. That should be the job of the people reading the financial statements, but the figures themselves would remain intact. I prefer hard figures with the familiar limitations to today's soft figures. Dutch businesses have been having their cake and eating it: with goodwill in the balance sheet but preferably without goodwill factoring into the calculation of profit per share. That is not a very consistent approach. What I would truly like to see is the presentation of figures for two years according to both the new and the old principles. Then we could make a comparison. But if this were done, many companies would show a negative shareholders' equity. They have therefore wisely decided not to take this approach.

'Further, the interest of the investor should be given more attention. Every company chooses its own target and ratios. Traditional companies without any major acquisitions focus on net profit. Companies which have made acquisitions focus on per-share profit before the amortisation of goodwill. Those with a positive cash flow state their targets in terms of EBIT and those who cannot even manage that focus on EBITDA. And the investors? They cannot see the wood for the trees. Financial reporting should not be like ordering à la carte, where one can opt for whatever is the most appealing or flattering. A positive EBITDA is nice, but do not forget that those taxes (T) and interest (I) still need to be paid and that depreciation (D) is often subject to mandatory replacement investments.

'We therefore find it high time that companies publish their quarterly figures. That initiative actually needs to come from the stock exchange. Those companies which we were able to convince to take this step are actually quite pleased with the results. After all, a quarterly information system also forces them to work more quickly and to stay alert. Problems can be placed under control more quickly. Moreover, companies in the year 2002 can simply no longer get away with reporting to their share-holders only twice a year. KPN recently made the switch. E-plus was actually acquired in 1999, although it was not reflected in the figures until 2000. It was not until April 2001 that they told us about the damage. It would have been nice to know that before. That is why we are so in favour of quarterly figures. Transparency also means being honest with oneself. And that is good for everyone, including the organisation in question.'

Chapter 16

The supervisory director: striking the right balance

An interview with Paul C. van den Hoek

Paul C. van den Hoek

Professor Paul C. van den Hoek (1939) was until 1998 attached to the controller course at the Free University of Amsterdam as a Professor of Company Law. He works for the legal firm of Stibbe. In addition, he is a supervisory director at various companies, including ASMI, Buhrmann, Ballast Nedam and Robeco Groep.

According to the Van Dale Dutch dictionary, the word 'commissaris' dates back to 1353. It originates from Medieval Latin and means more or less 'delegate' or 'deputy'. Today a 'commissaris' is understood as an authorised agent or representative (as in the Royal Commissioner or the Commissioner of Police) or someone who in the name of the shareholders supervises and counsels the directors of a company. In the last case, the 'commissaris' (or supervisory director in English) is a member of a supervisory board, an official body which oversees the policies of the management and the general state of affairs of an enterprise.

Not so very long ago, the image of the supervisory directors was 'striking', to put it gently: corpulent, prosperous men who met together every so often to sip gin, puff on expensive cigars, listen to the company management, and then give their nod. It was all a formality, nothing more. Without a doubt, it was a distorted picture. Since the 1980s, supervisory directors have come increasingly under fire, especially when the management has been given a too free hand and has taken some very consequential decisions without having to paying heed to any form of rebuttal or criticism. Obviously this is locking the stable door after the horse has bolted and the business has gone bankrupt. There have also been calls for the supervisory board to be held responsible for wrongdoing.

Nowadays, the supervisory board cannot be compared to a dozing hound in a sunny yard. The supervisory directors keep a sharp and vigilant eye on the state of affairs inside and outside a company; as a rule, they bring much business experience and the necessary objectivity to a company, are desirable and respected controllers and advisers as well as valuable interlocutors for the auditor. What does a supervisory director expect from the financial reporting? We asked Professor Paul van den Hoek. He is a supervisory director for several companies and knows the subject well.

Can a supervisory director perform his role properly with the present system of financial reporting?

Professor Van den Hoek: 'In general, the supervisory directors function as a Board. Although each supervisory director is very interested in the numbers, each also has a specific role to perform. This is especially true for a larger enterprise, which will often have an audit committee. The role of a supervisory director in financial reporting is determined to some extent by the specific role, which he or she performs on the Board. For example, I am a lawyer; my background is not financial. This is not a problem as long as there are also a few supervisory directors who have a good feel for the numbers and can interpret them well. Other supervisory directors have other specialisations: strategy, personnel management, marketing, contracts, etc.

'Nonetheless, internal and external financial reporting is more than numbers alone. Supervisory directors cannot do a good job if they are not well informed – and keep themselves well informed – on what business is going on. They should see the numbers, preferably every four weeks, presented in a standardised format in which the key ratios are prominent and can be readily identified. Comparisons, *vis-à-vis* the prior fiscal year and the specified budget, can then be made easily. The changes clearly stand out.

'Certain key figures are not of equal concern to every business and can be subject to trends. I am thinking now of cash generation. The analysis of cash flow is far more important now than ever before and it has also become more important than the profit and loss accounts. You must look carefully at the development of the working capital and the extent to which the cash flow is positive. Other indicators are also important. Furthermore, the supervisory director must remain objective and keep a distance from daily operations.

'Naturally, external financial reporting must be correct and complete. The same holds true for internal reporting; after all, that is how you settle up your accounts. In as much, this information is also important for a supervisory director, especially concerning a company which is quoted on the stock exchange and publishing quarterly results. Every three months you are confronted with figures which can arouse certain expectations. The supervisory director must act as a sort of gyroscope to find the balance between the expectations and the reality. In short, the bottom line has got to tally. The Board is responsible for keeping disappointments to a minimum. If there are disappointments, the supervisory directors, too, will be sharply rebuked by the public: they must pay better attention and take corrective action.'

How can the supervisory board be certain the financial reporting is complete?

Professor Van den Hoek: 'The supervisory director does not have much to do with the actual making of the financial report, with the exception of decisions related to the accounting principles and the assignment of provisions. One issue, which would concern the supervisory directors and over which they would have a say, is if you have charged the goodwill directly to shareholders' equity and you are not forced to capitalise and amortise it. The same holds true for the time frame for the write-offs: do you opt for 40, 20 or 10 years? Thus, if there are fundamental choices regarding accounting principles, it is up to the supervisory board or the audit committee to deal with them. If there are no choices, because the law or accounting principles specify a certain course of action, there is also no discussion. The supervisory directors are then given the annual report in draft, which is discussed with the management in the presence of an external auditor. It is, however, essential that the most critical items are highlighted and included in the document. The amount of available time and the expertise of the supervisory board must not be overestimated. The supervisory board is not a detective squad which investigates the numbers and uncovers the mistakes. That is not our job. Nevertheless, we will always study an annual report of some hundred pages thoroughly and compare it with the data from the prior years. That's how questions surface. However, if downright choices must be made or dilemmas must be solved, the management and/or the auditor must indicate them and answer our questions on them.'

And the directors' report?

Professor Van den Hoek: 'The directors' report is especially important for enterprises with external shareholders. They have a right to know what has been going on with the business. The tone is also significant. It must not be too optimistic, but certainly not too grim. In this respect, cultural differences can play a role. Take, for example, last year's annual report of the office product supplier Buhrmann. It was written up in English. Not only did the management work on the text, but also an external public relations firm and, of course, the auditor. It was a real co-production. The Dutch supervisory directors found the report too enthusiastic, too jubilantly worded. My two American colleagues found it acceptable. The American norm is more jubilant. According to them, there was nothing wrong with laying things on a little thicker.

'In continental Europe, we tend to be more reserved and shun exaggeration. In the USA, one is quick to label something "fantastic" or "extremely urgent" instead of using a more moderate expression. It's all in the art of communication. You also see these cultural nuances in the Orient. "No" is not said there, because the word is impolite or offensive. Consequently, "Yes" does not always mean "Yes" there. Here in the Netherlands, we try to word our text carefully, especially with regards to future expectations and forward-looking statements. Otherwise, before you know it, you are guilty of misrepresentation.'

How do you view the internationalisation (read: Americanisation) of external financial reporting?

Professor Van den Hoek: 'I am Chairman of the supervisory board of the Dutch semiconductor equipment manufacturer, ASM International NV (ASMI). The company has been listed on the NASDAQ since 1981 and on the Amsterdam exchange, AEX (now Euronext Amsterdam), for five years. It is included in the Amsterdam Midcap Index. ASMI has always published two financial statements. The original report is drawn up in accordance with US accounting principles, as required by the American SEC. However, since ASMI is a Dutch company and its financial statements must conform to Book 2 of the Netherlands Civil Code, a separate report with reconciliation is also made. Compared to the American version, the Dutch report looks very meagre. Anything not absolutely necessary is done as simply as possible. A good impression must be made on SEC and on the American investors. Consequently, that report looks magnificent. Nevertheless, the Dutch report, produced according to the Dutch system, is the version which is approved at the shareholders' meeting. I have never had any problem with that. It is only an omen that the US – by means of their accounting standards and the importance they place on the presentation of a report to the public – is setting the trend for Europe in general and the Dutch in particular.

'We must catch up with the US GAAP, which are much stricter than the flexible Dutch rules. In the Netherlands, as long as the financial statements are drawn up systematically and provide good insight (the general criteria of Book 2 of the Netherlands Civil Code), there is leeway. Consequently, with regards to external financial reporting, a company such as ASMI, which has already been subject to the US accounting rules for 20 years, is much further along than the majority of Dutch companies, which have only followed the Dutch rules. Look at their sections on options, remuneration systems, pension costs, goodwill, etc. The books are very detailed and open.

'In 1999, the FASB issued specific rules on revenue recognition. This can be fiddled with: machines for the manufacture of a chip are capital goods. Then there is also the grey area: What belongs in the financial year which is almost ending? What belongs in the next financial year? The introduction of this new rule on revenue recognition cost ASMI around USD 10 million in the first year. It was grin and bear it, because that money was gone. The amount must be spread out over a number of years. No matter how painful, it is a tough, but good rule in itself. It forces line management to be very disciplined with respect to transport, invoicing, and the fact that the client has accepted the goods. These are now the deciding criteria and must form the basis for management.

'Such rules greatly reduce the chance of errors and aberrations. It is noteworthy that the financial irregularities of the Dutch software and business services company Baan and the Belgian speech technology products firm Lernout & Hauspie were first exposed in the USA. The *Wall Street Journal* published information that was available from the SEC. In this respect, the Americans are much more advanced than the Dutch. Naturally, you don't have to agree with all the rules. Take the treatment of goodwill for example. The Americans have again come up with something new (the annual impairment test). Sometimes I wonder which interest is served with some of the new rules. Not every change is an improvement.

'All in all, there is great advantage to more uniformity in financial reporting. We are getting that here now too. We can soon choose between the international and the US standards. Those who, for example, want to invest in the automobile sector, benefit by being able to compare the financial reports of Ford, Daimler Chrysler and General Motors with each other. It is a logical aspect of the globalisation of financial markets, of stock exchanges, and thus also of financial reporting. No one can have anything against this.'

Is financial reporting too formal: too much form and too little content?

Professor Van den Hoek: 'Some facts and events are readily expressed in numbers, while others are not. Some numbers just can't be added, subtracted, multiplied or divided. In other words, numbers are not always "equal". Nevertheless, this does not bother me when I see financial statements. You must look through them. I try to understand what is actually going on by the way in which the executive board is answering questions, by watching how the directors deal with each other, by recalling the reasons for an acquisition and what has come of it. Furthermore, a supervisory director can ask anything he or she wants to about internal financial reporting. Internal reporting is not too formal; external reporting could possibly be too formal, but that doesn't bother me.'

What is the relationship between the supervisory board and the auditor?

Professor Van den Hoek: 'In my opinion, this relationship does not have to be intimate. You must keep a distance to be able to work professionally with each other. Some people feel they need to be "close" to be able to work with each other. I don't. I do not have to be on a first-name basis with someone to have a great respect for him or her and vice versa.

'However, there must be no barriers. You must be able to say things and to ask each other questions. The auditor must have access to the chairman of the supervisory board in order to tell him or her something important and perhaps too sensitive to be said in a meeting. The chairman must be "open". Nothing is gained by playing hide-and-seek. Once I had an auditor come to me to say that something was bothering him. It had nothing to do with the figures, but rather with the actions of the CFO. That was also difficult for the auditor to bring up, because that same financial director paid his fees and could discharge him from his assignment. The guy was walking on eggshells. It was therefore of the utmost importance for the auditor and the chairman of the supervisory board to trust one other. I need to have this relationship, because I want to know what the auditor finds out during his work. For whatever reason, the auditor has got to open his mouth too. If the chairman of the supervisory board is not aware of any trouble, sooner or later he will definitely be put on the spot. Some problems are better solved informally. As a rule, the informal way is much more practical than the formal channels.

'If you do not agree with the findings of the auditor, you can always call for another opinion. If a fundamental question is involved, the professional practice research department of the auditor's firm might have the answer. This situation could be potentially awkward for the consulted colleague, but you must always remain professional. For this reason, I advocate a professional distance between client and auditor.'

What problems are there in the area of external financial reporting and what are the choices?

Professor Van den Hoek: 'Segment reporting can be done according to sector or geographical area or whatever. Transparency makes you more vulnerable to criticism. You used to be able to report an increase of 2% without having to report that Saudi Arabia was responsible for a plus 20 and the Netherlands a minus 18. Thus, the more you segment, the more transparency there is.'

The attention paid to corporate governance seems to be waning. A few years ago you saw the recommendations of the Peters Committee (Committee for Corporate Governance 1996) in some annual reports. You don't see that anymore. Was it all just hype?

Professor Van den Hoek: 'I see two standards. One is the "hype", where the words "corporate governance" pepper every third sentence. The other is the reality. The hype puts forth corporate governance as a panacea or a holy commandment. Of course, that is crazy. The discussions of a few years back, however, have had a positive effect on the behaviour of management and supervisory directors. We are now, more than ever, inclined to give account for everything and whatnot. I will always remember the comments of the chairman of the executive board at a shareholders meeting some four years ago. At one point during the meeting, which had already been going on four hours, someone stood up and started asking even more specific questions. The chairman reacted grumpily: "We have already discussed that, and besides, those of us behind this table must get back to work now." Apparently he re-garded the shareholders meeting as an irritating interruption of his work, and not his work or a task he was hired to do. Whereas in fact, one of the most important tasks of the chairman of an executive board is to give an account of the money to the people who gave it to him. That was then. As a lawyer, I have attended meetings of the management of a company and have heard people speak disparagingly of the shareholders. In some cases, the shareholders had it coming to them. Sometimes they definitely did not behave like expert and discerning parties who had really analysed the books and who only asked questions which were absolutely necessary. The discussions about corporate governance have stirred things up, which is very good. I think that this trend will continue and the require-ments to justify the accounts will increase.'

On to the year 2005 and IAS: as a lawyer, do you find such rules a good idea?

Professor Van den Hoek: 'Yes, the efforts to harmonise financial reporting, particularly of large enterprises which borrow on the various capital markets, give reason to cheer. The rules are fairly flexibly formulated; therefore, they should not be so difficult to satisfy. Naturally, there will be some interpretation problems, but I remain quite enthusiastic.'

Should small and medium-sized companies have financial reporting requirements?

Professor Van de Hoek: 'External financial reporting is directed particu-larly toward two target groups: the creditors and the shareholders. From the financial statements, a creditor must be able to determine if a business is healthy or not and to evaluate its solvency. Whether the company is very large or medium-sized, does not really matter. Even though the interests in absolute financial terms are somewhat smaller in a medium-sized business than in a large one, the information still must be reliable and clear.

'As to whether a director-large shareholder must report to himself or herself, I don't know. As far as I am concerned, the rules could be reduced somewhat, but I don't know where the line is to be drawn. Nevertheless, I expect that more requirements will be established for smaller companies. After all, they must also report to the bank, the chamber of commerce, the tax authorities. A creditor wants to have information about the net equity and the like. That is also the rationale behind the European Directives. The creditor and other interested parties must be protected and not unpleasantly surprised. Consequently, it is not just about the bank, but also about the contractor that the company wants to hire and who goes to the chamber of commerce to see if the contracting party is bona fide and solvent.'

Will issues such as the amortisation of goodwill have an impact on company decisions?

Professor Van den Hoek: 'To pay goodwill for a company, capitalise the costs and write them down so that it is reflected in the future annual earnings is logical. The profit made from an acquisition is something to show off proudly. It is therefore also realistic to book the surplus value in excess of the acquired book value as the capitalised future profit (market value of the future earnings) by means of amortisation of the goodwill to the debit of annual earnings. To write down these costs over 20 years and record them against the profit makes sense to me.

'The impairment test can actually be a worthwhile addition. The amortisation of goodwill over a period of 20 years at 5% is somewhat static. If during the tenth year you see that the goodwill really no longer exists, should you do something radical? Issues of this sort naturally impact on business decisions. But if I look at the Dutch telecom company KPN, I can't help but say that they obviously have not quite realised that they have banked on the next generation. Nevertheless, there were probably some supervisory directors who advocated caution. Even if you capitalise the goodwill so that you can amortise it over a period of 20 years, it is still a hefty amount that is charged to the result every year if the acquired goodwill is high. That is a control factor, and rightly so.

'In the past, solvency ratios were always examined before an acquisition was considered and that can still be useful. Many factors play a role in an acquisition. I often ask for a pro-forma balance sheet and ditto 'profit and loss statement after acquisition'. If you analyse a similar scenario and see in the classic case that the solvency ratio drops below the level which it has always maintained, it can be a reason to cancel the operation. Similarly, if the management is not strong, that can be another reason to back away. That may also be the case with the presentation of future earnings and then thus EBIT – and not EBITDA – when there are such enormous amounts of goodwill to be worked off. There is a good reason why many companies have published their EBITDA in the last years. Then they are not required to show everything. However you must be able to look through this.'

What is your view on the future of financial reporting for companies? Will you also speak on the director's liability and the publication of the director's remuneration?

Professor Van den Hoek: 'Liability enters the picture when it appears that procedures have not been followed meticulously. You cannot blame a supervisory director if the company makes a loss. You can blame him or her if they have never contacted the auditor or if they have supported the appointment of someone who evidently was not qualified or if they collaborated on an irresponsible acquisition policy. I think that the increased complexity of financial reporting and the more stringent requirements for corporate governance have made the risk of liability greater. With regards to the remuneration of the supervisory directors, I do want to say that the compensation is very often too low, considering all which is asked of them. This is particularly the case for the chairman of the supervisory board. Much more is demanded from him or her than from the others.

'The disclosure of a director's remuneration will not lower his or her pay cheque. On the contrary, I think it might even increase it, because comparisons will be made each year. In any case, a good director will work as hard to do his or her best for one million euros as for two million. He or she will certainly not work twice as hard if they are paid twice as much. There is a limit though. I find it absurd that Mr. Eisner of the Walt Disney Company earns USD 200 million. Until recently, Dutch directors lagged behind their French, German, Belgium, and (let alone) American counterparts in terms of remuneration. However, as far as that is concerned, the equalising of income has had the desired effect. The reason fee payments in the Netherlands have risen so substantially during the past few years is because we are not an island or remote outback. We are part of a global market for managers, where fee rates affect each other.

As a citizen I say that there must be a certain limit. If I had such a job, I would want to be able look the doorman straight in the eye when I walked into the building in the morning. That would be easier if the pay scale differences were not so extravagant. On the other hand, a company could possibly lose its best people if their colleagues in England or Germany earned twice as much for the same amount of work and responsibility. The demands of the marketplace cannot be ignored.'

Chapter 17

Insurers are lagging behind

An interview with Lou Traas

Lou Traas

Professor Lou Traas (1934) studied in Rotterdam at the Nederlandse Economische Hogeschool, now the Erasmus University. He graduated in 1956. In the 1960s he held a variety of financial management positions at Philips, including head of the commercial economics department. In 1969 he became Professor of Business Economics at the Free University of Amsterdam. Since his retirement in 1994, Professor Traas has carried out numerous investigations. Furthermore he is in regular demand for committees such as those on insurance companies' financial reporting. Since the early 1980s Professor Traas has been involved with many courses of the VERA steering committee on business economics, either as lecturer or as a steering committee member.

In an age characterised by internationalisation, the call for uniformity of rules is ringing ever louder. For the sake of comparability and comprehensibility, there is a quest for standards which can apply everywhere. After all, were not units of size, weight and money the most significant stimuli for the unification of states? And this is also clearly the case in the EU with rules which apply to each member state – to say nothing of the introduction of the euro. The increasing demand for the standardisation of rules can also be seen in financial reporting. The 68-year-old 'éminence grise' Professor Lou Traas, Professor Emeritus at the Free University of Amsterdam, is calling forcefully for more uniformity in reporting rules, 'Provided that this is coupled with more thoroughness in the instructions and a higher quality of explanatory notes. Introduction of the IAS rules in Europe in 2005 will bring about this uniformity. This will take reporting into a new phase. Given uniform rules for the financial statements, the management's discussion and analysis section in the annual reports and the directors' report will receive more attention and will be extended. This will be generally beneficial for the quality of reporting.'

Professor Traas has published extensively on the quality of financial reporting. He is a member of the jury of the Henry Sijthoff prize awarded every year for the best annual report, covering both financial statements and directors' reporting. Another committee, which he is the chairman of and which accordingly bears his name, is concerned with the quality of insurance companies' reporting. The findings of this committee have created considerable commotion. Aegon senior executive, K. J. Storm, wrote in *Het financieele Dagblad* on 8 August 2001 that the recommendations of the Traas Committee would lead to poor reporting. Professor Traas replied to this with an article in the same newspaper (31 August 2001) entitled 'Aegon wants to drive looking through the rear-view mirror'. That was telling them!

What's your opinion about financial reporting of insurance companies?

Professor Traas: 'I do not particularly doubt the willingness of insurance companies to give the outside world details of the full extent of their activities and their financial position. Naturally, insurance companies' annual reports contain the necessary information on this and much can be gleaned from them on current and future management policy. But I find that their quality is disappointing on essential matters. Firstly, there is a lack of consistency. In the Netherlands, there is a fairly broad scope within which a company can choose how it wants to present its reporting. That does not make it any easier to compare companies' results. And comparison is not only becoming more difficult between companies – call it horizontally – but also between different years' annual reports from the same company – call it vertically – due to much switching between reporting methods in some areas. In general, companies do this so as to present their results as favourably as possible and so the user of the report has to be able to read between the lines.

'Secondly, many insurance companies are missing the point when it comes to earnings information. They are not giving details, as part of the result for the year under review, of what happened regarding investment results, what was received as dividends and interest or the movements in the value of their investment portfolios. Here too, we can see different companies doing different things. They first take investment results to a revaluation reserve, and subsequently release them gradually from the reserve to the income statement. This gradual release to the income statement can stretch over 30 years, which means that the results can appear exceptionally stable. You already know, as it were, in February what will happen for the full year to 31 December, and so the effects of the stock market crash of 2001 – strongly reinforced by the events of 11 September 2001 in the United States – are barely visible in the investment results reported in 2001's income statements. This crash will be spread out over the next 20 to 30 years and thereby reduced to a small blip. I do not consider that to be reliable reporting. But it is ideal for the business, which is able to present a steady earnings picture, with no surprises. In this way it can create great confidence with the financial market. But, of course, the problem is that an average figure over such a long period means little. The business can already be long bankrupt, while on the basis of the moving average it is still able to show a profit. Using a moving average would be possible if it were certain that insurance companies had an indefinite life expectancy.

'The idea underlying this spreading is that investment results should be appraised over an entire investment cycle. Some people think that you should look at a very broad cycle, such as the Kondratieff Wave, familiar from economic theory, which takes 30 years to go from peak to trough and then back again over the following 30 years. Therefore the averaging must be over 30 years, to cover the entire cycle. Now, if an insurance company was in fact immortal, there would be absolutely no problem in averaging over such a long period. But not even insurance companies last for ever. Vie d'Or for example turned out to be very fragile: the shocked policy-holders did not escape lightly after the mess had been cleared up.

'Conceptually, the annual reporting of insurance companies is com-pletely wrong as a result of averaging. In simple terms, the objective of annual reporting is to provide information on accountability, so that the actions of management and supervisory directors can be endorsed. But it is absurd to endorse their conduct for the past year on the basis of a moving average over the last 30 years. Annual reporting should also provide information for creditors, shareholders, employees, policyholders and other stakeholders to base decisions on; they need an idea of the state of the business. In general, the annual report should do this by presenting a picture of the company's ability to generate profits and cash flow; this enables investors to assess the market value of their shares. To get an idea of these things, we "simply" need detailed information about the most recent year – after all, it is the closest to the future.

'Averaging across a cycle makes absolutely no sense for financial statements. Philips makes many products which have their own life cycle, for example the video recorder. That, at least according to Philips, has just about reached the end of its 30-year life cycle. But Philips is not going to determine its results in that sector in its annual report by averaging them over the life cycle of video recorders or shavers, is it? The same also applies, for example, in the chips industry and for bulk chemicals. Everyone knows that these are cyclical industries which, every so often, go through a deep recession. Companies in these sectors simply report their annual earnings – sometimes high, sometimes low – but do not consider working with moving averages over half a cycle. So my criticism of insurance companies' annual reports is quite strong in this respect. Application of the so-called indirect yield method is not allowed anywhere on earth. Only in Canada is there anything similar, and even there they want to get rid of it. But because all insurers of any importance also report according to US GAAP the need for abolition is not so urgent. In the Netherlands there are experts, such as Professor A. Oosenbrug (see Chapter 21), who state with great authority that the system of averaging, in fact, conflicts with the law.

'Within a few years the IASB guidelines will become mandatory for quoted companies and for the consolidated reports of unquoted companies in the financial sector. We, as a committee, should not anticipate this. The IASB will probably recommend compulsory valuation at fair value for all balance sheet items. But should we just sit down and wait patiently for this to happen? No, in the meantime we can try to make improvements. Our committee has made proposals in that direction. We want more uniformity. We want to eliminate the variations which currently exist. Quality can also be improved – and not only in the insurance sector – by introducing the idea of "comprehensive income". This will create a solid link between the income statement and the balance sheet. The movement in shareholders' equity – between opening and closing balance sheets, if you exclude movements in capital – would then correspond with the bottom line of the income statement less any dividend. It would not be permissible for shareholders' equity actually to decline if at the same time the income statement is showing a profit, or vice versa. Insurers' reporting is failing in this area as well.

'Quality can also be improved by giving even more information on solvency, that is, the company's ability to meet its long-term liabilities. It should be possible to answer the question of how big an insurance company's reserves are to absorb losses and to meet their current liabilities.'

How will the insurance companies react?

Professor Traas: 'They do not particularly want to change, of course. It is the users of information who benefit from an improvement in quality, not so much the companies themselves. The insurance companies would prefer to wait until the IASB guidelines are compulsory, so that they can change everything in one fell swoop. I certainly understand that, but I do not think it is in the interest of policyholders, the financial market and other users of the financial statements to wait so long, because "fair value accounting" in all the areas the IASB is looking at is anything but uncontroversial. It may therefore take much longer for the IASB standards to be introduced than people expect. At first, 2005 was the expected date for mandatory implementation of IASB standards in Europe. But now 2007 is being talked about and, as I said, the substantive debate about fair value still needs to be resolved and this may well take more time. The important thing, however, is that our proposals will not need to be reversed when the IASB's work is complete. The report of the Committee on Insurance Companies' Annual Reporting is definitely not an informal document of recommendations and suggestions. On the contrary, it was sent to the Ministries of Finance and Justice, who have adopted the proposals on standardising the concept of profit, "comprehensive income" and more solvency information, and submitted them to the Standing Committees for Finance and Justice of the Lower House of the Dutch Parliament with a memorandum saying that they want to draw up a bill on the subject. Those Committees agreed and the bill has already been drafted. Ultimately, Parliament will decide. We shall see how that works out.'

The profit concept shows investments at market value on the debit side of the balance sheet. Shouldn't the provision for life insurance obligations on the credit side therefore also be at market value?

Professor Traas: 'The valuation of investments is a central issue in insurance companies' reporting. It carries through in two directions. On the one hand, the Committee wants realised and unrealised movements in the value of investments to be taken to the income statement. On the other hand, the liabilities standing opposite those investments must be valued. After all, an insurance company is not merely an investment company. It holds investments because it has long-term commitments which it hopes to be able to meet from the results of those investments. A balance sheet should balance. Now, the IASB guidelines currently under discussion aim at striking a balance between the credit and debit sides, between the valuation of the investments and of the insurance commitments. An assets-liabilities approach has been proposed, in other words the balance sheet is of primary importance, rather than the determination of turnover and costs. Under this new approach that is still under discussion, investments are carried at market value (fair value). The commitments should likewise be valued on the basis of the latest mortality tables, current expense forecasts and salary trends. While there are no approved IASB guidelines on this at the moment, a solution must be found. Our committee is of the opinion that investments in fixed-interest securities must be matched against insurance commitments. We see investments in shares and property as being matched against shareholders' equity. Broadly, the total amounts of both categories on the balance sheet will be in line with each other; certainly after recent falls in share prices. Fixed-interest securities are valued at historic cost, as are the commitments. This is current practice in most of the insurance companies. We see no imbalance in this, even though the insurance world claims otherwise. We only value investments in shares and property at market value, and changes in their value will thus be reflected in shareholders' equity (and in the income statement). What we do want is to standardise the valuation of fixed-interest securities at historic cost. Different methods are still being used, but we are calling for redemption value to be the only one permitted.

'Valuation of insurance commitments on an historic basis implies that their value was established on the basis of information available when the policy was taken out. And that could have been a long time ago. This can then raise the question of whether there may be deficits in the commitments, or even hidden reserves. We will have to wait for IASB guidelines for the valuation of commitments at current value, but an adequacy test can already be applied. Indeed, this already has to be done annually for the Pensions and Insurance Supervisory Authority of the Netherlands. [*Pensioen- & Verzekeringskamer*] Our proposal is that the adequacy test should be tightened and its result disclosed in the notes. The notes must clearly identify hidden reserves or deficits, or – as they say in the insurance world – whether there is any "fat on the bones". Therefore no question of imbalance appears in our report. It is a pity that some commentators have not read the report carefully enough and thereby drawn premature conclusions.

'What the insurers are making an enormous fuss about is the volatility in annual results which would occur if realised and unrealised movements in valuation are taken directly to the income statement without being averaged. They claim that this would totally disorientate investors. In my opinion this is a gross exaggeration. The days are long gone, if they ever existed, when a company could be assessed on a single profit figure or earnings per share. For a balanced judgement, you have to look at separate elements of the result and their significance as indicators of the company's future ability to generate profit and cash flow. Goodwill amortisation is a good example of this. This has meant that investors and analysts now look at EBITDA as well as the bottom line of the income statement. So in order to properly assess insurance companies' results you will have to look at how much is represented by investment results, and what the nature of these is. Insurers suggest that you should not draw too many conclusions from fluctuations in investment results, since everything will be all right in the long run. But of course this is not so. It makes a considerable difference whether reductions in the value of the investment portfolio are the result of falling prices of structurally overvalued stocks (such as hi-tech shares) which will never return to their former values, or in Enron-type enterprises which disappear through bankruptcy, or relate, for example, to oil companies facing tem-porary pressure in the market due to a fall in oil prices.

'Movements in value should be clearly and openly described – and not hidden away in an explanatory footnote – so that investors and analysts can ask the right questions (if the right answers are not already given in the analysis part of the annual report) and assess the quality of the profit. The opposite leads to totally implausible reporting. It is surely absurd – as happened in the last few years – to report that a company has seen a major increase in earnings per share when, elsewhere, the annual report states that the investment portfolio has fallen in value by billions.'

Is internationalisation affecting the quality of reporting?

Professor Traas: 'Definitely, and I am pleased about that. I find the trend towards uniformity in the shape of IASB rules a step in the right direction. Where possible this development must be encouraged. But I would make one observation: the question is how far European political opinion, that is, the European Parliament and other EU bodies, wants to go along with IASB guidelines without making too many changes because they are fash-ioned along Anglo-American lines. I find it difficult to imagine that Europe will simply accept rules which were developed largely in the United States. So I can see considerable difficulties ahead from a political view-point. Nevertheless I think this is an excellent development.

'An essential improvement is in comparability. Problems in this area will go away. Furthermore, the IASB guidelines are of excellent quality. I think it is a major benefit that all of the choices and nuances which can now be incorporated into reporting are being removed.'

So it is all good news then? Business economists could feel they have been put in second place by the dominant legal nature of the reporting?

Professor Traas: 'That is possible. Business economic nuances are not discussed so prominently in financial statements as was formerly the case. The IASB guidelines are, and will be, relatively rigid, legally-oriented provisions. What must be shown in the balance sheet, the income statement and the notes will be set out in detail. But still, you cannot bring about a high quality in reporting merely by standard-setting. This is clear from recent developments in the United States. In 1998 the SEC began a major campaign there against ''earnings management'', also referred to as ''income smoothing'' or ''hocus-pocus accounting''. The SEC believes that there is currently major collusion between senior management, external auditors and analysts when it comes to establishing profit figures at many companies. With nods and winks, the members of this cabal create a situation where ''profit'' does not so much reflect economic reality as the situation management wants to see. And what management wants to see is continuously rising profit with a predictable line on the graph which rewards investors with a high price/earnings ratio and consequently with a high market capitalisation. According to the SEC this development could be disastrous for the efficient operation of the American capital market. The SEC has entered the battle against this on two fronts. Firstly by encouraging stricter standards on provisions and premature recognition of revenue, but also by giving non-executive directors and, in particular, audit committees (where they exist) specific responsibility for the quality of reporting. Non-executive directors should state that the financial statements and annual report present a fair view of the commercial reality within which the company is operating. This is really a quality judgement which goes far beyond establishing that the financial statements comply with accounting standards. Beyond this, the economic emphasis and the accents which strategy, marketing, logistics, etc., bring, should be given a rightful place in the annual report itself (the directors' report), but it is not possible to develop strictly legal guidelines for these.'

So what, then, is the relationship between the auditor and the directors' report?

Professor Traas: 'In my opinion it has to be more thorough. At present it is still the case that the auditor only checks to see if the directors' report says things which are not consistent with the financial statements. But I see a clear tendency towards involving the auditor to a greater extent. The proposals in the United States, which I referred to earlier, would require the non-executive directors (or the audit committee) to discuss the quality and transparency of the reporting separately with the auditor before reaching their opinion. This discussion will go much further than merely establishing compliance with accounting standards. Something similar is on the horizon in Germany where the *Gesetz zur Kontrolle und Transparanz im Unternehmungsbereich* came into effect on 1 May 1998. This is a law that requires the auditor to express an opinion, in the annual report, on the company's risk recognition system and on the directors' report.'

How can directors' reports be improved? Which elements are missing? What are the shortcomings?

Professor Traas: 'I think it is not enough for directors' reports merely to summarise the year's events, without giving any explanation or context. Reading that a new factory has been opened or a new product has been launched does not in itself tell me much: I want to know what the local market is doing, I want to read about the company's prospects and competitive position. I find propaganda, and the exaggeration of positive elements and playing down of negative elements, reprehensible. The directors' report must be balanced and offer more depth. It must show me the context within which the company is operating. I want to know the strategy the company has chosen in order to capture a particular market segment or to maintain its position.

'In this area I would like to see the SEC requirements followed. The company should provide an analysis based on three years' figures and show from historical evidence the developments which have taken place in the market, also in the financial sense with regard to the resources available. Where possible such an analysis should follow a fixed format. For financing, for example, that would be the cash flow statement, showing what funds have been generated internally, what the requirement was for external funds, what they were used for, and forecasts for all of these items. The fixed format should form a basis for readers of the directors' report, and in particular for the shareholders, who should be able to take decisions about the future. It is very important that shareholders may presume "business as usual" unless management announces that things are going to change. According to the SEC, the shareholder would then be entitled to extrapolate. If it later transpires that things which could have been disclosed were not announced in good time then senior management will "hang", at least in the United States. But things are also moving in this direction in the Netherlands. What's more, management's vision should be embodied in an assessment of the business's current position and strategy. Future expectations should be substantiated with data. An idea should be given of the way management is running the company. And more significantly, which indicators are being managed. This all comes together in the so-called "comprehensive model": giving an idea of the way the management is running the business. The outside world wants to be able to look at the company "through the eyes of management".'

What do you think of the supervision of annual reporting, from your position as adviser to the Enterprise and Companies Court?

Professor Traas: 'The Netherlands adopted a kind of "whistle-blowing" system in 1970 meaning that anyone who has a complaint, or detects suspicious signs (and can clearly demonstrate an interest in the outcome), can go to the Enterprise and Companies Court. That inevitably creates problems. Firstly, it is not that simple for an outsider to know whether something is wrong with the reporting. Secondly, there is the question of what the complainant's interest is in the case. The Supreme Court has ruled that shareholders always have an automatic interest. Employees also have an interest, unless the employer can prove otherwise in a particular case; in effect a kind of reversed burden of proof. But beyond this, everyone – lenders, suppliers, whoever – must prove an interest. Thirdly, a case takes a lot of time, patience, energy and money. Consequently the "whistle-blowing" system does not in fact work that well. This is not the fault of the Enterprise and Companies Court; it does its best to run the procedure as quickly and efficiently as possible. For supervisory purposes, it would be better to have a Companies Authority, along the lines of the American SEC, which could perform random checks, thoroughly analysing financial statements from top to bottom.'

In 2001 the Limperg Institute carried out research into the quality of reporting. One of their conclusions was that the Enterprise and Companies Court does not in fact work well as a supervisory body. Either we need another body, or the Enterprise and Companies Court must act differently. You yourself are a member of the Enterprise and Companies Court. What do you think?

Professor Traas: 'I think that the Enterprise and Companies Court works perfectly, but few complaints are brought before it. I wonder why researchers who often make such a fuss about what is wrong with everything do not submit complaints themselves. If they have no direct personal interest, they can call in the Procurator General, who can bring a case in the public interest. Provided, of course, that the public interest can be demonstrated. If so, the Procurator General will be happy to act. But neither the Procurator General nor the Enterprise and Companies Court has an institution like the SEC at their disposal and so they are dependent on third parties reporting complaints to them. Until the Netherlands has a Companies Authority (if there ever is one) at its disposal, the Limperg Institute will perform a useful social function by reporting cases of substandard reporting to the Enterprise and Companies Court. It should not just shout from the sidelines that everything is so badly organised but take action and make full use of the ways and means that already exists.'

Chapter 18

Double Dutch in financial reporting: highly flexible = extremely judgmental?

An interview with Henk P. A. J. Langendijk

Henk P. A. J. Langendijk

Professor of External Reporting at the University of Amsterdam and Nyenrode University. Member of the VERA steering committee for Financial Reporting and instructor at External Reporting seminars of the VERA.

Though it is not politically correct for a Dutchman to observe this, let alone say it out loud, the cloying consensus implicit in the Dutch polder model has led to undesirable excesses. Whether it's the overly relaxed drugs policy, the anti-authoritarian upbringing of our children or the universally accepted practice of ignoring red lights, the fact is that society has not become any safer or happier over the past 30 years. Some claim that the Dutch accountancy world has now also caught the *laissez-faire* bug. 'In the Netherlands, anything goes; in the Netherlands, you can do as you please and in the Netherlands you can get away with everything. That's more or less the way people look at us too. That's what I call "hollanditis in external reporting".' This broadside comes from a fulminating Professor Henk P. A. J. Langendijk (1952), Professor of External Reporting (NIVRA-Nyenrode, Nyenrode University and

University of Amsterdam) and well-known for his publications about the quality of external reporting in the Netherlands.

Is that quality really so poor? Surely we, the Dutch, know what's what when it comes to accountancy, and not just accountancy for that matter?

Professor Langendijk: 'The Dutch are also well-known for their smugness, boorishness and generally misplaced arrogance. As soon as we feel superior to someone else, we make no secret of the fact. The Americans and Anglo-Saxons are a different matter: we look up to them and seize every opportunity to slavishly copy them or follow in their footsteps, but as for the others...That same misplaced smugness is noticeable in the field of external reporting. The American professor Frederick Choi once praised us for being "amazing accounting technicians and accountants". And "amazing" in this context was to be interpreted in the positive sense of "highly competent". Oh, yes, how amazingly good we were at external reporting.

'But since Choi wrote that in a publication 20 years ago, the quality of external reporting in the Netherlands has – in comparative terms – suffered deterioration, it has started to flake and crumble, so to speak. It's not just the actual practices, but also the external reporting regulations in the Netherlands that are now internationally viewed in a much more critical light than was ever done by Choi. Nobes – a highly prominent British professor of accountancy – uses the phrase "highly flexible, extremely judgmental". The latter term clearly carries a negative connotation. In other words: when it comes to reporting in the Netherlands you can go in whatever direction you consider convenient. And that's what brings me to describe it as "hollanditis in external reporting". Over the past 30 years the rule in the Netherlands has been: everything has to be possible and everything is possible. And anyone who objects or protests is a reactionary and out of touch with modern ways. Common sense has come under suspicion: let your imagination run riot; that was the watchword in the 1970s and some evidently believe these heady days are still with us. So why shouldn't we have that same freedom in the field of external reporting? It is a bitter thing for me to say that this is the image we project abroad. We now not only have the dubious reputation of being a Narcostate, but also a pirates' nest in the field of external reporting.

'The law of elasticity reigns supreme in our annual accounting practices. There is an awful lot of latitude; there are a great many degrees of freedom which you can use, but also abuse. No wonder that the Netherlands has its share of scandals with financial statements that turn out to be not entirely above board. Our former Minister of Finance, Mr. Zalm, is apparently also aware of the problem, because he produced a consultation document with a view to taking stock of the opinions of Dutch groups and individuals concerning the creation of a strict supervisory body for external reporting. He obviously has his reasons for making this proposal.

'Evidently something is wrong with external reporting in the Netherlands. A scientific study carried out by the Limperg Institute indicates that the quality of external reporting in the Netherlands is rather meagre compared to the standard in other prominent countries. The researchers are not terribly impressed by the performance of Enterprise and Companies Court as a supervisory body. In the 25 years or so that this court has existed, it has proved to be something of an ad hoc orchestra. It only responds to incidents. The court plays no genuinely active role as a supervisor that systematically scrutinises and sanctions financial statements. In other words: in its current set-up, the Enterprise and Companies Court really serves no identifiable purpose.

'To raise the quality to a level comparable to what is customary in the USA and the UK, we must create a supervisory body that can restore the public's faith in external reporting. This may sound rather bold, but the media make the same point. *Het financieele Dagblad* and the NRC national newspapers regularly publish articles about external reporting in the Netherlands. These invariably centre on the application of the bookkeeping rules, as they call them. And time and time again, our external reports are found to be "unreliable to a certain degree". Accountants should take that observation to heart.'

So the Netherlands is pricing itself out of the international market?

Professor Langendijk: 'Of course we can go on pretending to ourselves that we are the ones who are right, but the world is much bigger than our country. There are too many degrees of freedom in our external reporting, and that leaves a lot of scope for abuse; particularly compared with the countries around us such as Germany, France, Belgium, the UK and, a little further afield, the USA. The IAS are also stricter than the Dutch rules. So I welcome the fact that Dutch regulations are being adapted to the IAS and that this is to take place, as proposed for the listed companies, before 2005. This will improve the quality of external reporting in the Netherlands.

'Another major step forwards, if you ask me, would be to scrap Article 362 Section 4 and thus get rid of the derogatory effect of that section. Now that really would help to improve the quality. I always call that article the escape clause. The fact that you need to diverge from the detailed provisions of the law to give the required true and fair view is asking for trouble in my opinion. That article is a monstrous anachronism; it's more than half a century old and stems from the good old days when the world was still a happy and straightforward place and Mum knitted you a jumper for Christmas. But come on, all that's long ago... So: stricter rules and an efficient and consistent supervisory body that goes about its task in a systematic manner with a large high-calibre staff and lots of clout in terms of supervisory sanctions. And, if the company fails to adhere to the rules, the auditor must simply say so in his or her report. That way, you get the clarity you need. But, as things stand, there is still no such transparency in the existing structure.'

Okay, tighter rules. But surely these can also impair the quality?

Professor Langendijk: 'No, really they can't. Entrepreneurs are an imaginative lot and will always explore the boundaries of what's possible. If you draw unclear lines for them, you bring the problems upon yourself. They'll simply think they can get away with anything. So once again: stringent rules.

Actually we should really move towards a system with a single method of valuation, a single method of estimation, and so on; no more options in other words. Stringent rules must also be introduced for the profit and loss account. Only then will you know that you're on the right road towards quality. And only then will you be in a position to compare. Which is absolutely essential in a world of ongoing internationalisation. The purpose of external reporting is to provide a true and fair view of the organisation's financial position and result as well as of the composition of that result. That is vital information for investors, banks, stock exchanges and everyone involved in a company. Insistence on uniformity of regulations is by no means a passing fad or obligatory talk. Far from it: it is a precondition for entrepreneurship, commerce, the economy, the financial system and the banking industry, for the social structure, for the cohesion of society as a whole. And stringent rules quite simply leave less room for tampering with the figures and their interpretation.'

In a special issue of VERA-Actueel *that appeared in mid-2001, you were rather critical about earnings management in the run-up to the VERA Congress entitled 'Creative accounting and fraudulent reporting: accountant, keep your back straight'. Do you think these flexible regulations encourage such practices?*

Professor Langendijk: 'In a certain sense I do, yes. As long as people abide by the law, there's not much wrong with it. Apart from the fact that I find the regulations too loose, of course. But in principle you can present earnings in lots of ways while still remaining within the legislative and regulatory framework. But in cases where people break the law and take more liberties than legally allowed, I speak of earnings manipulation and that of course is extremely reprehensible. Before you know it, you're careering down a slippery slope towards the realms of fraud. That is obviously not on. So I think that what went on at Lernout & Hauspie was really totally out of order. They simply made up invoices and customers to beef up sales and improve their creditworthiness. That is downright deception. And everybody finds that reprehensible.

'It supports my case for tightening up the regulations. As soon as you give people room to "shift" the figures around, you've let the genie out of the bottle. People can then lose sight of the legal and also the moral limits. In such cases you often see that all sorts of front men are instructed to pay non-existing invoices just before the accountant is due to come round. That money is then paid back plus a bonus as soon as the accountant has left. Things like that really cannot be tolerated. The legislator in the United States goes a step further. An accumulation of earnings management practices with premeditated intent is also considered manipulation there. So even if you remain within the laws and regulations, but change your accounting method ten times in a year and deliberately use all sorts of tricks, then that is considered to be manipulation. They call it "aggressive accounting", but whoever does that runs a very real risk of being prosecuted; even though according to our standards they have not actually broken any laws or regulations. The view they take is that the figures have not been truthfully presented. In my opinion, that kind of aggressive behaviour must also be openly denounced in the Netherlands. So earnings management in itself is fine by me, but if it leads to all sorts of earnings management practices involving substantial amounts of money with far-reaching consequences, then it must be rigorously dealt with.

'As far as I can see, there is less latitude for earnings management with the IAS. These rules are clear, tight and transparent. The IAS provide for a system with a benchmark treatment and an allowed alternative treatment.

Whoever opts for the allowed alternative treatment must justify this choice. In practice therefore, companies will tend to opt for the benchmark treatment. But that's not the way our laws and regulations work. These still leave too much room to do as you please. Here we sometimes have as many as 10 or more methods for a single item. As I said, the IAS has only two: the benchmark and the alternative, where you have to provide justification if you want to use the latter. That makes sense to me.'

'But more stringent rules and strict supervision alone are not enough. Accountants too must take their public task seriously. In addition, analysts must follow companies critically and give investors recommendations based on their critical analysis. The Powers Committee found in the Enron case that the company's financial statements for 1999 and 2000 were not in compliance with US GAAP. The Powers Committee is also critical of the role that the accountants played at Enron (and the external reporting of Enron in particular). If company managements fail to prepare their external reports according to US GAAP, if accountants no longer correct their clients in this field (or modify their report) and if analysts no longer follow companies critically and only give their customers buy recommendations, then stakeholders will naturally be in constant doubt about the quality of the presented figures. This can eventually have a disruptive effect on society. Entrepreneurs and accountants must therefore ensure that reports are reliable and truthful and analysts must give investors their honest and critical opinion of these reports.'

'Fair value accounting' is very much in vogue at the moment. This means that everything is stated at market value. But isn't that very subjective? And won't it merely encourage even more earnings management?

Professor Langendijk: 'It means that the accountant is increasingly becoming a value appraiser, which is really partly a new profession. But if there is no hard market value, the stated amounts become more and more fluid and therefore easier to manipulate. Accountancy training around the world should therefore devote a lot more attention to financing and capital markets discipline.'

If you manage earnings by releasing provisions, everyone can see what you've done. But if you manage earnings by making a slight modification in the 'fair value approach', nobody will notice. Isn't that much worse?

Professor Langendijk: 'No, but it is necessary to explain clearly and extensively what the actual valuation is based on. So the financial statements must be accompanied by appraisal reports. This also applies to the valuation of intangible assets, derivatives and goodwill, particularly in the case of items that are of capital importance to the balance sheet. What this basically boils down to is an entirely new method of reporting. This new valuation method therefore requires detailed clarification, with statements of movements and all sorts of other statements. They must be multi-year statements as these give you many more analytical options. And it also allows you to see what the value appraiser thinks year on year. You can then also see whether and how the system remains consistent. And a comparison over several years also makes it easier for you to assess how the real estate or intangible assets are valued. A year is only a year, but a period of say 10 years is a totally different matter.

In addition, a true and fair view of the financial position and of the result is of great importance. The actual value method is of course in the first instance a solution for giving a true and fair view of the financial position. After all you are trying to approximate the organisation's market value. An accountant will not hesitate to claim that he or she can give a true and fair view of the financial position. No doubt this is so – according to the accounting rules, that is. But if you leave the accounting rules out of consideration, there is not a single company that gives a true and fair view of its financial position. Because that's simply not possible with the historical cost method. What fair value does, above all, is provide a solution for giving a true and fair view of the financial position as stated on the balance sheet. The result, being a derivative of this, can consequently also be considered to be largely reliable. But this too will leave opportunities for earnings management. After all, the company management can now influence the market values year on year. Historical costs are "harder" and therefore easier to check for an accountant. With market value, the accountant is walking on thin ice, because he is having to base his or her judgement on a whole host of different appraisal reports. What's more, the objectivity of the appraisers is open to question; they after all are not only engaged but also paid by the company management, which will expect them to deliver accordingly. This incidentally is an objection that will not sound unfamiliar to accountants.

'So there are tensions here. And I hope that the accountant will pay closer attention than ever to practices involving the management of earnings and the financial position. "Fair value accounting" will only make things even more difficult for the accountant. Against the advantages of offering a truer and fairer view of the financial position and the result at a given moment, it also opens up opportunities for manipulating these two entities. But I expect that companies who are found to be guilty of incorrect reporting will face a severer backlash in the coming years than is currently the case. So that will keep everyone on their toes; and this, I think, is only to be applauded. In that sense I am not opposed to "fair value accounting". But we have to remain vigilant, because the spectre of capital and earnings management is always lurking somewhere in the background.'

But surely there are not that many reporting scandals in the Netherlands?

Professor Langendijk: 'The fact that shareholders don't go to court or call the company management to account is not necessarily because the reports are so tremendously good and sound. Whether shareholders are sufficiently knowledgeable and critical to see through all the smoke-screens and illusionary tactics is highly debatable. In addition, any suspicions of wrongdoing have to be put to the Enterprise and Companies Court. That procedure takes years and it doesn't earn you any money or honour. The maximum you can get out of it is that the management is rapped on the knuckles and possibly motivated to do better next year. But civil action or disciplinary proceedings against an accountant also take a long time; even if only because it's hard to provide strong evidence and because of the defendant's endless appeals in an effort to win time and exhaust the other party. You not only need a great deal of patience, but also sufficient financial stamina, because legal proceedings cost a fortune. And substantial risks are attached to court action. That's why shareholders are inclined to let the matter rest. In other words: the fact that there are not many cases doesn't mean everything's hunky dory.

'It's a different story in the USA where if the management of a company is juggling the figures it will immediately find the SEC breathing down its neck. The SEC is the stock exchange watchdog – some would even say stock exchange bloodhound – and it has teeth to match. Court proceedings can be initiated in no time and the entire judicial procedure for cases like this is a good bit faster than in the Netherlands.

So we need something like the SEC in the Netherlands?

Professor Langendijk: 'I'm warmly in favour of that. Former minister Zalm has already described such a supervisory body, complete with extensive sanctionary powers. Excellent. Such a body should bone and fillet the external reports of a few hundred companies every year and give their verdict on the quality. It is absolutely essential that such an organisation has top-level employees and is able to deliver top quality. This need not be confined to the Netherlands but could also – and perhaps preferably – be set up in a European context. You need reporting specialists for this, and accountants would certainly be eligible for this role. These accountants should then be in the employ of the supervisory body (modelled on the US example).'

So we need more specialists in the reporting field?

Professor Langendijk: 'Definitely, because it is vitally important for such an institute to build a brand name. It is vitally important for it to hit the target each and every time. And if there is any reason for doubt, let the matter rest. That's how you establish a reputation.'

If a supervisory body is set up, would the Autoriteit Financiële Markten (Authority for the Financial Markets) be a likely candidate for that role?

Professor Langendijk: 'Yes, but the village character of the Netherlands as well as the lack of specialists here means that we are simply too small: you keep moving around in the same circle. So the operation must be controlled from EU level. A supervisory body for the EU could work well. It could also maintain ties with the EFRAG. It should in principle be able to audit between 100 and 500 financial statements of listed companies in Euroland every year. The Dutch will then automatically get their turn. Almost all companies publish an English-language annual report. So that cannot be the problem. And if too little expertise is available, then it simply has to be hired. The experts must be properly rewarded, because unless the reward is interesting, you won't get the best.'

What kind of experts do you have in mind?

Professor Langendijk: 'People with a demonstrably high quality in the reporting field, people who are at home in company and criminal law, good business economists, good financial experts, you name it. So you need a team with lots of experts; not just people who know everything about external reporting.'

You are not an accountant yourself. How do you perceive the accountancy profession?

Professor Langendijk: 'It is a unique and fascinating profession. The accountant is at the centre of opposing forces. He or she is the first to see a company's figures – sometimes actually prepares them. He or she has dealings with small and medium-sized businesses, big companies, middle market companies, listed companies, government institutions, non-profit organisations. In fact, who doesn't the accountant have dealings with? There is virtually no sector of society where the he or she does not have a role to play. He or she is almost constantly under pressure: everyone wants to come up with a splendid set of figures and the accountant can help them do that. But no matter what way you look at it, the accountant fulfils an extremely useful task. It could be an idea to have accountants paid by the government and not by private customers. An institute should be set up to supervise companies on the government's behalf, a kind of cross between a Court of Audit and a chamber of commerce. But with many thousands of accountants, naturally.'

Do we have good accountants in the Netherlands?

Professor Langendijk: 'Our accountants have had the benefit of a thorough theoretical grounding as well as extensive practical training. There is a good umbrella accountancy organisation, there is good education and good further education through the VERA.

'Moreover, these days they are also required to go through a practical traineeship, so that too has been institutionalised. You cannot but conclude that in terms of training and experience our accountants can hold their own internationally. Many of these people, in fact, ultimately end up in senior positions at large companies. That is no coincidence. But the structure could do with some changes. The problem with the selected structure, after all, is that the accountant has to send the bill at the end of the month. And they want to be invited back next year. That is a commercial dilemma that bedevils the entire accountancy profession. Accountants often have to put themselves in the customer's shoes; otherwise the customer won't want them back next year. When you're advising a company in your capacity as an accountant, that's no problem. Nor is it a problem when you provide administrative support, as consulting accountants frequently do. But as soon as you have a social responsibility to fulfil as an auditor of financial statements, you have a problem, because you are being paid by the audited party. So there should be a strict separation between auditing and consulting for organisations subject to audit requirements (that is, not just the public interest entities).

Accountancy firms should only provide auditing services or consulting services to these organisations, but never both. A combination of the two at such an organisation creates confusion regarding the incentive structure of accountants in their dealings with companies. Both nationally and internationally there seems to be a movement in this direction, and I applaud that.'

Chapter 19

The auditor is gratefully back on his pedestal

An interview with Pieter T. Lakeman

Pieter T. Lakeman

Pieter Lakeman (1942) studied economics and founded Stichting Onderzoek Bedrijfs Informatie (SOBI) in 1976. He has numerous publications to his name, such as 'Binnen zonder kloppen', a study on the costs and benefits of immigration. In addition, he has instituted many financial statement proceedings, which have generated the necessary jurisprudence.

'I am grateful for the sternest criticism, as long as it remains businesslike,' stated the 19th-century German Chancellor Von Bismarck. Not that this ultimately highly embittered statesman had much reason for gratitude. Criticism is not always welcome, but sometimes the truth has to be uttered. But what is truth?

Someone who has never minced his words and has never been overly impressed by established reputations is Pieter Lakeman. As Chairman of the SOBI, a Dutch foundation that investigates business information, he has been analysing financial statements and monitoring the corporate sector critically and persistently for over 25 years. Where necessary he will bring proceedings against large corporations and organisations. After his (once again) controversial study *'Binnen zonder kloppen, Nederlandse immigratiepolitiek en de economische gevolgen'*

('Entering without knocking: Dutch immigration policy and the economic consequences') in 1999 things went quiet for some time.

But Lakeman is still 'alive and kicking', providing evidence of that vitality with proceedings against the telecom company KPN, which had built up debts of some EUR 25 billion through incompetent management.

We have not heard much about you recently. What are your main activities nowadays?

Lakeman: 'Things did indeed go quiet for a while. During the 1990s I invested some 5,000 working hours – or a net four years – in the Friesland-Coberco project (the former Heino Krause). We are acting on behalf of over 200 victims of this dairy giant and its accountant Ernst & Young. That project has nearly been completed. I have indeed initiated financial statement proceedings against KPN. In the summer of 2001, I was looking for the AEX stock that had made the greatest error in the recognition of share options (which in my view should, under Dutch law, have been booked as personnel costs right from 1971). To my pleasure I recently noted that Unilever had introduced this method of entry in its 2001 financial statements. In my view this recognition follows directly from the Dutch legislation since 1971 under which companies are obliged to provide insight into the composition and size of the result. At a certain point Baan Company had several tens of a percentage point outstanding as staff and management options that had not been recognised as personnel costs. I consider that to be incorrect.

'My eye was however drawn to the financial statements of KPN. These struck us as curious and containing major errors. The errors are on a much greater scale than previously encountered in the Netherlands. This was not something we could ignore. In addition, there were the interim injunction proceedings instituted against KPN and the State of the Netherlands for providing insufficient information to shareholders upon the most recent share issue. As is known, that information was then provided after all. The proceedings were so successful that the leading financial daily *NRC-Handelsblad* declared me as winner of the year 2001.'

In the early 1980s you published your book 'Het gaat uitstekend' ('Things are going very well') – a cynical title. This put the auditor in the dock. Has much changed since then?

Lakeman: 'I still stand by it entirely. It was on top of the bestseller list for three months and was highly influential in various areas of Dutch society. Ultimately the hitherto fairly uncritical public began to place question marks against the auditor's report. But the effect ebbed away in recent years. Everywhere I went people would say innocently, just as they did 20 years ago, "But wasn't that approved by the auditor?"

'The auditor came in for little critical examination in recent years and gratefully climbed back up on his pedestal. Whether I regret that is not important, but it is what I have observed. However, since the Enron affair – or strictly speaking the Arthur Andersen affair – the public has swung round entirely again and, as established recently in a Dutch survey, there is now widespread suspicion in the Netherlands concerning the independence of auditors. This affair will undoubtedly determine the atmosphere and opinions concerning the operations of external auditors for a number of years in the Netherlands. Recent research has indicated that as many as four out of every five entrepreneurs do not believe in the independence of auditors. The latter finding is particularly revealing since practice indicates that entrepreneurs use external auditors as a shield against the criticism of shareholders and works councils.

'What is certain is that the auditors were shocked by the commotion that my book aroused at the time and have gone into overdrive. Since then – and not just because of my book – the large accountancy firms have gone full-tilt down the commercial road. Sometimes it is as though they are ashamed of their core business: the external auditing of financial statements, or at least regard it as not commercially justified to portray themselves as external auditors. Instead, they increasingly present themselves as financial consultancy firms or service-providers in a general sense.

'The large accountancy firms in the Netherlands have now become full-scale commercial service-providers and, on account of their oligopo-listic privilege of auditing financial statements, have a big competitive lead on other international organisations and consultancy firms. An advocate or consultant can only wait and see whether he or she will be invited to enter a beauty contest, but the auditor automatically has the entrepreneur's ear. He or she sweeps in and, like an accomplished commercial traveller, sells a range of products that are often not related to the industry. The partners of the big five (now four) have consequently become rich and prosperous – so rich in fact that the Council of the Dutch Central Bank recently proposed that they publish their incomes. That is not in fact required since everyone knows that they earn between EUR 0.5 and 1 million.

'For myself I'd draw a distinction between two kinds of accountants in the Netherlands: on the one hand, the thousand or so partners of the largest firms, who make big money from trading in services and, on the other, the remaining accountants, including the non-partners in the big firms and all the accountants in other firms, which are often less extensive in nature and also stick more closely to their core activities.'

Has the quality of the annual report in the Netherlands improved in recent years?

Lakeman: 'Initially, in the 1980s, it did. The companies provided more detailed information, so that the annual reports had greater informational value for connoisseurs, although less well versed investors sometimes complained that they couldn't see the wood for the trees. But that just has to be regarded as the flip side of the fine coin of extensive information. The second key point is the question as to whether the information is also reliable and accurate. Here – particularly in recent years – we can see a major decline in quality. I feel flattered by the thought that as an 'awkward' private watchdog, SOBI, helped ensure an improvement in the quality in the 1980s and early 1990s by conducting annual account proceedings. That action has also been consistent with what was stated recently by the jury of the Sijthoff prize for the best Dutch annual report in the financial daily *Het financieele Dagblad*: "Just observing the rules is not enough; there must also be a body checking whether this is being done in the right way." In recent years the spur of annual account proceedings has clearly not been used enough, with a noticeable decline in quality.

'But a "natural" enforcer such as the Public Prosecution Service which, since the Financial Statements Act in 1971, has had the ability in the public interest to refer a set of financial statements to the Enterprise and Companies Court for annulment, has shamefully neglected its duty. When the Public Prosecution Service appointed a special Advocate General in the late 1980s to conduct financial statement proceedings the latter got around to just one case (compared with 25 largely won cases by SOBI, including cases against banks, insurers and large contractors). The Advocate General started a case against the largest shipping line in the Netherlands, NedLloyd. It was ultimately declared inadmissible by the Supreme Court since the public interest was not at issue, while the

Advocate General's demands had already been substantively rejected by the Enterprise and Companies Court. That was a poor start. Since then nothing further has happened. In my view that is primarily due to lack of expertise. As Advocate General you need in the first place to know when the public interest is at issue and secondly you must be able to recognise genuine shortcomings in financial statements. NedLloyd was not in any way open to reproach. A number of ships that had lost value on account of economic obsolescence were additionally written off (what we would today refer to as application of the impairment test), but such appraisals of the book value of productive assets against the operational value, on top of and not instead of the regular depreciation, have in fact been compulsory in the Netherlands since 1971. In this regard the Netherlands has anticipated the United States by several decades. I regarded the additional write-down by NedLloyd as excellent. The Public Prosecution Service did not, however, because the extra write-down meant that less could be depreciated in later years, so that the profit in those years was increased. That was indeed the logical consequence of the additional write-down, but it was a correct consequence of a correct action.

'An annual report by an insurance company, bank or utility is more of a candidate to be tackled in the public interest than that of a shipping line. For what, seen historically, could be more private than a shipping company? Shipping lines have for centuries been pioneers, free merchants, who never bothered about the interests of third parties. No: tackle a public utility, a Dutch energy trader listed on the stock exchange. If you look at the absurd growth of Dutch energy traders, who purchase and sell an identical product in this market, there could easily be little Enrons running about in the Netherlands.'

Could the official role of the Public Prosecution Service not be taken over by another official body?

Lakeman: 'That would be entirely possible. A new agency is currently getting off the ground in the Netherlands, namely the Authority for the Financial Markets – a kind of appendage to the Social and Economic Council. In my view, this body should obtain the right, just like SOBI, to approach the Enterprise and Companies Court in order to enforce compliance with the rules. Unlike SOBI, the authority should not however be obliged to buy a share in the company concerned first. Like the American SEC, however, the authority, which has grown in the space of a few years from a staff of 50 to 350, is seeking to issue concrete instructions to companies concerning the way in which financial statements should be prepared, bypassing both the courts and the auditor. For the Netherlands, the exclusion of the Enterprise and Companies Court as the final court in the adoption of financial statements would mean a big step backwards. The Enterprise and Companies Court provides the parties with all the procedural guarantees forming part of normal civil proceedings. This is the state under the rule of law in optimal form, about which one hears so much, not least in the Netherlands.

'The signs are that this European – or at least Dutch – system is also superior to the American system in another respect. The American system is characterised by the frequent amendment and imposition of new rules, which I regard as a major disadvantage for the users of financial statements. Now, while I am on the subject of the SEC, I must confess that I used to be a major admirer of it, particularly since there was too much freedom in the valuation of means of production in the Netherlands, as in the rest of Europe. I was and am an advocate of strict rules. The American SEC, however, has developed from a body exercising strict rules and control into one that amends guidelines on the slightest whim and which furthermore only turns out to have exercised control over small firms, on the argument that we can be sure everything will be in order at the big firms. By contrast, we consider it makes more sense to look at the big firms first.'

What is SOBI concentrating on?

Lakeman: 'As it has always done, SOBI is seeking to promote correct reporting by Dutch companies. We are therefore looking at the new financial statement procedures. There is ample choice: among the 25 AEX stocks, more than a handful of financial statements contain significant errors (such as writing losses off against the reserves instead of the result, which is at variance with legal judgments in respect of SOBI against Aegon, Slavenburgs Bank and HBG) and/or misleading representations of facts.

'In recent years we have also been concentrating on the correct promotion of interests of individuals or legal entities who were penalised by misleading information. This can happen to suppliers when their Dutch customer has not yet paid and goes bankrupt (a percentage of bankruptcies in the Netherlands have a fraudulent odour) but also to shareholders in family companies, or company councils. We are working on a couple of projects in which subcontractors worked on the basis of what turned out to be flawed information in the financial statements of main contractors. We conduct an examination of the facts, draw up a report and help lawyers win their claims.'

What is the state of financial reporting in the Netherlands?

Lakeman: 'If I am to believe the media, one legal reporting system appears to be tumbling over the other. That is hardly transparent on the part of companies that profess "corporate governance" and other high-sounding ideals. I am also obliged to say that the media are not entirely transparent: foreign financial statements legislation and private financial statements legislation – of which I regard IAS as part – are presented in the press as equivalent to or even superior to Dutch law.

'In my view it has now become generally accepted that strict regulation is vital for accurate reporting. This makes it possible to compare the results and performance of companies and even industries more effectively. Social and economic life only stands to benefit from this. Firm regulation is particularly vital for the treatment of goodwill, as this concerns such huge items. Particularly in recent years the entire result can stand or fall on the question as to whether or not it is written down. And if so, over how many years? This must be the subject of clarity. I would consider it acceptable if the legislation or regulations used different amortisation periods for different types of goodwill. But these must be fixed periods without the possibility of exceptions, which the IAS favours. Everyone must know where they stand. In international terms one of the worst developments has been that the rules are changing ever more rapidly. This complicates the comparability over time and insight into the development of a company's results.

'As far as this is concerned, the Dutch statutory system is also superior to the American system. The relevant Dutch Act is based around the fact that financial statements must provide a correct insight into the size and composition of the result and the assets. This is the basic section of the Act, and weighs more heavily than the more detailed sections. This has been evident in a number of legal actions and our demands for the amendment of financial statements are accordingly often based on this basic section without reference to all sorts of detailed sections later in the act. And with success, for a good many judgements had been handed down by the Enterprise and Companies Court on the basis of this general section.'

What are the key points in the KPN affair?

Lakeman: 'In the first place the mismanagement – the payment of over EUR 10 billion in goodwill for 77% of E-plus, a comparatively unknown German telephone company that has yet to record a profit, and the purchase of a UMTS licence in Germany for EUR 8.4 billion. And on top of that the incorrect Year 2000 financial statements. The result was negative but was made positive by recognising the payment by a third party into the share capital of a participating interest as profit. In my view that is incorrect. If you and I have a company and each decide to pay in an additional EUR 5,000 into the share capital, we can't say next year that we've made a nice profit of EUR 10,000. That is an inadmissible device.

Another objection to the KPN year 2000 financial statements is that an exit scheme for a minority shareholder in E-Plus, BellSouth, was capitalised as goodwill in the balance sheet for a sum of EUR 7.5 billion. I find that very odd. Furthermore, equity and borrowed capital have often not been clearly distinguished.

'It is further claimed that the book value of the goodwill (acquisition less regular amortisation) was assessed at the going concern value, with the conclusion that the book value was not too high. But nowhere is it stated in the financial statements what the assessment involves and how it was carried out. The valuation principles have, consequently, not in my view been set out as required under Dutch law. We are demanding an explanation of the assessment, so that we can assess the assessment itself. Otherwise anyone at all can say that they have assessed the value of their assets against the indirect realisable value. Given the importance of the issues at stake, a proper explanation (going beyond a simple reference) of this assessment is vital. If the assessment should show that the value was lower, the goodwill would already need to be written down in the year 2000 financial statements and not just in 2001.

'Furthermore, it is curious that the purchase of E-Plus, which took place in December 1999, was not recognised in the financial statements until 2000. The matter becomes even more curious when one considers that the exit scheme was valued in the 1999 financial statements not at EUR 7.5 billion but at EUR 2.6 billion.'

Is a new form of reporting needed for businesses in the 'new economy'?

Lakeman: 'Nonsense, for a brief while some people thought that the laws of economics had suddenly changed. A fast telephone service had arisen called the Internet and suddenly the entire economy was said to be shuddering on its foundations. I never believed in this. Although the Internet meant an extra one-off rise in labour productivity of several percentage points, there was a great deal of to-do and hype which even leading people believed in. An example was Cees van der Hoeven, now

President of Ahold who, as a KPN Supervisory Director, genuinely be-lieved in a total revolution in the field of economics. In March 2000 he privately paid EUR 120,000 so as to be able to buy extra shares upon the flotation of World Online, whereas the price was based on EUR 2,000 per Internet subscriber and each subscriber could transfer to another Internet provider without paying a cent in severance premium. What sort of mass hysteria was this? I would not want to devise any new accountancy rules for this kind of madness. You can get a long way with ordinary goodwill. There have of course been profitable dot.com companies and new ones will be added too. If you buy such a company and it is worth more on the basis of realistic plans and achievements than the disclosed net asset value, you then pay a bit – or if necessary a big chunk – of goodwill for it. But you do need to treat that as ordinary goodwill. I can't see any reason whatever for drawing up special annual reporting rules or tolerat-ing unusual practices.'

Hasn't shareholder value – the dogma of a few years ago – had a negative influence on the reporting, particularly if the top management is dependent on the company's financial results? Surely, they will after all do all they can to present the results in the best possible light?

Lakeman: 'Yes, of course! That has undoubtedly had an enormous influ-ence. Except that until recently it was impossible to demonstrate this. But in May 2002 a thesis was published in the Netherlands by J. G. Van Rooyen, with statistically significant findings demonstrating that com-panies issuing large numbers of share options to the top management do more to jack up the results than companies in which fewer options are issued to the top management. I must say that this is a highly inter-esting conclusion – not so much in the sense that the conclusion itself is interesting (everyone in fact already knew this) as the fact that it has been shown to be statistically significant. A company director is after all just a human being who is more concerned with his or her own interests than with the general interest. That should not be a matter for surprise; that's just the way most people are. You can trust the cat to keep the cream. If their remuneration is made partly dependent on the share price – well, what would you do? You would try to inflate the price and you would dress things up to look better than they really are.

'But other questions should then immediately be posed. Does one have to go along with this? And if not, how can you protect managers against themselves? And then it ends up again as a matter of enforcing the rules.

'The most important thing is to have a set of fixed rules that apply to everyone. You sometimes hear complaints that it is all becoming overly detailed. That criticism applies especially to the SEC in the USA but, at least at present, such complaints cut no ice in the Netherlands. Fixed rules provide clarity. It also means that a firm cannot continually switch systems over the years.

'I do however fear the worst in the coming years. When you read the reports about the continually changing content of the IAS and the European regulations from 2005 onwards, it raises fears that the regulatory juggernaut of the SEC will also be implanted in the Netherlands. This, complete with the annually changing content of the rules, meaning that the act will be at risk of becoming an arbitrarily filled in framework act, with the loss of any capacity for sequential comparison.

'It is highly important that all the financial statements of various companies should be fully comparable with one another, at least in the same industry. That was also the aim of the European Fourth Directive of the 1970s. That aim was not achieved at the time, partly because the mistake was made of allowing various valuation systems to exist side by side. In the case of the Netherlands this meant the two main approaches of historic cost and replacement value. Each of the systems can be defended, but admitting both of them was a mistake, and naturally put paid to comparability.'

What recommendations would you make in the field of reporting?

Lakeman: 'In the first place, rules without room for exceptions, so also just one method of valuation. Secondly, no continuous amendment of the rules. Thirdly, not too many details, with primacy attached to the right insight into the size and composition of the assets and the result. Fourthly, regulations that are included in their entirety in the act so that the changing wishes of interest groups do not determine the content of the act, as is at risk of happening now by making the IAS rules compulsory in Europe. Fifthly – and also for other countries – regulations whereby interested parties are able to force amendment of the financial statements in the courts. It should not be forgotten that stock exchange authorities generally have little involvement with the financial statements of unlisted firms, whereas it should also be possible to enforce the observance of the rules by those firms.

'Furthermore, an impairment test should never replace regular depreciation but should just act as a supplement. The write-up of means of production or goodwill by means of an impairment test is in my view fundamentally wrong. Although theoretically that possibility might look a big step forward and to be unquestionably superior, its application in practice would be extremely arbitrary and undermine the comparability of financial statements. If impairment tests can result in write-ups, or can replace ordinary depreciation, financial statements will lose any genuine significance for users and become degraded to material for the writing of theses. Particularly if, like KPN, you do not explain the impairment test applied in the notes to the balance sheet and maintain that refusal before the court on the grounds that competition-sensitive information would otherwise be disclosed.

'In essence the impairment test resembles the old system of replacement value, but limited to the balance sheet valuation, as used before particularly in the Netherlands. Just as with that system the impairment test is, theoretically, a superior system (of which I used to be an advocate). But just like the replacement value system, the impairment test is in practice entirely at the discretion of the management. I would be glad to drop the theoretically superior system in favour of one that is less arbitrary in practice.'

When will 'Things are going very well', part 2 appear?

Lakeman: 'I am working hard on other projects. I have no time for a follow-up to 'Things are fine'. What I do want to have on my agenda is a booklet on disciplinary rules for auditors in practice and theory. I think that this could provide a good deal of clarity that is currently lacking. I have the impression that many people are unaware of what is going on. My target group for this booklet consists of individuals or legal entities with a complaint against a Dutch auditor, in relation to both their conduct and the work performed. In brief, we are right back in the saddle again.'

Part V

Fair Value Accounting

Chapter 20

The irrepressible advance of Fair Value Accounting

An interview with Martin N. Hoogendoorn

Martin N. Hoogendoorn

Professor Martin Hoogendoorn RA (1959) is a partner at Ernst & Young, where he is head of the Professional Practice Reporting department. In this context he is concerned with financial state- ment issues. Furthermore, he is involved with a number of large financial companies as account manager. He is Professor of Financial Accounting at the University of Amsterdam and, since 1 October 2001, Chairman of the Council for Annual Reporting. He is a lecturer on VERA External Reporting courses.

The year 2005 will be a milestone in the history of the Dutch accountancy profession. That is the year in which IAS will come into force in the Netherlands and accountants will thus no longer be able to avoid valua- tion according to the fair value. Although there is a throng of supporters of the fair value approach, the opposition to it must not be underestimated. We talked about this with Professor Martin Hoogendoorn.

Will fair value become the 'standard' of this century?

Professor Hoogendoorn: 'Yes, IAS will come into force in 2005 and fair value will be a dominant standard for reporting. Here I refer mainly to financial instruments and to obligations and provisions. It will perhaps apply rather less to buildings, machinery and the like, but valuation according to fair value will certainly also apply to tangible and intangible fixed assets in the longer term. A different form of profit determination will also emerge, a kind of "performance statement". It is therefore better to not refer only to net profit, because there is no longer a traditional profit and loss account. Such a performance statement will consist of countless components, one of which can be our traditional profit concept. Furthermore, a difference may arise between the consolidated and company financial statements. The profit in the company financial statements will then be more prudently determined, with the realisation principle playing a role. An important question in this respect is: What can you distribute to shareholders, what can serve as a basis for the levying of taxes? I cannot preclude the possibility that a stronger link with the calculation of profit for tax purposes will arise. In the consolidated financial statements, however, all kinds of unrealised value changes, both increases and decreases, will emerge in the performance statement. The effect of exposure to market risks, currency risks, interest rate risks and the like will thus be expressed.

'In addition, I would like to say that there is now already a tendency to value a few isolated balance sheet items in terms of fair value, thus separately from the other balance sheet items and even separately from the entire financial position of the company. Fair value is already applied for quickly realisable investments, for example listed securities. Banks do this, for example, for the trading portfolio. For the listed securities of non-banks, the law prescribes valuation at cost or lower market value. This is a prudent principle. So if the market price has fallen, you must write down, but if the price rises, you don't have to increase in value yet. But on this point the Council for Annual Reporting has already decided in favour of fair value, as a departure from the specific statutory provisions, by stating that these investments are carried at market value and all (unrealised) value changes are looked upon as profit.

'You also see valuation in accordance with fair value in the case of real estate: valuation of this is often at appraised value. This is also much more logical than valuing a property that you bought for EUR 250,000 some 20 years ago at cost less depreciation, while it is now perhaps worth 10 times that amount. This does not provide enough insight into the net worth. We rarely see fair value in the case of liabilities, no more than in the case of most tangible and intangible fixed assets.'

Will fair value become the basis for valuation of all financial instruments and elements in the financial statements?

Professor Hoogendoorn: 'Ultimately, yes. The next step will be that the valuation in accordance with fair value will also play a role with non-financial items. As a capital-intensive company, Corus, the metals group, has a lot of tangible fixed assets on the assets side. The entire factory complex is actually the company's most important asset. This is, of course, financed with loan capital. Now it would be rather strange if you valued the liabilities at a kind of fair value – so if there are interest rate fluctuations, the liabilities move with them – while the tangible fixed assets are fixed at the historical cost less depreciation. There is after all a direct relationship between them. It would therefore not surprise me if the tangible fixed assets, the stocks and even the intangible assets were to be measured at fair value. In this context, the development in the United States with respect to the non-depreciation of purchased goodwill is interesting. This is in fact a step in the direction of fair value.'

And so fair value will therefore also apply to non-financial assets in the financial statements, thus on the debit side?

Professor Hoogendoorn: 'Yes. A balance sheet should reflect an equilibrium, with the same principle for assets and liabilities. I also see another development: in the case of the valuation of all assets and liabilities at fair value, the shareholders' value does not reflect the value of the company. After all, the company is also faced with all kinds of factors that do not appear on the balance sheet. I refer to the intellectual capital, the infrastructure, the brand name, the expertise of the personnel. These should actually also be put on the balance sheet, and we refer to this as "own goodwill". The more own goodwill, the more risky the company.

'To give a simple example: if a company only has liquid assets, that is the value of the company. There is no own goodwill, and no uncertainty about the value. But this is different for Internet companies. If you are to believe the stock market, they consist almost entirely of future expectations. There are absolutely no "hard" assets present. It has therefore become apparent that these kinds of companies are much more vulnerable. The larger the "own goodwill" item, the greater the risk. In my opinion, this really does have a considerable information value. Own goodwill closes the gap between the book value and the market value of a company. Incidentally, I believe that fair value for these kinds of items will only be used in 2010. For the time being, the valuation in accordance with fair value will be introduced in stages: financial items in 2005, tangible items in 2007/2008 and perhaps own goodwill in 2010/2011.'

How will provisions be included?

Professor Hoogendoorn: 'The "Statement of Financial Accounting Concepts 7" was published in the United States in mid-2001. This document covers the use of present value in accounting measurements and also represents a breakthrough for the valuation in accordance with fair value. After all, present value and fair value are directly connected to one another. The present value of future revenues of liabilities, in the case of provisions on the basis of a weighted average of opportunities and results, is in effect "fair value". This view is also employed in IAS. You must include a provision at present value. If, for example, you perform a reorganisation that is accompanied by substantial costs, for the valuation of the provision it is important whether you expect to pay the expenses next month, or stretch them out over two years. The present value then makes a difference. Stretching the expenditure out over two years obviously means a lower provision. This is in essence an element of fair value. And this method of valuation also makes itself felt in the provisions.'

Where financial instruments are concerned, the valuation of debt based on fair value is controversial and particularly the effect of the change in the 'credit rating'. What is your opinion about this?

Professor Hoogendoorn: 'This is one of the weak points of a partial application of fair value. Suppose that a company has taken out medium and long-term loans and pays the bank 7% interest on these. If the situation deteriorates for a time and the company has to borrow money at market rates, for instance 9%, it has an advantage *vis-à-vis* the already agreed 7%. But does it therefore make a profit? Is it therefore worth more? If a company's performance deteriorates, should this be expressed in the valuation. This is where we see the flaw with the partial application of "fair" value. The problem with "credit rating" is that it is regarded too much in isolation as merely financial assets and liabilities. Therefore, the intangible and tangible assets must be included in the valuation, and the fair value of these has probably decreased. If we also include the own goodwill, there is a disadvantage on balance.'

Fair value may be a fine concept in theory, but does it work in practice?

Professor Hoogendoorn: 'That is where the problem lies. In theory, the method is useful and relevant for users, but the information must be reliable. If the fair value is unreliable, if it is possible to fill in all kinds of values and if there are enormous intervals, is the information then adequate in a qualitative sense? The reliability of information is essential. As long as the valuation relates to listed shares, the information is fairly reliable. But it already becomes slightly less reliable if you have to determine the fair value of mortgage loans. And for real estate it is even more difficult. And how do you value the fixed assets of companies like Corus, the ships of Nedlloyd or the refineries of Shell? In part, these are unique assets. On the other hand, there is increasing expertise in the valuation of property and companies.'

Profit is a rather subjective concept. How do you get to grips with it?

Professor Hoogendoorn: 'It can be incredibly confusing for private investors. There are often various kinds of profit concepts, such as net profit before the amortisation of goodwill, EBITDA, etc. In itself, this is not a problem, these are the components of a performance statement, as long as the content of the concepts is unambiguous and equitably communicated to investors. The public at large has problems dealing with a profit concept that includes all unrealised value changes. The reason is that this leads to high volatility in the bottom line of the profit and loss account. The fear is that the public will misinterpret these kinds of figures. A lot depends upon the moment at which you report. If a company has a lot of shares and the stock market has sharply increased, while it takes a nosedive the following year, you see a substantial profit one year and a reduced return the next. Only by providing clear explanatory notes is it possible for a company to prevent the public from drawing the wrong conclusions. This is also the argument in favour of providing explanatory notes. Transparency is the watchword.

'The bottom line is not the only profit concept that is important for the evaluation of the performance; another aspect is that there are, of course, more measures of performance than just the "bottom line". I have already referred to the EBITDA: the earnings before interest, taxes, depreciation and amortisation of all tangible and intangible fixed assets and goodwill. The development of a company just cannot be grasped with only one performance measurement. Furthermore, net profit is not the only way of measuring performance. Operating cash flows, for example, are also important criteria for establishing how a company has performed. Solvency ratios are very important, as well as interest cover and the like. But you must make it clear to the public exactly which measures you use. Otherwise, confusion arises.'

What will audits look like in five year's time?

Professor Hoogendoorn: 'Audits will not be any easier when the fair value system comes into force. The value of a company will then change from year to year. Indeed, if there are interim figures, these will continually show different values. The auditor will have to provide an opinion about the acceptability of the valuation. This can lead to discussions with the company's management. I think that auditors will increasingly have to turn to external experts, such as chartered valuators, assessors, actuaries and other specialists, in order to be able to establish the value of particular items as objectively as possible. The audit will thus more than ever before become teamwork with the auditor becoming the co-ordinator and "main contractor" for the engagement. Auditors will obviously continue to bear responsibility for the approval of the financial statements. They will also have to rely upon the professional skills of their advisers. But they cannot take refuge behind them. The opinion of the external expert has therefore become their opinion. This means that they must have a more than superficial knowledge of the fields for which they have enlisted help.'

The business community in the Netherlands acknowledges the principle of shareholder value. This also fits in with the 'corporate governance' model. Will financial statements become more transparent with the implementation of fair value?

Professor Hoogendoorn: 'Yes, as long as companies adequately explain the assumptions underlying the valuation. They not only have a moral duty towards users to do this. After all, shareholders have entrusted their capital to companies, which will then have to render an account of how the capital is used. Fair value fits in perfectly with this. You show what something is worth right now. Whether or not it is worth more or less in the future, this a risk that we all have to face. The financial statements are thus not a guarantee for the future, but a diagnosis at a particular calibration moment. Part of the responsibility is therefore also shifted to the users because they are much more conscious than ever before when they make a decision. If things turn out wrong, they can't blame companies since they have been very open and honest. Companies must therefore not be so afraid about openness. The more they cover up and disguise, the more vulnerable they become. I would therefore advise an open and honest discussion of risk management policy with the shareholders. If they are in agreement or do not make any objections, they cannot reproach the management as they have been consulted. Running a business means taking risks. Furthermore, you cannot cover everything. And no-one knows in advance how something can best be covered.

'I believe that transparency is always a sign of strength. A company that dares to be open shows courage and self-confidence. Those that behave evasively will have something to hide and will therefore be a risky investment. That is why I applaud all "fair value developments" and believe that it fits within the model of corporate governance, shareholder value and transparency. And with Enron you can see what happens when the transparency is inadequate.'

From profit smoothing to a true and fair presentation of profits at insurance companies and pension funds

An interview with Alfred Oosenbrug

Alfred Oosenbrug

Professor Alfred Oosenbrug RA AAG (1960) occupies the endowed chair for Financial Institutions and Financial Services Reporting at Erasmus University, Rotterdam. He was a member of the Traas Committee, which advised the ministers of finance and justice on short-term measures for improving the view provided by the financial statements of insurance companies. He is Chairman of the Association of Actuaries (AG), which he also represents in the NIVRA-AG Platform Committee (PCNA).

In times in which people stand up for their rights and demand an explanation and accountability from those parties responsible for looking after their interests, some attention to pension and life insurance management is called for. Certainly if Professor Alfred Oosenbrug makes the dry remark that company pension funds, which once blessed their parent companies with billions, are now suffering huge losses because of the fall in share prices.

Are our pensions now in danger due to possible mismanagement? Should the parent companies return that money to the pension funds, even if they themselves are facing considerable deficits? Or is the answer to charge employees higher premiums in order to cover this overly enthusiastic pension management?

Professor Oosenbrug: 'Those are quite some – somewhat tendentious – questions. I referred in that radio interview to a press release from *Statistics Netherlands* dated 29 November 2001. It reported the fact that insurance companies and pension funds had seen as much as EUR 55 billion of their investments go up in smoke in the third quarter of 2001. That is the heaviest blow ever received in a quarter. Now we have to realise that the towering investment profits achieved in the past 20 years were naturally absurd. After 20 – and not seven – years of plenty we had dozed off and now we were being shaken awake. A few quick calculations and an analysis of the facts show that pension funds have now achieved an average funding rate of 120%. That is 20% more than is necessary. During the past 20 years, however, investment returns of 15–20% a year were not uncommon. That is more than twice as much as the return needed to cover the accrual of liabilities based on the regular discount rate of 4% plus the inflation rate. So what have they done with all that money?

'Well, some of it was indeed returned to the parent companies. That's what Progress (the pension fund of Unilever) did for Unilever, for instance. Yet, more generally, premium stops and discounts came into play instead. The payment of premium was no longer deemed necessary, since the pension reserves kept on growing during the past period of prosperity. Since people had become accustomed to all those windfalls and saw them as "normal", people are aghast now that no more "goodies" are parcelled out in the form of extremely low pension premiums or even stops. Those always used to be the exceptions – not the rule. It is now that the situation is normalising and we are returning to normal investment situations that the premiums seem so high. Yet they are not any higher than what they would have been in the absence of a bull market in the past 20 years. And, if a year-long premium of 3% or 4% suddenly rises to 10%, we can naturally say that it has skyrocketed. But on the other hand, one can also say that we were paying 6–7% too little for all those years.'

Genesis 41 in the Bible relates the story of seven years of plenty and seven years of famine. In times of prosperity one must build up reserves: that's the lesson to be learned. Yet it looks like these reserves were never set aside. That can scarcely be called good management. Shouldn't proper financial reporting have revealed this earlier – isn't that what financial reporting is for?

Professor Oosenbrug: 'Of course, and there have been plenty of warnings. But financial reporting by pension funds is still in a prehistoric phase. No-one had insight into or could have known what was actually happening. People were simply given a sop.

'Specific rules for financial reporting are the sole domain of companies – and therefore not of the pension funds which administer their pension contributions right beneath them. The best they can do is to adopt the international rules, which do not fit as well into the Dutch context. Take, for instance, draft Directive 271 from the Council for Annual Reporting, which was derived nearly one-to-one from IAS 19, Employee Benefits. Here we find ourselves in the international arena. That means taking part in global harmonisation – clearly in response to the fact that financial reporting in respect of pension provisions was below standard on all accounts. But that immediately gains momentum. An international standard is enthusiastically embraced in order to impose upon companies a well established and highly detailed and complex system of reporting requirements. And this all takes place in a situation in which reporting by pension funds, that is, the professional pension administrators, is completely free in the Netherlands. It's liberty hall, as far as that goes. Companies that do business by filling and selling jars of peanut butter are now suddenly forced to satisfy extremely detailed reporting requirements concerning their pension situation, while the pension fund to which they are tied and which is assumed to have a good understanding of pensions and their valuation – and rendering accountability in this respect – is free to decide on its own what to report on and how to report it.'

What is the most essential shortcoming in pension fund reporting and how can fair value accounting help?

Professor Oosenbrug: 'Apart from the huge lack of transparency, the main problem is a structurally overly rosy depiction of reality. The fair value project naturally focuses on creating more uniformity and a fair representation and on using these factors to achieve more transparency in financial reporting. The steady application of fair value accounting was chosen as *the* instrument for reaching this transparency. In that respect, it is alarming now that the idea has risen in the framework of the insurance project to replace fair value accounting with entity-specific values. This threatens to bog the reporting process down in that extreme degree of subjectivity, which was precisely the reason behind the failure of the economic concept of profit to penetrate into the practice of financial reporting. The experiences already amassed under the strict systems of accounting rules, with earnings management and hocus pocus accounting seen in practice, paint a disturbing picture of the future. Within fair value accounting we will need to base ourselves on realistic forecasts. The present practices of using arbitrary or much too optimistic discount rates will, in principle, need to be relegated to the past.'

How do you see the developments in the IAS insurance project? Where is it going?

Professor Oosenbrug: 'In a certain sense, the IAS insurance project is very dramatic. It's back to the basics of the principles of financial reporting. It revisits the issue of what the basic principles of reporting are. And remember, insurance companies and pension funds have always been in the last wagon where financial reporting is concerned; one could even say that they've been running twenty metres behind the train. And now, suddenly, they find themselves up front in the locomotive. What a change! All of a sudden they have been made the pioneers for setting up a system of financial reporting standards based on new foundations – all under the motto of fair value accounting.

'In fact, this implies a complete switch from terms like accounting profit and equity to the general economic or microeconomic concept of equity and profit. That is revolutionary. This is why some hard work is required at insurance companies and pension funds to fathom and introduce IAS. Ultimately, this remains a long and difficult project. That was even one of the topics at the VERA-PCNA seminar on IAS Insurance held on 22 November 2001. Is fair value accounting on for the insurance industry and, if so, how can we prepare? Well, of course it is on. The only question is what timescale do we have in mind. The European Commission has said that the new IAS rules shall apply to all European listed companies with effect from the financial year 2005. Incidentally, national governments are at their liberty to expand upon its mandatory application. The Dutch government has announced that the requirements – concerning insurance companies at any rate – will not be limited to listed companies. All insurers and banks will – if the European Commission so deems – be faced with a completely different system in 2005. Since the figures for 2004 will be required in 2005, companies will, in fact, need to have their systems up and running from 1 January 2004 with a view to implementing the new reporting method.

'The question is whether the wishes of the European Commission can be honoured. The IASB believes they can and has planned that the IAS project for the insurance industry must be completely finished before 1 January 2004. A definitive financial reporting standard needs to be ready for use then. Whether this schedule is realistic, however, is another matter. Is it realistic to assume that European and national legislation and regulations – in respect of financial statements *and* in the area of the prudential supervisory authorities – can be amended and ratified all within one year? Just look at the legislative process in the Netherlands and bear in mind that the mechanism here can even be considered high-speed in comparison with what is customary in the rest of the EU. Many people agree with me that 2007 – which date Minister Zalm also mentioned in Parliament – would be substantially more realistic.

'Moreover, in a practical sense insurance companies and pension funds have been asked to perform a miracle. How can they possibly make the dramatic and, thus, time-consuming changes to their operating systems on time if they do not even know yet – and probably will not know until sometime in 2003 – the final form of the applicable financial reporting rules: standards that will signal a radical departure from current concepts, mind you!

'The next issue is how to set up such a project. One option would be to make a preliminary move in the direction of IAS to avoid having to sort out the whole lot in 2007. On principle, one could also justify getting a head-start. It would not hurt to curtail the present liberty hall attitude among insurance companies. There is a great diversity of financial reporting systems, particularly where reporting on investment results is concerned. Some companies average out their results over 30 years, others refrain from disclosing setbacks in their results and still others hide their results in their capital to reveal them later – in one go – upon realisation.

'The figures that are presented are completely incomparable. That is a pity, for comparability is the only way to help people understand performance and loss. In this way, we can filter away the impact of those external circumstances which no-one can influence. Yet if no comparison can be drawn, those figures mean nothing. A check must be placed on this situation.'

Some insurance companies see little in the recommendations of the Traas Committee. They see more in fair value accounting.

Professor Oosenbrug: 'I don't understand their reasoning. First they opposed full fair value accounting and now they are appealing to it to support their claims, since they are completely against the recommendations of the Traas Committee. In fact, they are saying, "Let's not make any changes, since there's no avoiding fair value accounting anyway, even though we're not particularly chuffed with that either."

'I fail to comprehend their tentativeness. They are afraid of giving a true and fair view of reality, while that remains the key to reporting. Reality shows results – certainly in the area of investment – which are not always optimistic. Yet that does not license them to cover up that volatility solely under the premise that no-one can explain it. In fact, they would prefer to sketch out – carefully, with the greatest caution – a picture of stability, as if volatility never even figured in the equation.

'That is a common debate which was held years ago in the banking industry in respect of reporting on the provision for general banking risks. Banks used to have the option of creating a secret provision to cover contingencies. That was more elegant than having to admit a clanger. They were afraid that such an admission would spark a run on the bank and the practice was eventually brought to an end. If such setbacks are explained to the public, they will be able to appreciate them. After all, life is full of risks. And if such blunders cannot be explained, the public is entitled to know what happened.'

But can volatile results be explained to the average investor, who prefers seeing nothing but an upward trend in performance?

Professor Oosenbrug: 'The way that people have reacted in recent times to announcements of financial setbacks shows that investors in the year 2003 do indeed know how to distinguish between explainable setbacks, such as those related to a slow economy, and unexplainable setbacks caused by a lack of control over a company's development. For example, huge operating losses at Ahold sowed panic on the stock exchange, while disappointing results at insurance companies – the logical response to 11 September 2001 and the generally poor equity market performance in 2001 – scarcely raised an eyebrow. On the other hand, ING's initial boldly optimistic estimate of the implications of 11 September 2001 for the claims incurred by Reliastar did provoke a response from the stock market. And that had nothing to do with the size of the incurred claims but rather with the apparent lack of insight into its own portfolio and exposure.

'Incidentally, various Dutch pension funds have been showing their total return on investment directly and fully in the statement of income and expenditure. This, without causing the slightest panic among members stemming from their supposed inability to interpret volatility in the investment results in the proper manner.'

The European Commission has since decided in principle to adopt IAS. Do the recommendations from the Traas Committee fit in with the international trends?

Professor Oosenbrug: 'They certainly do. The international community strongly condemns the practice of hiding volatility and sweeping it under the carpet of the law of averages. No, the fundamental point is to give a true and fair view of reality. As soon as that view fluctuates, that needs to be shown. That applies not only to investments but also to insurance. The tragic events of 11 September 2001 in the United States is a clear example of this. Everyone understands that such a huge disaster is a tremendous blow to an insurance company and that the insurer is bound to suffer financial losses. It would therefore be idiotic to camouflage volatility by "averaging it away".

'Yet that is exactly what all manner of Dutch insurance companies do with their investments. Volatility is averaged out over a period of no less than 30 years. Former minister Zalm spoke out on this topic in the Dutch Parliament. According to him, we do not refer to financial statements as the annual accounts for nothing. Otherwise they should have been called the "thirty-year accounts". Insurance companies need to cease their rearguard actions and face the facts. The Netherlands is no island. It is better to work together constructively on the future than to keep defending the past.'

What is the best way for an insurance company to present its results?

Professor Oosenbrug: 'What has been common practice in the USA for years and what the Traas Committee also proposes is the presentation of comprehensive income. That is ultimately what investors care about: total results. After all, that is the criterion that investors use to determine how well they have done.'

But not all companies are keen on letting the rest of the world see their results.

Professor Oosenbrug: 'Well, that's no use, is it? All they talk about is transparency...where others are concerned. In the past, no-one was keen on letting others take a look behind the scenes. Management information was the privilege of a select group. Yet transparency, not only for financial reporting, but also in respect of capital markets and such, means that one must be honest about business. And if the CFO wants to see a reliable picture of the company's affairs and if that is also the definition of transparency, financial accounting and management accounting must be equal or be made equal.'

Should the government prohibit pension funds from investing in shares – because of the risks?

Professor Oosenbrug: 'We live in a free country. No-one can simply be forbidden from investing in shares. The point is, pension funds should only proceed in this direction if they have sufficient buffers in place to cover potentially bad investments. It is a fact of life that share prices are more volatile than fixed-yield securities. This has to be accepted. If one believes that equity investments can produce higher returns in the long run, one should be given the chance to make that come true – as long as one provides transparency and is thus willing to account for what one does with other people's money. If one has failed to maintain buffers or has taken unacceptable risks, there will certainly be some explaining to do.'

Chapter 22

Introduction of Fair Value Accounting: little if any haste

An interview with Kees J. Storm

Kees J. Storm

Business economist and registeraccountant Kees Storm RA (1942) was appointed as Chairman of the Board of Management of Aegon in 1993 and began in 1978 at one of Aegon's legal predecessors. He retired as Chairman on 18 April 2002.

The new reporting rules do not leave insurers untouched. In particular the treatment of goodwill and capital gains indicates how differently insurance companies and other companies approach this subject. A conversation concerning IAS, how this fits in with the US GAAP and the proposals of the Traas Committee was conducted with K. J. Storm, who handed over the chairman's gavel of the Aegon Board of Management on 18 April 2002 and took retirement as from 1 July 2002. Recently Aegon (which came into being in 1983 as the holding company of one of the five largest listed life insurers in the world, measured by market value and assets) decided to set up a joint company with China National Offshore Oil Corporation (CNOOC). The partners will each have a 50% stake in this new company, which is to sell life assurance in China. Both parties will be injecting the same sum of EUR 13.5 million. The head office is to be established in Shanghai and activities will get under way during 2003.

How will the reporting of insurance companies develop internationally and is it heading in the right direction?

Storm: 'That's hard to say, for a great deal is changing in a short space of time. For years in the Netherlands the treatment of goodwill in financial statements has been such that you could write it off in one go against shareholders' equity. In the United States this had to be done over a period of 20 to 40 years. We then changed tack in Europe and decided to follow the Americans. Whereupon the latter at last woke up and noted that it was in fact odd to write goodwill off against the result, thereby making the result more difficult to understand. Something was being charged to a particular year, even though there was no charge whatever in that year. And so there has been a turnaround in the United States: now they do not want to write anything off and want to use an impairment test to examine whether there has been any change in the value. In theory this is an excellent proposal, which I see as ultimately leading to goodwill being written off against shareholders' equity. And then we will be back to where we began.'

Is fair value accounting a good thing?

Storm: 'The notion that the insurance world should apply the same system of valuation as other companies, thereby improving the comparability of the figures of insurance companies, is in my view a good and admirable ideal, and one I fully support. Where I have greater reservations is the fact that fair value accounting is comparatively new and that no framework has as yet been created for it. While it may therefore look as though we will be using a single system in 2005, this is just the appearance, as the underlying assumptions can differ totally. I am thinking, for example, that the percentage at which the future cash flows are calculated at present value will differ. The discount rate is highly subjective. The unsuspecting user of the financial statements needs to bear this in mind. And then the discount rate is a highly visible factor: much less visible differences in assumptions will make things even more difficult.

'In the United Kingdom reporting is based on the embedded value, a related valuation variant. And what do we see: certain British insurance companies do not attribute any equity or take-up of capital to new production in a particular year, whereas others do. This makes an enormous difference to the valuation of the new products. That value is particularly important – as indeed it is in the case of fair value accounting – because analysts are concerned not so much with the value embedded in the portfolio as with that of the new production or growth. That they regard as a growth potential. Such growth will be made to look as high as possible by the insurance companies. The fewer costs assigned to the new production and the more costs assigned to the old portfolio, the higher the value of the new production becomes. These kinds of underlying matters will play an important role. All this is something that will be beyond the average user of the financial statements; nor is it something that can be made explicable with all kinds of additional information.

'To take another example: long-term pension contracts are generally renegotiable after five years. Is that new five-year period the new production for that year? Or is it an ongoing item that has been running for already 30, 40 or 50 years? And does it form part of the embedded value? You will see that companies will try to place the emphasis as far as possible on the value of new business, that is, the value of that one year. In short, there are all sorts of items that will lend themselves to arbitrary treatment in the future. That will not always mean the highly desired comparability of company figures.

'We must continue to be constructive. This was also something I hammered away at in my address at the Ernst & Young Insurance Day on 18 December 2001. Taking the US GAAP as a firm frame of reference will in my view remain an important point for the future. I think that the United States, with the SEC in the forefront, will not give up their valued and cherished GAAP. And why should they? I therefore think that the best thing would be for us to make a start with fair value accounting, but that we must build up our experience with it by providing the information not in the financial statements themselves but in the notes. I therefore challenge actuaries and auditors to develop and test standards during that phase.'

Why the scepticism towards IAS?

Storm: 'As insurers, the IAS reporting standards are of no benefit to us. In the first place, fair value in the financial statements is not conceptually the most obvious reporting method. Secondly, the proposed change is simply too comprehensive to be assimilated and introduced during the period up to 2005. We are by no means against change. We are for example also not against the US GAAP, but we do consider that there needs first to be total clarity and agreement on the issues concerning the fair value standard. Only then can such rules be applied to the financial statements. Like anyone else we consider that the accounting treatment must be harmonised and that we must all strive towards a complete standard accepted worldwide instead of an incomplete standard that may need to be changed again in the short term.

'If the current proposals are introduced without any special provisions and without due care, that will send the wrong signals to our policy-holders, shareholders and other stakeholders. That will place the share price under pressure, increase the costs of raising capital and complicate the necessary comparability between companies such as ours. To that you can also add incomplete information as it will be impossible for IT systems and software to adapt in good time. That does not mean that we fail to see the advantages of fair value accounting. If applied correctly this is certainly something from which the management can benefit considerably. It is however questionable whether it is in the interests of financial reporting.

'As long as no standards have been agreed, you have to make do as best you can with what you have, in this case the only available working system that deals with the recognition of insurance contracts. If those principles are included in the IAS for insurance contracts, a worldwide harmonisation comes into prospect. So we are not so negative about IAS. A number of important preconditions do however need to be fulfilled.'

Shortly before your retirement you took grave exception towards the amortisation of goodwill. What are your objections towards the way in which goodwill should be written off according to the US GAAP rules and charged to the profit and loss account?

Storm: 'Goodwill, I have argued, is not just a simplified, but also an artificial, difference between the acquisition price and the net asset value of a company. The US GAAP rules want this difference to be written off against the profit and loss account over a certain period. I consider that wrong. If I buy a particular consumer durable, that will become worn and worth less as time goes by. But if I take over a company, it is quite possible that its value may rise as time goes by. Why then should you amortise it?

'The FSAB then introduced an edict under which goodwill may no longer be written off against the profit and loss account but must be held on the balance sheet, unless it is evident from an impairment test that the value of the capitalised goodwill has fallen. Only then may this diminution in value be recognised as a loss in the profit and loss account for that specific year. Fine, but how do you determine the value of an acquisition after it has been absorbed and blended into your own company? And how do you then know whether that value has risen or fallen?

'And, as I have said before, if you write off goodwill over a totally arbitrary number of years, a loss in a particular year often doesn't represent any charge at all for that year. In other words, you are providing an incorrect representation of the results for a financial year in order to provide greater insight into the "real" equity position of the company. And how can you obtain a realistic picture if the elements making up that picture are incorrect?

'The argument is often advanced that the equity position of a company is regarded as an indication for the value of the company. That is incorrect. If companies capitalise goodwill and write it off, that will always be adjusted by analysts. They simply deduct the capitalised amount from the shareholders' equity. There is therefore no reason not to do so oneself from the start.'

How then should you treat goodwill?

Storm: 'There is no way that is ideal for both the profit and loss account and the balance sheet. But if you have to make a choice, choose the treatment that provides the most insight into the actual results during the reporting period.'

Is it true that you also had quite some objections towards the treatment of capital gains and capital losses?

Storm: 'Yes, the Traas Committee recommends showing the realised and unrealised capital gains in the profit and loss account. And if one chooses not to do so, the US GAAP approach would be preferable. That only takes account of realised capital gains. But the question is first of all how one can reflect realised and unrealised differences in value in the profit and loss account and whether that also holds good for insurance companies.

'In the first place, it is notable that life insurers and pension funds generally have different obligations from investment institutions. We have obligations with a long life and invest in the long term. Our investment policy is to obtain an optimal return for the policyholders. So what do we do? We spread our investment as far as possible. The portfolios also contain shares and property, the value of which can fluctuate considerably from year to year. For example, 1999 was a particularly good year,

Figures 2000

NOK millions	Published net results	**Unrealised** capital gains/losses (after tax)	Net results before **unrealised** capital gains/losses (after tax)
2000	705	−5,606	6,312
1999	3,500	5,464	−1,964
1998	442	−1,894	2,336
1997	1,008	9,051	−8,043
Average	1,414	1,754	−340

Figure 22.1 Published net results, unrealised capital gains/losses (after tax) and net results before unrealised capital gains/losses (after tax) of Storebrand.

2000 was reasonable to good, but 2001 was highly disappointing when compared with the preceding period. If we were obliged to represent all these differences in the profit and loss account, we would show a highly fluctuating picture that would not provide the user of the financial statements with a true insight into the quality of the assets, the results and the financial position of our company. The balance sheet and profit and loss account are drawn up at the end of each year, and that is just a snapshot in time, particularly if you take our long-term investments into account.

'Adoption of the Traas Committee proposal leads to some bizarre figures. This type of method is employed in Scandinavia. An example is provided by the Norwegian company Storebrand. If you examine the figures (see Figure 22.1), it is instantly clear that they do not tell us anything.

'The differences also serve to obscure the correct picture in the case of the Swedish Skandia (see Figure 22.2). What kind of information does such an approach add if the results for the financial year are obscured by more or less accidental fluctuations in the investment portfolio? This system does not work and the best proof of that statement is that the Scandinavians also do not care for it. What is more, it is not used anywhere else.'

Figures 2000

SEK millions	Published net results	**Unrealised** capital gains/losses (after tax)	Net results before **unrealised** capital gains/losses (after tax)
2000	2,826	−409	3,235
1999	3,456	−1,009	4,465
1998	1,242	−715	1,957
1997	3,403	1,359	2,043
1996	1,140	1,141	−1
Average	2,413	73	−2,340

Figure 22.2 Published net results, unrealised capital gains/losses (after tax) and net results before unrealised capital gains/losses (after tax) of Skandia.

Nevertheless you are not entirely happy with US GAAP?

Storm: 'If only realised capital gains are reflected in the profit and loss account, this can lead to manipulation. And that's what we find in practice too. The management wishes to publish good results and instructs its own investment department to sell off certain assets. These generate a profit and, hey presto, the management has performed well, for a profit has been made. Yes, but not with the core activities. And if the portfolio manager should object to the sale, he or she will be instructed to buy the assets back on 2 January the next year, if necessary at a loss. That's what I mean by manipulation. We don't want this kind of yo-yoing, which is why we have introduced a system that is transparent and reliable for shareholders and policyholders. It does not provide any opportunity for manipulation of the figures.'

That calls for explanation surely?

Storm: 'We lump together all realised and unrealised results on shares and property in a single pot. We apply a 30-year average to the indirect

Capital Gains

Euro millions

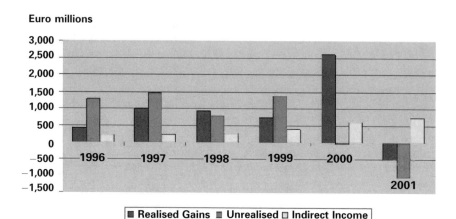

■ **Realised Gains** ■ **Unrealised** □ **Indirect Income**

Figure 22.3   Capital gains: realised gains and losses, unrealised gains and losses and indirect income from 1996 to 2001 for Aegon.

return on a portfolio with a seven-year average and often release that indirect income to the profit and loss account, solely in so far as that indirect income is derived from profits that have genuinely been made. Our system is new and has not yet been widely implemented, but it has already demonstrated its merits and deserves to be taken into consideration if new international standards are being drawn up for the financial statements.

'Over the past five years we have paid in a larger sum into the pot each quarter than we have withdrawn from it as indirect income, with the exception of three quarters in 2001. And that produces a highly reliable picture (see Figure 22.3).

'According to our own bookkeeping standards – and I continue to utter the word bookkeeping with pride – the net earnings since the introduction of our system of indirect income look as follows according to US GAAP (see Figure 22.4). All the differences have been included in the figure and consist primarily of the difference in the amortisation of goodwill and in indirect return in relation to realised capital gains.

'With the exception of the last year the earnings do not differ and are published each year in our annual report with an analysis of the differences. We could therefore readily live with US GAAP if the latter were to

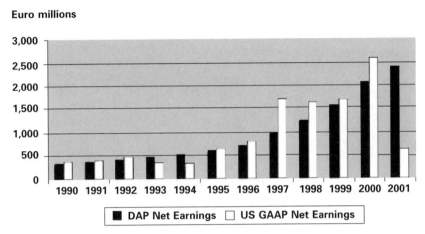

Figure 22.4   A comparison of Dutch Accounting Principles (DAP) net earnings and US GAAP net earnings from 1990 to 2001 from Aegon.

become the international standard, but it would need to be modified with rules for the treatment of goodwill and the recognition of indirect income in the profit and loss account.'

Aegon is an organisation that is highly oriented towards the United States. What will the relationship with US GAAP be?

Storm: 'If one switches in the Netherlands to IAS we will of course follow suit. But we have already been publishing financial statements according to US GAAP since 1984. We really won't be changing that. In addition, we will be presenting the results according to the directives applying at the time in Europe. People will therefore be able to choose. I would regard that as transparent.'

Fair Value Accounting will result in less transparency and more volatility in banks' financial reporting

An interview with Bert Bruggink

Bert Bruggink

Professor Bert Bruggink (1963), head of the Control Directorate of the Rabobank Group, has worked at Rabobank Netherlands since 1986. Since 1998, he has been part-time Professor in the Technology and Management Faculty of the University of Twente, teaching on Financial Institutions and Markets (Management Control).

Not only is the accountancy landscape being rearranged by regulation but the banking sector is also being faced with far-reaching rules. Concepts such as 'Basle-1' and 'Basle-2' are spoken of with awe, while the unwary seem to think that they refer only to river levels in that Swiss city on the Rhine. Basle-1 is a first attempt to standardise capital adequacy regulations and Basle-2 is a further refinement, based on risk-sensitive policy. Cynics say that a bank will lend you an umbrella when the sun is shining and ask for it back when it rains. Understandable, for while the thunder clouds of Basle-2 are gathering threateningly, the lightning bolts of IAS are still in the air. A weather forecast from Professor Bert Bruggink, head of the Control Directorate of the Rabobank Group.

How concerned are banks such as the Rabobank about, say, IAS 39?

Professor Bruggink: 'To start with, I have to say that it is inevitable that reporting based on IAS will land on us, whether we are talking about IAS 39 or the "full fair value" that may follow soon behind. Only the timing of its introduction is not certain, but it will definitely happen. That does not mean that we should not look at it uncritically. If, to start with, I restrict myself to IAS 39: one of the main objections is that its provisions are one-sided. In other words: a number of instruments on the asset side of the balance sheet are automatically subject to marking to market. As this is not emulated on the liabilities side of the balance sheet, this in itself results in a greater degree of volatility in results and/or shareholders' equity.

'From that you can argue, as proponents of IAS 39 also do, that it is opportunistic. And it is, for there are indeed instruments with a given market value. But the great objection to IAS 39 is its provisions on hedge accounting. The proposals on this conflict so much with banking pragmatism that there need to be some serious amendments. Professor M. N. Hoogendoorn underlined this, although he is a great supporter of these developments. It is stated that hedge accounting should only be done on an item-by-item basis. Well, suppose that a bank like ours grants mortgages based on financing in the form of savings. Everyone knows that this represents a "mismatch position", an interest risk position. In other words: you have a EUR 250,000 mortgage at a fixed interest rate for 10 years. It is financed by savings. That is an interest rate risk you can cover by hedging. If you now have to include a derivatives transaction to deal with the risk on each separate mortgage, one by one (and we have hundreds of thousands of them), it could take quite a while. Currently we do it in a different way: we take the entire mortgage portfolio, assess the composition of the financing and note mis-matches. We then cover that risk in one go with a single large transaction. In practical terms, it is completely pointless and inefficient to do this item by item. That is in fact the greatest objection to IAS 39.'

And 'full fair value accounting'?

Professor Bruggink: 'I have mixed feelings about this. On the one hand, "full fair value accounting" can have a positive effect in the light of risk management, especially with RAROC-type concepts and economic capital concepts. There, it is almost necessary to work on the basis of a market value. On the other hand, I don't think that this applies for reporting. In my experience, reporting has a purpose other than management control and risk management. On balance, the objections attaching to "full fair value" are too great merely to base the financial statements, both the balance sheet and the profit and loss account, on it.

'The principal objections attach mainly to those items where it is difficult or impossible to determine a market value. What is the market value of savings? What is the market value of current account balances? You can approach this purely theoretically, using discount rates to get a present value. But the assumptions you have to make to arrive at the discount rates or present values, have such an influence on the outcome that I dare say that strictly speaking any result could be created and justified. And in that case I do not think the argument that it offers so much transparency is all that convincing. I would go even further. I dare to argue that "full fair value accounting" will result in a reduction in transparency and that, in fact, an organisation's performance will be less clear. At least, if the financial statements are used as the source of information. In short, IAS is inevitable. Are we happy? Well, for internal use we have no problem, but for external use, in my opinion, it is a disaster.'

In the past there was the 'Provision for General Banking Risks', the VAR with a V. Now we have the 'Fund for General Banking Risks', the FAR with an F. Will this particularly Dutch phenomenon fit in with 'fair value accounting'?

Professor Bruggink: 'No, they are past their best. Fair value will raise the FAR for discussion. As soon as you have set the market value for the assets and liabilities, by definition what is left is a market value for shareholders' equity. The FAR is part of that, and so it does not really make any difference whether you call it equity or something else. The issue is whether the market value of shareholders' equity is adequate for the capital requirements set elsewhere. The composition is not that important. There are historical reasons for why the FAR developed, but its time has passed.'

The Dutch Bankers' Association (NVB) has issued a response to 'Basle-2' on behalf of the Dutch banks. Does the Rabobank hold a different view?

Professor Bruggink: 'No, I think we can say that there has been closer co-operation between the financial institutions and the supervisory authorities with respect to the Basle 'Consultative Paper' than in any previous case. Even the smaller players have been very closely involved with the responses compiled on the first paper. The document is very comprehensive. It is only 10% of the size of the "Consultative Paper" itself, that runs to almost 600 pages. In short, it is a very extensive memorandum with comments on behalf of all the banks and represents the opinion of the Rabobank as well. In addition, we have very regular technical consultation with the Dutch Central Bank (DNB) which, in my opinion, is well represented by its staff in Basle; for example, in the various working groups, shaping Pillar-1 (credit risk, operational risk, etc.), Pillar-2 (supervisory review) and Pillar-3 (disclosure, transparency). The Rabobank and the other banks can put forward their opinions and viewpoints, known as technical consultation, properly through the channels open to us.'

Although the Basle document maps out many subjects comprehensively, the 'operational risk' section, where there are very significant risks, is vague. How does the Rabobank deal with this?

Professor Bruggink: 'In the autumn of 2001, Basle published a document on operational risk which suggested a capital buffer for operational risks of 12% of the total capital requirement; much lower than the original 20%. Furthermore, and I think this is both significant and disappointing, this applies to the "standardised approach" and that the "advanced approach" (operating with internal models for operational risk) could result in a 25% discount, which is not very much, only 3% of the requirement.

Basle-2 presumes that operational risk could be the main category of risk. A decision has been explicitly made to have this element as part of Pillar-1 despite the fact that it is very underdeveloped theoretically. This should, however, encourage the banks to form a theory and suchlike, as we have seen for market and credit risk in recent years. But then there should be a reward and banks should be encouraged to develop such models. What is the reward for the bank? I believe 3% is not enough. Of course, many will claim that you do more than just meet external obligations. You can be sure that, where there are explicit adverse operational risks, banks will definitely have taken their own measures. Perhaps not in a structured and model-based way, but there will be a reaction. It is also the case that banks react appropriately to situations and, for example, revise processes, provide additional staff training or undertake additional research through accountants or the DNB. In short, we have always had plenty of measures, procedures and mechanisms which lead to identified operational risks being tackled. That will not change in the future. So the only thing that is new in this context is the capital requirement. And, in my opinion, the encouragement that the Basle document seems to give is too little to get banks to make additional investments in developing theory and models for managing operational risk.'

What does this mean for the Rabobank?

Professor Bruggink: 'Unlike in 2001, when we were still talking about 20%, we see no significant reduction in the capital requirement if we move to internal models. At 10%, we are still talking. Let me give you an example relating to the Rabobank. We have EUR 15 billion in equity. Let's assume that this is equal to the capital requirement. Of that, EUR 1.5 billion, 10%, is certainly a substantial amount. If we are talking about 3%, we are left with EUR 0.5 billion. If we allow for the "cost of capital", one and a half billion at (say) 7%, we are talking about an annual investment of EUR 100 million. You can do a lot with that. If I assume EUR 500 million as an additional requirement, times the cost of capital, then I am talking about an amount that is only one third of that. You can do a lot less with EUR 30 million. It is not just the Rabobank that is making these calculations, but the other banks too. I think that the high expectations we recently had and which many consultancy/accounting firms set up practices for, can be put on the back burner and considerably amended. On the one hand that is good, because some really wild ideas were put forward. On the other hand, it is unfortunate as it hampers ongoing thinking about a model-based approach to operational risk.'

Operational risk can cover extreme disasters, such as the terrorist attacks in the United States on 11 September 2001. J. P. Morgan suddenly has a big problem with this. How do banks in general and the Rabobank in particular react to that type of threat?

Professor Bruggink: 'There were disasters before 11 September 2001. Operational risk management always existed implicitly or explicitly. But back-up and contingency facilities now need more attention than before. We must of course pay more attention to this and work on it, but it is not new. We will go through all the documents and facilities once again with a

fine-tooth comb. We must assess very critical processes carefully. Naturally, we always assume the worst, but on 11 September 2001 real life
showed that things can always be a degree worse. You wonder then
whether it makes sense to be prepared in terms of risk management or
capital requirements or in some other way. To put it another way: if you
end up in such a situation, it is more a question of survival than one of
properly running procedures that in theory and in the models are always
the solution and which always run smoothly, but which in practice prove
inadequate or which are not applied as intended.'

*Supervision in the Netherlands has three angles: the
Dutch Central Bank (DNB), the Authority for the
Financial Markets and the Pensions and Insurance
Supervisory Authority of the Netherlands* (Pensioen- &
Verzekeringskamer). *Former minister Zalm has said that
he wants to raise the operation of supervision for
discussion to arrive at a different structure. What are
your thoughts on this?*

Professor Bruggink: 'Good supervision is good for us all. The fact that the
Netherlands is well known as a country with strict banking supervision,
can sometimes be a little difficult in operations, but in the end we all
benefit from it, including the banks. The simple fact that the Rabobank
is supervised by DNB creates a number of benefits with respect to reports
by rating agencies. Good supervision is, therefore, exceptionally important. We are also happy with the current supervisory structure. Nevertheless there is a movement under way, prompted by a number of
situations and developments, where we see a consolidation of supervision. This is most obvious in the United Kingdom, where all the supervisory authorities have been merged. That is in the line with what the EU
wants. Joint supervision is on the horizon. The current model in the
Netherlands is in any event open for discussion.

'Supervision has two components. Paul Koster discussed them earlier
(see Chapter 11). On the one hand there is the more traditional prudential
supervision and on the other hand business-conduct supervision. As far as
I am aware, prudential supervision is not under discussion. If a financial
institution is being supervised by the DNB, it will simply continue to be
so: by the DNB. In addition there is business-conduct supervision. This
did not exist 10 years ago, but it is becoming more important. Business-
conduct supervision covers communications, the financial information

leaflet on financial products. It also covers assessing proposed managers and shareholders, combating money laundering and suchlike; certainly now that the war on terrorism has taken on this extra dimension. This has gradually ended up with the supervisory authorities.

This has all resulted in a debate on whether it is possible or sensible to place these issues with the same supervisory authorities. There are very different opinions. Some people are quite adamant about this: you should not make a supervisor, operating from the prudential standpoint, responsible for these matters too, since they are of a different order. More so, they can be in conflict. That creates for example, the Australian model with the two supervisory tasks, prudential and business conduct, being separated. That means two supervisory authorities working separately. I have some sympathy with that but, because there are many overlaps between the two types of supervision and a need for communication, a single supervisor would also have a good chance. In the United Kingdom, where the decision was for complete integration, the model in which supervisory authorities are combined is not working. It may be teething troubles or start-up problems, but it has not worked for years. I should also note that there is no European model yet. So why should the Netherlands again be ahead of the game, with a real chance that the supervision model will have to be replaced at some time by one approved by the European Union? And that will definitely happen; within 10 years. It doesn't make sense to come up with a local model which has loads of institutions which will need to be reorganised, set up differently or even disbanded. That costs huge amounts of money and energy and brings unnecessary friction and destruction of capital. These are considerations that have to be weighed up. There are serious discussions under way between the Ministry of Finance, the supervisory bodies and the bodies under supervision. And that discussion is far from complete.'

Organisations like banks face high fixed costs. How do you arrive internally at sound and accurate pricing?

Professor Bruggink: 'That is a difficult question. Allocation of income and expenses to different customer groups has always been tricky. On the income side, it is mainly the allocation of interest income, where technically you have to use the system of relevance. But which discount rate is appropriate? This has been discussed in the professional literature for about 25 years and no definite solution has yet been found. There are certain categories where there is no optimal solution and where the word "option" is more appropriate. And a choice is by definition subjective.

The position on expenses is similar. It is true that we have a large range of expenses that seem to be fixed. But I think that you can regard a good proportion of them as "common" costs. That is an old and familiar concept for me and one that those who have read van der Schroef will recognise. A characteristic of common costs is that they cannot be allocated objectively. So if you are thinking of allocation, it has to be done subjectively, even though some choices can be more easily and better justified than others. That is what a bank is involved with.

'Some years ago, my colleague, Jan Bos, and I wrote a number of articles and a book on management control and more specifically on the issue of costs. We referred to a system we called the "Einzelkosten 1 method". In fact we were working with a set of layers to separate various allocation levels. A not inconsiderable part of the expenses can be defined at the very lowest level (product level, individual customer level or distribution level). But there are also those which are very difficult to profit from at that level. Then you go a layer further, starting from the core. Now you are referring to a product or customer group or a business unit. In short, there is a sort of hierarchy of calculation objects, four or five layers or as many as you think necessary. Costs are allocated to the various levels. If you do that, you are no longer able to set an integral cost for each product. Which is a pity if that was your final objective. However, if your aim was to introduce a cost control system, a hierarchy of calculation objects and allocation to the level where influence is possible, it becomes much more interesting. I have the impression that for many banks this is more important than a uniform system of cost calculation. Generally speaking, cost calculators are not the best tools for cost control.

This does not answer the question. I think that there are tools that are more useful for the banks, at the present time, when cost reduction is definitely back on the plate of the management. In my opinion, this is a more important issue than the problem of arriving at a clear cost calculation.'

The relationship with auditors: we know about the information memorandum from the DNB which clearly defines a function for auditors which is different from the one applying to the rest of business. What should the auditor's role be?

Professor Bruggink: 'Internal and external auditors each have their own specific functions. A bank's internal auditors must perform all kinds of operational audits and associated work. That is the main component.

They also do a lot of preparatory work for the financial audit which is signed off finally by the external auditor.

'However good external auditors are, they are limited by the simple fact that they are not involved in the business every day. That is a handicap, as institutions like the Rabobank – and this also applies *a priori* to other institutions – are so complex that it is pointless to suppose that an external auditor can have detailed insight into what is happening in the organisation. Consequently, external auditors must be able to rely on the preparatory work of internal auditors. And that implies that internal auditors must have a sufficiently objective role within the organisation that the external auditors can depend on their work. And not only the external auditors. Supervisory authorities are increasingly relying on the work of internal auditors.

'We were just talking about Basle. You see that the external supervisor's role has clearly shifted from what was done in the past, assessing output in the form of monthly reports and other data, to what has happened since the mid-1990s: looking at processes in the form of models and trying to agree them. This approach is confirmed by Basle-2. Large parts of the business are described in the form of models and the supervisor focuses primarily on answering the question of whether the models are indeed adequate, and then checks them against criteria such as regularity of the scenario analysis, back testing and suchlike. If the model meets the requirements, the output is obviously a result of it and it is no longer necessary to look further in detail. The internal auditor is engaged to assess whether the models are up to the mark. And so the supervisory authorities are also relying more on the preparatory work of the auditor.'

Which business developments do you see coming in the banking sector?

Professor Bruggink: 'There are two very specific developments which are of vital importance to banks and where the role of the controller is central. Firstly, Basle and, secondly, "fair value accounting". To put it another way: Basle integrates risk management and control. It would not surprise me if there are no risk managers or controllers in five or 10 years. The two functions will be integrated. Risk and financial performance are two sides of the same coin and that is now increasingly being confirmed by all systems.

'Fair value accounting also fits into this. Marking to market is very sensible for risk management, management control and internal situation management. But I think reporting is different and so integration of risk management and "financial control" seems inevitable. At the same time I have to say that complexity is growing. Not so much because we cannot do our work; it is that transparency is more difficult to achieve. Volatility is increasing: things are based more and more on complicated models. You can say what you like, but Basle-1 was extremely simple. I could explain it to first and second year students in half an hour. You cannot handle Basle-2 in a single lecture. In a manner of speaking, it is a separate subject and even then it will be difficult to grasp all the principles. In other words: only a select group will be able to follow it and that has affected developments.

'Do not underestimate the effects of Basle-1: the derivatives business grew directly out of it. Lending has also been under pressure as a result of Basle-1. Basle-1 had major commercial significance. Some products disappeared, some appeared. Securitisation arose purely from the Basle concept. Basle-2 will also have a great influence. Those banks able to understand the new rules from the beginning and realise their implications, will have a big advantage. If you start from there, controllers and the financial-economic departments within a bank must "understand" the complexity of the issues to get a grip on them. For this, they must be able to transfer the acquired knowledge to as many people as possible: not only directors, other colleagues and whoever else, but also to customers. If we succeed in that, we will be in the first division. If not, we risk dropping a long way behind. It is very important that we try to reach the highest degree of quality. Only the best succeed in this and those lagging behind will be swallowed up and no longer exist independently in 10 years. Controllers will have a vital role for the time being.

'We are already seeing financial institutions working with concepts based on Basle-2 and basing strategic decisions on them. Certain activities are being sold off. That is not a coincidence but is being done very consciously. I, therefore, expect that the positioning of banking institutions in 2005 will be very different compared with now. We are getting new types of "near-banks" and "non-banks", institutions not under direct supervision. I will risk a prediction. I expect that many financial institutions will close their leasing companies. Barclays is doing it and others will follow. And why? Because those who don't will be hit by Basle-2. I am convinced that the aim will increasingly be for "structured investment vehicles". That means that activities will be transferred to unsupervised, associated or independent parties. It's not impossible that the Rabobank, which currently has a balance sheet total of €180 billion, may only have €18 billion in 10 years' time. That does not mean that the bank will be 10 times weaker. No, it means that it will have "piggy banks" all over the place.'

Chapter 24

Financial statements are a result of policy and not a factor informing policy

An interview with Joost G. Groeneveld

Joost G. Groeneveld

Joost Groeneveld (1944) is a director of Wingman Business Valuators and as such is a 'business valuator' for corporate financing, transaction management, valuations of shares and loss adjusting. He also lectures at Rotterdam Erasmus University, Financial and Management Accounting group. He is involved in regulation and legislation on financial reporting and for more than 20 years has been a teacher and member (since 1991 chairman) of the VERA steering committee on Business Economics.

Marking to market (fair value) is making reporting more dynamic and less consistent, say many experts. Information must be reliable, but if there is a chance that valuations can be arbitrary, fair value definitely cannot be regarded as an improvement and the valuation of certain assets will become pure guesswork. In short, the fair value system will not make the audit simpler. The stock exchange value of a company will fluctuate from year to year and if interim figures have to be presented, those fluctuations will only be greater. If the auditor has to express an opinion on the acceptability of the valuation, he or she will have to refer to external specialists, such as "register valuators". One of these is Joost Groeneveld.

Will a lot really change for the auditor and the 'register valuator'?

Groeneveld: 'I think so. Certainly in respect of the quality of reporting. According to section 362(2) of the Netherlands Civil Code, the balance sheet must present a fair, clear and systematic view of the net assets.[1] And the expression "fair, clear and systematic" is repeated in paragraph 3[2] with respect to the profit and loss account. The same quality requirements also apply to the notes. Of course, there was a reason for that section being formulated in this way. Society has every interest in a company's position being presented fairly. You have to be able to rely on the view, since you make important investment decisions based on it. I emphasise this point, since so much is invested in companies. The reporting must also be clear. I regard that as the vital element: a company must aim for clear and unambiguous communication with all stakeholders. And then there is systematic. That means that you cannot swap systems from year to year. In business, the true and fair view in the financial statements is paramount. The financial-economic view must be worked on. The moves towards applying fair value can be seen in that light.'

Will financial reporting still add value?

Groeneveld: 'It depends on what you want to use it for. I have to say that I think the expectations are too high. The need for the results of the past year is completely different from that for information to base certain decisions on: financial statements are not meant primarily for that. Consequently, I prefer to see reporting in the context of accountability, of management. I think financial statements are more a result of policy than a factor informing policy. To me, that is the difference.

'Financial statements are very important for accountability and management. Although financial statements work less well in other possible

---

[1] Article 362: (...) 2. The balance sheet and the notes thereon shall fairly, clearly and systematically reflect the net assets and composition of the assets and liabilities at the end of the financial year classified in separate items. The balance sheet may reflect the net assets in accordance with the appropriation of the profit or the treatment of the loss or, where this has not been determined, in accordance with the proposal therefor. The heading of the balance sheet shall state whether the profits have been appropriated therein. (BW 2 : 363[4], 364 v.)

[2] The profit and loss account and the notes thereon shall fairly, clearly and systematically reflect the result for the financial year and the items of income and expenses upon which it is based. (BW 2 : 363[4], 377) (...)

areas of application, this does not mean that they should just fade away. You cannot expect more than a report can provide. You should not develop policy on it. If you want to change the contents of financial statements, you lose sight of the fact that in principle they are structured around realised cash flows: receipts and expenditures which have happened and not those which may occur in the future as they depend precisely on policy which does not exist but which still has to be formulated.

'What I am alluding to is the use of marking to market. In my opinion, "fair value applications" are necessary for the operation of financial statements. I have always put that in the category of unsolved problems, phenomena which do not fit the criterion of realised cash flows. If that criterion is applied without possible valuation based on fair value, significant elements – vital for a true and fair view – would remain "off the balance sheet". For example, the development of new financial instruments makes the challenges too great, too important and too material. I think that the application of fair value should meet certain conditions.'

Should financial statements give a better impression of the value of a company?

Groeneveld: 'As I have mentioned, I think that financial statements fail when it comes to information to base policy on. If you want to gather information for that, you will need more. When the shares of a listed company are well in excess of the book value, people get concerned. When stock-exchange prices and book values are fairly close to each other, no one gets excited. We saw this at the time of "inflation accounting". When inflation was under control, interest in inflation accounting quickly ebbed away.

'No, there is a practical problem when prices rise too quickly and book value lags behind. If you see that as a problem, you have to present or structure financial statements differently. And I think that is going a little too far. You damage financial statements with the argument of a value gap (stock exchange value – book value). What do you do if prices fall quickly? You will have to alter your reporting quickly to remain in step with the fall in prices on the exchange. That will look chaotic and panicky and does the company and all its stakeholders a disservice. I, therefore, call for keeping accountability in the financial statements and quotation on the stock exchange strictly separated.'

Does the future of the auditor lie in the hands of the valuators, as some say?

Groeneveld: 'The valuation of assets and liabilities is indeed a subject of its own, but I see it more as complementary to accountancy. A valuator should not want to move into the auditor's field or vice versa. If everyone is aware of his or her capabilities and limitations, there can be excellent co-operation and that co-operation will offer clear added value. I myself am both a *registeraccountant* and a "register valuator" and can, therefore, speak for both groups. In my eyes, an auditor is essentially a checking and certifying specialist. A valuator is a valuation specialist.'

Is today's auditor sufficiently equipped to meet the challenge?

Groeneveld: 'It is a problem that value is so variable. Values can fluctuate. And I am not just talking about the stock-exchange prices we face in 2002, but of value differences. External circumstances can create huge fluctuations as we have seen recently. The question is whether an auditor is in a position to issue an opinion on a sharply changing picture. On a snapshot or a movie. One is static and two-dimensional, the other perhaps fragmentary. I find it very difficult and I can well understand that there are auditors who avoid it.

'Another thing is that value can be very subjective. Something of great value to one person may be worth little to someone else. It is the relationship between object and subject. It is exactly these value differences that you use in transactions, in economics. You use value differences to justify transactions. They are the reason for transactions. You have to be able and willing to use them. In accountancy, you often see arguments from a type of supposed objectivity.'

Is it to be welcomed that IAS will apply to everyone from 2005?

Groeneveld: 'I have my doubts. It is as if everyone will soon be walking round in Chairman Mao suits. I am not a supporter of uniformity and loss of identity. Can a view still be true and fair if it lacks identity? Of course, in theory, it is excellent that there will be a single set of rules, but if the suit does not fit, it will have to be altered. This is where I see a trial of strength for the audit profession, which, while maintaining the true and fair view, will have to move from bespoke to off-the-peg. That demands care and responsibility. Auditors will have to be sure of themselves; certainly in a society where people are quick to sue. I foresee risks, and things will certainly not be easier for auditors.'

Should we perhaps have specific standards for small and medium-sized enterprises?

Groeneveld: 'Such enterprises include every type of business: mature and young, a bit of everything. As a result of the heterogeneity of this sector, you may fail if you want to squeeze every business into the straitjacket of a single set of rules. And such enterprises have their own problems. In any event, they should not be subject to the same publication requirements as listed companies. Their legal form often differs from listed companies. The separation of management and ownership is often less significant or even absent. That could justify specific rules.'

What does fair value mean to you?

Groeneveld: 'It is a good, but unclear, American term; after all, what is "fair"? The term is often translated into Dutch as market value, which is confusing since market value is the value based on market listings, on prices. Provided that markets are well organised, open to everyone, transparent and efficient, there is no objection. Prices will then give a good indication of expected cash flow. You can then also base value on the listing. That is market value for most people. Strictly speaking, however, market value alone is not an indication of value. After all, which market are we talking about? A procurement market? A stock exchange? A property market? If the thing is to establish the market value of a company, it is given that the value is derived from different prices on different markets, including procurement markets. But there is more. Even if you restrict yourself to shares, you see that it is not just the exchange, but also the market for corporate control. As a rule, control is not traded on a stock exchange. Companies occasionally disappear temporarily or permanently from the stock exchange. That means that there is arbitrage between the stock exchange and the market for corporate control. This says nothing about market value. In other words: if we talk about market value, we are in fact referring to current prices on markets. They do not have to be the same as commercial value or the value in the books. So in that sense it is not the balance sheet or book value or whatever you want to call it. In practice, fair value may well be approximated by market values, but in principle it is still seen as the commercial value. It is a value derived from the future, as an economist does it. A discounted cash flow value would then be the fair value.

'With reference to a legal component, one should beware of confusion between fair value as a commercial value and "open-market value" which could have an element of market value. The "open-market value" is the arm's length price in the best transaction that can be achieved. Fair value relates to the future. Even a museum that owns many valuable objects gets its significance not from the fact that a given picture was painted 300 years ago, but from the fact that visitors will come and see it tomorrow, and that there will be interest in it tomorrow, the day after and in a year from now. Commercial value is derived from the future. In that sense, value is an expression of doing business. No-one knows the future with certainty. It involves expectations, risk assessment, investment in the future. I readily accept that society is sometimes so dynamic that you can doubt reasonable expectations and that risk can sometimes be dominant. That causes me some concern, of course. In the extreme, the expression is that it seems to be a lottery. As soon as the other famous expression "What a fool would give" becomes dominant, I withdraw. But I must add, for my own peace of mind, that I have never met that "fool". People try to be sensible with their money and weigh up decisions carefully. Even when circumstances are very changeable and uncertain, they base their lives on certain expectations. That sometimes involves certain risks, but life is like that; certainly for a businessman. Accepting risk is a condition of a businessman's existence. Perhaps it is precisely that element – based on realised cash flows – that is by definition missing from financial statements.'

What are the basic principles of fair value for financial instruments (IAS 39)?

Groeneveld: Up to now, it has always been a choice between "off the balance sheet" and fair value. But I think that goes too far. If it is material, it must not be off the balance sheet. Otherwise, you do not have a true and fair view. That leaves fair value. But you have to be sure that the markets are indeed (virtually) perfect. In other words: standard products, efficient markets and meeting places, efficient tools with efficient markets. They are the conditions I had in mind earlier. Then it is possible. Then you have prices that are good indicators of the actual value.'

Does that also apply to property?

Groeneveld: 'Yes, property is appraised at market value. Hidden reserves are revealed without having to worry too much about the property's legal status to the company. If property is valued at the price per cubic metre in a first-class location at current market prices, the current value is not being treated properly, since the property in question is not going to be put on the market. That may not happen for perhaps 60 years, at the end of a long lease for example. In other words: if you value faithfully, using cash flows, you should not look at what a property of that size in that location would "make" now. Because the circumstances simply do not exist. It will not be put on the market, it is not vacant possession, which depresses the value. You, therefore, have to apply many assumptions (what could this building, including the rights and obligations on it, provide in cash flows in the legal context?) to come up with a good valuation.'

And the valuation of brands and other intangible assets?

Groeneveld: 'If you determine the current value of that type of asset, you are in fact doing what has always been done. In social-cost issues, you attribute the revenues to that one asset, regarded as vital or irreplaceable. If you still want to know what that one brand is worth, you must try to trade it separately. Is there a market for it? If so, can you separate out what is available for it and is it realistic. Otherwise, tangibility is not that important to economists. It is always "goods and/or services".

'The valuation of "human capital" is linked strongly to individuals. You see this in large stock-exchange listed companies, where the share price often seems to be partly based on up-and-coming talent or the person who is leaving or a combination the two. In small and medium-sized enterprises, the personal link is even stronger. Transactions often specify that the owner/director selling the company has to stay on for a couple of years. He or she is regarded as vital and in fact forms the value of the business.

'I am not sure whether you should include these as separate assets in the balance sheet. You are still not tackling the complex value. In fact it is a bit of a *Fata Morgana* to try to include all these separate assets in the company's value or the shareholder value in the balance sheet. That will not work. And in that sense, I think that financial statements, traditional as they are, still offer their own clarity. Perhaps you should include all these other components not in the balance sheet but in an additional statement, separate from or as part of the annual report.'

Do you view the future as sombre?

Groeneveld: 'Not at all. I even see traditional financial statements being restored to honour on the basis of realised cash flows. Using the realisation principle. Nothing is simple though, but there are recognisable criteria. What does not fit in the financial statements, can be disclosed separately.

'What we have to watch out for is that each company has its own identity, serves different interests, and that each transaction is, therefore, different. It is important not to look too mechanically to the models – such as the financial statements – which present such entities and events. They always add up on paper. But reality is much more interesting. If you want to recognise and give a place to the people in this mechanism, our profession is an excellent one. Because in the end it is about people.'

Chapter 25

Financial reporting and the search for truth

An interview with Dirk M. Swagerman

Dirk M. Swagerman

Dirk Swagerman is attached to the University of Twente in Enschede, Deloitte & Touche Amsterdam and the Controller's Training Course of the Eurac/Erasmus University Rotterdam. Recently (15 November 2002) he was appointed Professor at the Economic Faculty and the Faculty of Business Economics of the Rijksuniversiteit Groningen (RUG).

The interview we had with Professor Dirk Swagerman revolved around the relationship between financial reporting and the search for truth. A bridge was thus built between accounting, financial reporting and corporate finance. Swagerman believes that the interaction between his practical work at Deloitte & Touche and the more theoretical approach at the university is extremely valuable.

> *There is ever-mounting pressure towards the standardisation and codification of regulations. Couldn't this reduce the accountant's role to that of a mere 'rule checker'?*

Professor Swagerman: 'Before I can answer that question we must first indicate what type of accountant we are referring to. If we are speaking of a "rule checker", then it must be about the – future – certifying accountant. It is clear that regulations are undergoing a process of standardisation and codification. On the one hand, uniformity of regulations improves the transparency. That is a good development. On the other hand, this could lead to the construction of an overly restrictive normative framework. I think that the latter point sometimes gets short shrift in the current discussion and therefore merits further explanation.

'A shift is occurring from a normative approach centring on profit and capital, which is the typical territory of accountants, to a more subjective approach which looks at the value of the company. In the latter case the financial statements should provide insight into and information on the company's ability to generate cash flows. The rationale here is that positive cash flows are a precondition for value creation. Questions about the value of companies belong to the realm of corporate finance. As a consequence, specific groups of users such as financiers, banks and providers of capital are increasingly asserting themselves in the domain of accounting regulations. In the past this was the area where the accountant played a key role. Now other parties are coming forward and demanding a say in the discussions about the regulations.

'The central question is whether the financial statements are an accountability document or an instrument for making decisions on corporate finance matters. These, in my view, are two separate things that are often unjustifiably lumped together. If the annual report is intended to be an accountability document, then information based on historical cost is perfectly adequate. But if it's supposed to be a document for decision-making purposes, then a strong case can be made for the fair value approach. You see, accountability implies explaining and justifying actions carried out in the past. In other words: the prime focus is to provide information about the application of capital rather than to make a statement about future profits. This then means that the accountant by definition forms an opinion on the basis of historical accounting information. The financial statements – as an accountability document for clarifying the past period and determining the moment of settlement with shareholders and the Inland Revenue, and complete with auditor's report – are increasingly being seen as a "commodity" which should by preference be as uniform as possible to promote comparability. The accountant can of course be asked to express an opinion about the possible purposes for which the financial statements can be used. But in that case a different normative assessment framework is being assumed.

'The requirements of the international capital market simply demand regulatory uniformity to ensure capital allocation takes place as efficiently as possible. The mutual comparability resulting from this uniformity will conveniently allow users to form a more balanced picture. The capital market is increasingly dictating the norms for shaping and designing the regulations. There isn't much against that in itself, but a shift can be discerned from the primacy of the company's "own nature" to the significance of capital as a production factor. A similar difference in approach can be found incidentally between the company financial statements where capital maintenance regulations make their presence clearly felt – in the form of the maintenance of statutory reserves – and the consolidated financial statements where prudential control is a more prominent concern.

'A good directors' report seeks to bridge the gap between these two separate domains: on the one hand, it attempts to explain all sorts of events that have occurred in the past period; on the other hand, it contains the prospective element about what the future holds in store. Basically, many directors' reports are still too limited in scope to allow the reader to form an opinion about future developments. That's why we are now slowly but surely seeing the concept of the "comprehensive model of business reporting" appear on the horizon. This model is very broad in scope and offers ample room for an informative section on the future outlook.

'Let me return briefly to what I just said about the company's "own nature", a term that finds its origin in the "typology of applications" as first developed by Starreveld. The concept of the company's "own nature" is all about recognising essential differences between organisations that can't simply be lumped together. These differences entail that each company must organise its processes efficiently and effectively in a manner that best suits its specific needs. The administrative organisation of a virtual Internet company, for instance, is of a completely different order from that of a family-owned metal-processing company. So taking account of the company's "own nature" means that financial statements are prepared in the light of the accounting policies that are appropriate to the business in question. In that way, sufficient latitude is created for recognising differences between various types of organisations, particularly in relation to such important items as goodwill, intangible assets, valuations, provisions, etc. At a virtual Internet company that has obtained a stock exchange listing (either organically or via acquisitions), for instance, the size and significance of the intangible assets will be of much greater importance than at a family-owned metal-processing company.

'The notes to the financial statements explain the methods used to account for the company's specific characteristics and also indicate the accounting consequences of using these particular methods. The differences that exist between companies are not easy to capture in a ready-made set of uniform rules that can be applied to all organisations. The financial statements must give a true and fair view of the economic reality. The imposition of a normative set of rules puts severe constraints on the entrepreneur's freedom of expression and will make it impossible to give an accurate picture of that economic reality in all situations. An added difficulty is that the economic reality is undergoing constant change.'

What is the consequence of this line of reasoning?

Professor Swagerman: 'As I said, a specific company's "own nature" may not be done justice in cases where the economic reality cannot be adequately presented with a set of uniform rules. Assuming that this observation is correct, then the annual report does not provide the accurate reflection of the financial position that we are aspiring towards. If more emphasis is placed on uniformity and codification, then some alternative means must be found to express those differences between organisations that receive little or no attention in the financial statements. That's why I think the directors' report can play an important role: because this is where specific attention can be devoted to the company's "own nature".

So are the financial statements an appropriate instrument for presenting an accurate picture of the company's value?

Professor Swagerman: 'Here you are referring to the use of the financial statement and the information it contains for decision-making purposes. From the financing theory and corporate finance perspective, strong emphasis is placed on the fact that the company's value is based on the discounted value of the future free cash flows. That is the well-known DCF method, which I believe is a perfectly good approach in itself! At the moment, however, I think we are inclined to use this method a little too hastily while neglecting other possible approaches. The DCF method confronts you with its own specific problems. These particularly concern determining the level of the discount rate, making an accurate assessment of the expected cash flows, weighting the cash flow duration, estimating the residual value and finally the denial of possible flexibility. All these aspects need to be recognised. And once you do that, it becomes clear that there is a tendency to overestimate the importance of using expected free cash flows for calculating a company's value. Usually the DCF calculations overstate rather than understate the value. I would also like to note in this context that the value of financial statements based on historical information cannot be completely dismissed. They can help to form an opinion on the net asset value.

'If we apply accrual accounting properly, and more specifically the matching principle, then – barring direct movements in shareholders' equity – value creation will be shown in the profit and loss account while the way in which value creation takes place is shown in the balance sheet. If you follow a very strict line of reasoning, no future-oriented information can be derived from financial statements other than that there are no continuity problems at the time of publication. Even so I think there's a lot to say for using financial statements as a starting document for value determination purposes and against focusing too facilely on the DCF method. I think that the significance of the profit and loss account will diminish in the future. This is due to the subjective interpretation of the profit concept. The cash flow statement, on the other hand, will be given more weight while the nature and composition of the capital – based on fair value – in the balance sheet at a given moment will be looked at more closely. Finally, I think that if you make a really thorough analysis of accrual accounting versus the DCF method, then accrual accounting will be found to be conceptually much trickier.'

How do you see the relationship between analysts and other external financial parties (that is, the valuation in the market) on the one hand and internal accounting policies and a consistent line of behaviour for the financial statements (that is, the internal valuation) on the other?

Professor Swagerman: 'Analysts are under pressure at the moment. Doubts are being raised here and there as to whether they are really independent and whether their recommendations are really based on in-depth analysis. The chances are this group of professionals will find themselves more emphatically at the centre of attention in the coming period. Financial statements are an important source of information for this group. So here we see the financial statements serving as a source of information for decision-making purposes. The analyst processes that information and, in so doing, performs some of the intellectual tasks that the decision-maker can undertake. Statements are thus made about the future finance ability of the company. The analyst can never draw these conclusions exclusively on the basis of the financial statements.

He or she must also consult other sources. The arrival of fair value accounting will bring about many changes. The user of the information will have to get used to the greater volatility, particularly of the result. Fair value accounting will also make the interaction between valuation on the balance sheet and the rating by a rating agency much more dynamic and difficult to manage. This is of crucial importance for organisations that make frequent use of these agencies' services, because there are a number of underlying technical problems at work here that need to be properly understood. Investor relations could provide the answer.

'Apart from the aspects that I have mentioned about the essence of financial statements, there are also those of timeliness and accuracy of information. That's why there are developments towards providing information on a more frequent and continuous basis. The Internet could become a vital link in the reporting chain.'

There is a lot of talk about all sorts of value elements surreptitiously creeping into the financial statements. Where are these most clearly visible?

Professor Swagerman: 'The most important current issue is the debate about the introduction and significance of fair value accounting. This discussion is usually believed to be about a technical modification of our financial reporting practices, but that is not completely correct. The adjustments stem from a change of ideology involving a new emphasis on the primacy of the shareholder value philosophy, which has consequences for the corporate governance model and the associated reporting requirements. The central tenet here is that the company's value is basically nothing other than the discounted value of the future free cash flows. If we assume a different ideology, then the shareholder value philosophy makes way for a very different type of thinking. We find this at insurance companies and pension funds, for instance. They attach more importance to "prudence" than to shareholder value as a characteristic of the company's "own nature". As a consequence, they have a lot of trouble giving the fair value approach an interpretation that is appropriate to their circumstances.

'One important point is that intangible assets in particular have become so dominant in our economic production process but that this prominence has not yet been adequately translated to the balance sheet. It should be observed that one of the main underlying reasons for adopting the fair value approach is precisely to arrive at a more faithful presentation of the company's financial position. The discussion can ultimately be traced back to the well-known differences between the objective and subjective value theory. The value of a commodity is obtained in the transaction process between supply and demand. The value of a commodity is not determined by the accumulation of costs and sacrifices. So we are hovering between the objectivity of determining costs and sacrifices and the subjective value that comes about in the market. The market price in turn is then an objective given, but we won't go into that here. A related theme concerns the granting of staff options. Until recently these options were exclusively mentioned in the notes to the financial statements (is there any other appropriate place?), even though they can have a substantial impact on the future wealth of shareholders. In other words: the total "pot" has to go round more people.

'One of the problems is the difference that must be made between the net fair value of the assets and liabilities and the value of the company. The difference between these entities is determined by the goodwill that the company itself has generated. What then does this self-generated goodwill consist of? It is largely made up of the intangible assets. Now this brings us to an extremely interesting problem. If the company is to be sold in "the market for corporate control", then the buyer will state the acquired goodwill at fair value on the balance sheet. If the company continues to operate as an independent entity, then its value can only be approximated by means of an estimation. The intangible asset, after all, is not stated on the balance sheet. There's nothing wrong with this in the case of the family-owned metal-processing company we mentioned earlier, but it is most definitely a problem for a virtual Internet service provider with lots of professional staff on its payroll. There have been suggestions that the future role of the accountant will be confined to checking whether the accounting rules have been complied with. The reality will be totally different; the accountant will have to form his or her own opinion about whether the presented value is acceptable or not. Value determination, more than is currently the case, is set to become a completely new domain for accountants and therefore also for the accountancy firms.

'This brings me back to objective of financial statements. As we have seen, financial statements will in the future increasingly be used as a document for making decisions. The "IAS framework" also confirms this. First of all the framework says that "the objective of financial statements" is to permit "making economic decisions", and subsequently "also [to] show the results of the stewardship". Where the financial statements are to serve as proof of good stewardship, fair value plays a much more subordinate role. On the other hand, if the financial statements are to be used as a decision-making document, then the search for the company's value – which is constantly subject to change – takes a more central place. After all, the stock exchange can collapse or the company can suddenly come up with a product that takes the market by storm. Actually something paradoxical is going on here: we state the market value, while we don't know exactly what the selling value would be, but we are expected to make sound and reliable estimations of that value. This opens the door to let other and new subjective elements into the financial statements. I think that by introducing such elements we will ultimately fail in our objective and actually end up with less harmonisation and less mutual comparability! The financial statements may then become a mixed bag of different accounting policies with different objectives, which will obviously not increase the transparency. These are all problems that need to be recognised and addressed.

'Another problem that crops up with fair value concerns the objective determination of the company's "performance". The following example should clarify this. When an entrepreneur is confronted with changes in the market value, his or her result will also change. However, it will not be possible to attribute this change to specific – internal – business economic reasons. With historical cost, the results are determined on the basis of an objectively ascertainable entity. But with fair value, the presence of lots of assets with a volatile market value, such as financial instruments, can necessitate a considerable adjustment to the result that is not based on the company's economic activity. The entrepreneur is thus confronted with a new type of risk, namely the risk of a change in the result due to the application of fair value. I suggest we use the term "accounting risk" to indicate this risk of an unpredictable change in value and all its consequences for external accounting purposes.

'Financial accounting will have to be based on more criteria than just the profit figure to provide insight into the company's "performance". In this connection, I foresee a glittering career for the balanced scorecard that will enable companies to take other performance criteria on board in the assessment, even if only as an ultimate remedy and for the sole purpose of enabling them to generate a positive cash flow. Another consideration is that a change in value need not coincide with the reporting interval. This lack of synchronisation, in turn, will have consequences for the value that the users attach to the information. More financial information will have to be provided on an ad hoc basis: not just the notorious profit warnings, but also other types of information that can help the investor to make his or her decisions.

'In short, we are still a long way from getting to grips with the consequences of applying fair value. This whole discussion is also interesting from a scientific perspective: in my opinion a shift is taking place from the well-known normative accounting theory, which currently has the upper hand, to the positive accounting theory, which is concerned with management choices and stakeholder behaviour in relation to the accounting process.'

What will an entrepreneur get out of a changeover to IAS reporting principles? Put differently: does it matter to the entrepreneur, as the preparer of the financial statements, whether the reports are based on 'Dutch GAAP' or on IAS?

Professor Swagerman: 'The most obvious answer is that IAS reporting will permit greater comparability between reporting elements. The preparer can thus benefit from increased transparency. As for the entrepreneur, IAS may make earnings management a more difficult proposition. So entrepreneurs who use that as a "management tool" won't be too happy about the arrival of IAS. This would basically answer your question. But I think IAS accounting also has further advantages to offer. It may sound a bit paradoxical, but I expect the changeover to IAS to actually create opportunities for the entrepreneur. Value will be created thanks to the improved and increased transparency! As a result, entrepreneurs who converge from "Dutch GAAP" to IAS accounting will be rewarded with a premium. This premium will be expressed in the increase in the value of a (unlisted) company relative to companies of the same class that have not converged to IAS. Entrepreneurs do not have many opportunities to boost the value of their company, so the benefits of this premium should outweigh the costs of making the administration IAS-compatible. This argument might even stimulate IAS adoption among entrepreneurs who are not obliged to use IAS but who are keen to create additional shareholder value. These entrepreneurs can then try to achieve further benefits by means of regulatory arbitrage and engineering.

'In this context I would also like to point to the growing range of ICT tools that will greatly promote mutual comparability. The development of the various XBRL taxonomies is a case in point. Finally, I assume that the increased transparency resulting from the improved mutual comparability will also make a positive contribution to the quality of accounting.'

What developments do you see as desirable?

Professor Swagerman: 'As you can gather from what I have already said, the search for value is central. In this connection I think that the concept of "comprehensive income" and the moves towards introducing this concept into the financial statements will be developed further.

Everything that can assist our efforts to obtain the true and fair view, in other words a view that restricts the possibilities for influencing the profit figure, is scientifically interesting. The concept of comprehensive income is helpful in this connection and should therefore be further elaborated and be applied on a wider scale. Basically the comprehensive income is the "net income" and the sum of all changes in the shareholders' equity in so far as these are not related to transactions with the providers of shareholders' equity. The background to this development is the increased importance of fair value as a valuation principle for assets and liabilities. This then raises the question: How must the changes in the assets and liabilities be shown: in the profit and loss account or charged against shareholders' equity? The concept of comprehensive income is based on the "all inclusive approach". But the pure all-inclusive approach (clean surplus) has been "contaminated". All sorts of changes in the financial position are not accounted for directly through the profit and loss account. These changes are either only made visible after a time lag or are not shown in the result at all. The comprehensive income is thus less sensitive to the manner in which a company accounts for realised and unrealised increases and reductions in the value of the assets and liabilities in the financial statements. Unfortunately, there is still insufficient agreement about the best way of presenting the comprehensive income.

'I also believe it would be desirable to rein in the growing tendency to use such terms as EBITA and, what is worse, EBITDA. Their use frequently leads to an inaccurate picture. Companies that have actually suffered a loss, because of high interest charges for instance, can put a favourable gloss on things by reporting a positive EBITA. And EBITDA distorts the presentation to an even greater extent because it allows companies to omit the amortisation of goodwill. In other words, the goodwill is stated on the balance sheet, which may be perfectly justified in itself, but the amortisation component is left out of consideration.

'A small digression is in order here: if fair value is introduced, it is not directly necessary to write down the goodwill, but the "impairment test" – which strikes me as a rather theoretical device – will then come into play in the near future. It is worth bearing in mind that this test can lead to substantial abrupt changes in the value of the goodwill on the balance sheet. We need only look as far as KPN to see what the consequences of this can be. Careless use of EBITA and EBITDA may give a cursory reader the misguided impression that things will work out alright for the company. The correct use and the correct interpretation of the profit and loss account simply do not permit the use of these new measures of performance. Finally, I think there should be more clarity about the financial targets that a company sets itself. Information on the targets is often below par. The way in which the company proposes to realise vital targets should be disclosed in a much clearer manner than is currently the case. Adequate information will make it possible to establish how much shareholder value has been created.'

What will the agenda for the coming years look like?

Professor Swagerman: 'I can only answer that question partially and from my own perspective on possible developments. I won't try to give a neat summary of events in order of importance, but rather an overall picture of what lies ahead in the coming period.

'The most important development in the field of financial accounting in Europe will be the changeover to IAS accounting, both for organisations who are obliged to do this and organisations who want to adopt IAS voluntarily. This changeover will be a major and costly operation, but it can't be started too soon. The accounting systems have to be adapted. So this is the third administrative-organisational change confronting organisations in only a short period of time. First there was the millennium bug, then the euro and now, for a number of companies at least, the changeover to IAS accounting. The next development of this kind is the introduction of fair value. We are still only in the initial stages of this development. The fair value model has not yet been fully elaborated for entire financial statements. The question, therefore, is whether its scope should be extended to all items and within what timescale. Fair value not only has consequences for the technical presentation of the items in the financial statements, but particularly for the use and interpretation of financial statements based on fair value.

'For financial institutions, in particular, the consequences of IAS accounting can hardly be overestimated. Banks will be confronted in 2005 with the simultaneous introduction of IAS reporting and Basle 2. Under the corporate governance model of Basle 2, banks that do their best to reduce their risks will be rewarded with a lower capital requirement. In the past "the rules were the rules" and the situation was fundamentally static. But the proposals of Basle 2 entail that organisations can become eligible for a more favourable regime by undertaking certain actions on their own initiative. Better risk management will thus be rewarded with a lower capital requirement. This approach deserves to be applied on a wider scale! In line with fair value accounting the emphasis is on the presentation of prospective information. The directors' report will have to present the company's outlook on future developments more adequately than is currently the case. I also think that in view of the growing pressure to counter money laundering, corruption and terrorism, the directors' report should set forth the steps that the organisation is taking to address these issues. In this connection, the accountant will have to devote more attention than at present to the "accuracy" of the information rather than to its "completeness".

'Globalisation, too, will induce further harmonisation of the regulations while also increasing the need for mutually comparable annual reports. The typically Dutch accounting method will largely disappear in a step-by-step process, starting with the introduction of IAS accounting. Finally the small and medium-sized business sector will also have to accept the consequences of this harmonisation. These aspects apart, ICT is also having an influence on the financial accounting process. The ongoing advances in the field of ICT mean that the reporting interval can be shortened. The financial logistics of virtual companies already extend beyond the confines of the internal organisation and this can lead to virtual accounting. And, as I have said, the further introduction of the XBRL taxonomy will promote the comparability of information.

'The voices calling for the inclusion of non-financial information in the annual report are growing in volume. In this connection a draft bill ("Koenders – Rabbae") was submitted to the Dutch Second Chamber in September 2001 with a view to getting internationally active companies to report on aspects of social entrepreneurship in line with OECD guidelines. Though the Confederation of Netherlands Industry and Employers, VNO-NCW, is not particularly enthusiastic about this draft bill, I do think these developments are just round the corner! But have accountants, controllers and financial directors already equipped themselves for this task?'

What, in your opinion, is the significance of the Enron, Worldcom and Xerox affairs for financial accounting?

Professor Swagerman: 'The US GAAP system contains elements of the "form over substance" principle, which explains why the rules and their interpretation are described in such exhaustive detail. The customary US stance is that the full and consistent application of US GAAP will automatically lead to a "fair presentation". However, the fact remains that problems can always occur which the existing rules are unable to deal with. The problems at Enron illustrate this point. Dutch GAAP and IAS accounting are premised on a different principle, namely "substance over form". The difference between the two systems, however, does not lie in "substance over form" versus "form over substance" but in the "true and fair overriding principle". The US approach actually helps to create circumstances in which disasters such as the Enron affair can occur, because the formalisation inherent in this approach imposes too many restrictions on the accountant's freedom to form a professional opinion. In view of the manner in which the IASB has given shape and substance to the "overriding principle", our approach should be given preference over the US system.

'I think that the consequences of Enron will have an enriching effect on financial accounting and the organisation of accountants. For many years to come this case will be used to illustrate how volatile profession-alism can be. In the event, Arthur Andersen was completely dismantled within a mere nine months. As for the consequences for financial ac-counting, I think that the calls for the creation of a Dutch SEC will only grow louder. This could be done either by widening the tasks of the Auth-ority for the Financial Markets or by setting up a Review Panel Board responsible for forming an opinion on the quality of financial accounting.

What is your final message?

Professor Swagerman: 'I think that all our efforts are ultimately aimed at constantly increasing transparency in order to create a global level playing field. As a result of all these developments, risk management will gain in importance as it casts light on a company's vulnerability and may well become more relevant than financial statements based on fair value. Perhaps this is where the challenge for the future lies!'

Chapter 26

Warning signals about the application of fair value for financial instruments

An interview with Tricia O'Malley and Petri Hofsté

Tricia O'Malley

Tricia O'Malley FCA (1949) was appointed to the International Accounting Standards Board in January 2001. In October 1998, she was appointed as the first full-time Chair of the Canadian Accounting Standards Board. Before this appointment, she was a partner in the National Assurance and Professional Practice Group of KPMG where she consulted with partners and staff on complex client accounting issues. O'Malley was a member of CICA's Emerging Issues Committee from its inception in 1988 until 1997, when she was appointed Vice-Chair of the Accounting Standards Board. In her role as Vice-Chair, O'Malley represented the Canadian Board at the meetings of the 'G4+1' and the Financial Instruments Joint Working Group of national standard-setters. She was Chair of the Ontario Securities Commission's Financial Disclosure Advisory Board from 1992 to 1999, has been a member of the Independent Advisory Committee on Accounting and Auditing Matters of the Auditor General of Canada (since 1993), and is a Past President of the Canadian Academic Accounting Association.

Petri Hofsté

Petri Hofsté RA (1961) has spent a substantial part of her professional career at KPMG, primarily at KPMG in the Netherlands where, until last year, she was a partner in the Financial Services group, focusing mostly on banks. As of 2001, she has officially been one of the partners in the KPMG IAS Advisory Services group in London, her role especially being to deal with financial instruments accounting and the financial services industry. Hofsté is also a member of the Implementation Guidance Committee on IAS 39, which was set up by the IASC, and is a member of the FEE Banks Working Party. In the Netherlands, she is involved in the standard setting on financial instruments accounting, being one of the project supervisors for the implementation of IAS 39 within the guidelines issued by the Netherlands Council for Annual Reporting.

In this double interview, Tricia O'Malley and Petri Hofsté explain that banks are not convinced of the benefit of IAS 39 on financial instruments for banks. This equally applies to the banks in the USA and Canada. Banks particularly see problems with hedge accounting. They also point out that further study is required into the problems that arise with the application of a full fair value accounting model for banks. One of the problems they see with this model is its reliability. Furthermore, accountants must co-operate far more with financing specialists and acquire more knowledge of capital markets. For banks, it is important that the rules permit the valuation of portfolios of instruments and therefore that valuation does not have to be applied individually. The rules for financial instruments must apply to all banks, whatever their size.

Have banks already been convinced that IAS 39 is useful?

Hofsté: 'At a recent seminar we asked the banks what they thought about IAS 39 and whether they wanted to implement it. Their immediate answer was no. Banks fear the IAS 39 hedge accounting issues and are very much aware of IAS 39 recognition issues, which they think prevent them from conducting certain kinds of business. In the Netherlands in particular, the banks do not like IAS 39 because of the very strict rules surrounding the held to maturity portfolio and the major changes with respect to dealing with exchange results. What the banks fear most of all, however, is a full fair value model, which follows on behind IAS 39. What I have seen up until now is that the implementation guidance and the ensuing discussion about the interpretation of a number of issues has actually produced a lot more understanding of the ideas behind IAS 39. We have made it clear, for example, that the standard is not intended to prevent all hedge accounting. What we want to do is create the right atmosphere and establish the right criteria so that we can be assured of proper presentation with respect to the application of hedge accounting and we do, of course, want to prevent abuse.'

Are US and Canadian banks more willing to move towards full fair value accounting?

O'Malley: 'I would hesitate to say too much about US banks, although watching from a distance over the border in Canada, I think they have been fairly vociferous opponents of every single step that the FASB project has taken on financial instruments directed towards fair value, starting with the disclosures in 107 all the way through 133 on derivatives and hedging. In Canada, the banks have by and large not been as outspoken as those in the USA because there is no comprehensive accounting standard on the fair value of financial instruments. They have been focusing more on the Joint Working Group proposals because the Canadian board has been participating with the IASB on a joint project on financial instruments since 1987 or 1988. The chair of the Joint Working Group is a former chair of the Canadian board and we have provided the majority of the support staff, so our institutions in Canada are more focused on the long-term solution. In general, I would say that the reactions of Canadian financial institutions to the moves towards fair value have been exactly the same as the European institutions and everybody else; I don't think there is any difference worldwide in the views expressed.'

How do you convince your clients that changing the standards is not just an exercise in employing a lot of people, but actually a useful step for everyone in the field?

Hofsté: 'First of all, I should say that the financial services industry is the biggest user of financial instruments and also faces the greatest variety and complexity where these instruments are concerned. In that sense, therefore, the financial services industry stands on a different platform to other enterprises, which potentially will not face the same level of complexity when shifting from the current measurement system to a full fair value model. Nevertheless, if banks, which do have full value information available because they use this internally for their position making, say that they are not yet ready to produce full fair values on each and every item in the balance sheet, then we should perhaps examine whether the Joint Working Group has been given the right objective. More research and discussion may be required about what the users expect and therefore the introduction of full fair valuation could take longer than originally anticipated.'

Is there not a danger that you will create less transparency by transforming accounting standards?

O'Malley: 'It is now incredibly difficult for anybody who is not a specialist to try and figure out the results of the accounting for financial instruments, because there is a mixed model within financial instruments accounting. Where accounting standard 133 in the USA is concerned, there are qualified accountants who specialise in just one particular paragraph of the standard because it is so complicated. The draft financial instrument standard has an elegant simplicity with everything being valued on the same basis, thus eliminating all the complicated rules about how to classify this, that or the other. Almost all of the capital asset pricing models that we are familiar with start off by saying that the first thing that we need to do when analysing a company is to take all the financial instruments that are held and put them to market. We assign a multiple of one to the result, because it's already at fair value, and then value the rest of the business and add the figures together to produce the business value.

'In my opinion, the real issue here is the reliability problem. The Joint Working Group has done its best to resolve this, but a lot more work and research is required, especially with respect to the economies with smaller, much less efficient and less liquid markets than, for example, the economy of the USA. Another major problem with the Joint Working Group proposals as far as I am concerned is the income statement presentation. Frankly, we just didn't have enough time to deal with the issues in more depth because we were under enormous pressure from the sponsoring organisations to complete our work before the end of December. Work still needs to be done on performance reporting. This is an incredibly difficult issue because no work has ever been done in this field. I don't think we will see a full fair value model implemented until we have sorted out performance reporting.'

Could you say something about the market value of debt and credit risk?

Hofsté: 'Theoretically, a full fair value model should also include credit risk. The question is whether this is possible at the moment. Of course, if the value of a liability decreases, there is a decrease in the value of fixed assets, which is covered with impairment losses in the current model. There can also be internally generated goodwill that we don't see on the balance sheet. If this decreases in value, it counterbalances the decrease in value of the liability. The discussion on the subject has not yet been finalised and I'm sure that the Joint Working Group will receive a lot of reactions from the market.'

O'Malley: 'The majority of the members of the Joint Working Group wanted to leave the change in the entity's own credit out of the fair value of liabilities. There are practical difficulties in trying to leave this out because it exists when the debt is issued. If you want to leave out the effect of this change in a full fair value model, you first have to figure out what your own credit risk spread is on the issuance of the financial instrument. You must then isolate it so you can get back to a risk-free rate. In terms of the fair value changes, all that you are then dealing with is perhaps a risk-free rate and the industry spread, for example. Once you have isolated the difference, you have to figure out what you are going to do with it over time and how it meets the definition of an asset or liability in terms of a conceptual framework. The problem is therefore how to deal with the presentation and that is why I think that the Joint Working Group called for separate disclosure of any gain that resulted from a change in own credit risk. It is not the case that you always have a change in the value of your business or your assets, even though your credit rating may have changed. When a company's credit rating declines, you can still capture its value as long as the underlying value of the company itself is sound. As people become more familiar with the derivative products that are available, it becomes easier to explain why the information on value changes is relevant.'

Hofsté: 'Once people become more familiar with derivatives, the quality of market prices will get better. Because there will then be a deeper market, you can only do one thing, and that is grow towards the full fair value model. The issue as far as I am concerned is when have markets and when have enterprises got to this particular point? A major challenge for the IASB is to determine the objective and to establish how and at what pace we will reach this objective.'

As accurate market prices are not available most of the time, will the profession of accountant have to change to the profession of valuator?

Hofsté: 'Certainly the shift towards using more fair value information has already led to two major developments in the profession. Firstly, there is more emphasis on the education of accountants, on learning about finance and learning about financial markets. Secondly, there is greater co-operation within the firms between auditors and valuators. The skill set of auditors is now already quite different than it was 10 to 15 years ago.'

O'Malley: 'Accountants certainly need a better understanding of finance and capital markets. A number of years ago, I was on a CICA Vision Task Force and a key recommendation was that the profession as a whole needed much more background in these topics and since then there has been a significant increase in the finance component of the education programme for chartered accountants in Canada. However, based on what we saw when we implemented the Canadian version of IAS 32 on presentation and disclosure, I have some serious doubts about whether we have the accounting competence in financial instruments to actually implement a full fair value standard. Profession-wide I just don't think that we have enough finance knowledge. The knowledge about the standards and about the instruments is concentrated in such small numbers of people because the standards are so complicated. I do not believe you can sensibly practice accounting without having a reasonably good understanding of capital markets and of how the instruments actually work. The implementation of new standards will not only require a huge investment in education in the profession worldwide, but the user community itself must also improve its understanding of the markets.'

Is there not a danger that the quality of financial information will decline because of the gap between the standards and the level of understanding of accountants?

Hofsté: 'It is not only the level of understanding of accountants that is important. Those enterprises that are currently unable to come up with a fair value for a certain derivative instrument should not enter into them just because an investment banker comes along and tries to sell it to them. They must understand what the instrument does and what the risks are and what effects of changes in the market circumstances have on the value of that instrument.'

Doesn't that imply a significant increase in the cost of accounting for companies?

O'Malley: 'I do not believe that the cost of moving to a full fair value model will be significantly higher than the cost of trying to implement the mixed measurement system. I would like to re-emphasise the point that has already been made: if you can't figure out the value of the various instruments, then perhaps you should not enter into them. The simple instruments are not very difficult to value, it is the derivatives that are very complicated.'

Hofsté: 'I think that financial services enterprises, which already trade and perform transactions in many different types of financial instruments, do have the knowledge to value them. A shift from current traditional accounting to IAS 39 is a major issue in terms of processes and systems, but I would also expect this to be the case with a shift to a full fair value model at this point in time. The reason for this is that the current system picks up cash flows and calculates shifts in fair values in very broad terms, rather than trying to come up with sufficiently accurate fair value information to go into the financial statements.'

O'Malley: 'One of the first questions that the Joint Working Group had to deal with was whether we should talk about the fair value of individual instruments or about the fair value of portfolios, because the value of portfolios is clearly different from the value of instruments. I don't think that there is any particular expectation that people would have to value individual instruments, but I think the disclosure requirements allow you to bundle like instruments together and value the portfolio as a whole, particularly where the market price of the instrument is actually that of a portfolio and not for an individual instrument anyway.

'Some institutions in Canada that we talk to believe that it's going to be almost impossible to implement the new Basle approach to regulation without having a pretty good fair value model to deal with the risk management issues. Some of them are starting to build systems that embed fair value on the balance sheet on a much more frequent basis. There is an awful lot of change taking place, not just because of the accounting, but because of the way the markets themselves and the regulators are working.'

Because everything with regard to financial instruments is so complicated, should the standards only apply to listed or large companies?

Hofsté: 'No distinction should be made between listed and unlisted or small and large companies, because if you are big enough to enter into derivatives, if you are big enough to enter into complex financial instruments, then the standards should definitely apply.'

O'Malley: 'I entirely agree with my colleague. If a small company employs complicated financial instruments, it is even more important for them to understand what they are doing and they should be able to explain themselves.'

What is the added value of the new IASB compared to the IASC?

O'Malley: 'The added value, the most important change as far as I am concerned, is that the IASB has brought all the national standard-setters together. All those participating have agreed to put the same topics on their agenda that the IASB has. They have agreed to try and talk about the various topics simultaneously and work as hard as possible to come up with one set of international standards so that international companies wanting to access the capital markets do not have to apply different standards for each of their national subsidiaries. The long-term goal is to produce one set of international standards that can be used without reconciliation in all the world's major capital markets. We have been working this way with the national standard-setters for some time and improvements have been made already, but the IASB is the catalyst that is focusing everyone's attention.'

What is the significance of IAS 39 for the financial services industry and what developments do you expect?

O'Malley: 'The final version of IAS 39 will not be the same as the standard that exists now, because a number of improvements will be made, particularly in the area of derecognition. I don't think there will be many changes in the underlying principles, but a lot of clean-up work still has to be done by the Implementation Guidance Committee. The insurance contracts project has been put on the priority list and everybody on the board is well aware that we must have a standard in place for insurance by 2005. We cannot leave a major European industry without any standards; a huge chunk of their business, that is, the liability side of the balance sheet, must be covered and the policy liabilities must be dealt with in order to create a "balanced" balance sheet.'

Part VI

Capita selecta: external financial reporting and law

Chapter 27

IAS: right or wrong?

An interview with Hans Beckman

Hans Beckman

Professor Hans Beckman (1944) is Professor of Annual Reporting Law at the Erasmus University Rotterdam. He is also a lawyer in Amsterdam, a partner in Stibbe, an editor of the corporate law journal Ondernemingsrecht, *a member of the editorial board of MAB and a member of various editorial committees of loose-leaf publications, including* Compendium voor de jaarrekening. *He has been a member of the VERA Law steering committee (along with Professor Dick Degenkamp) since it was founded in 1978. He continues to lecture at VERA seminars.*

Dutch accountancy's origins in the dim and distant past were in business economics whose genetic material can still be found in Dutch accountancy practice. In very many other countries, however, the accountancy profession's roots were in the legal domain and there accountancy's 'linkage' is significantly more obvious with the law than with business economics. This is not to deny that the accountancy profession has left its cradle a long way behind and become a fully-fledged profession which is independent in every sense of the word. According to Professor Hans Beckman, however, there is a 'natural' relationship between accountancy and law. The question to him is whether current developments in the law on annual reporting are taking account of the backbone of the Dutch economy, small and medium-sized enterprises (SMEs).

Is there not an urgent need for a separate regime for SMEs?

Professor Beckman: 'I really could not agree more. It is too stupid for words to apply every kind of standard that an international – that is, Anglo-American – body wants for stock-exchange listed companies to all Dutch businesses, regardless of size. We are happier immediately implementing what we think is wanted elsewhere. Meanwhile American companies, for example, only have to apply the detailed standards of US GAAP if they are listed on a stock exchange or subject to an audit. And us? We want to have the most detailed rules, and the more American the better. It is as if we cannot or will not think for ourselves. The Council for Annual Reporting [*Raad voor de Jaarverslaggeving – RJ*] has become a sort of translation agency for IASC, now IASB, standards. At the same time, the RJ is seriously overestimating itself, partly through regarding its own views or IAS standards as more important than the requirements of imperative law. We see the same thing in day-to-day practice: accountants who insist on applying IAS rules or RJ guidelines under the threat of not issuing an unqualified report. I will give you an example. A large firm of accountants insists that a stock-exchange listed company should consolidate a non-group company as indicated by IAS or RJ guidelines, while this is clearly in conflict with imperative Dutch law and European Community legislation. There are in fact very few weapons against this type of abuse of power by auditors. It is an incitement to break the law. It then becomes incomprehensible that accountants emphasise in their reports that the company's management are responsible for preparing the financial statements.'

The law's influence on financial statements is growing. Is it not time for certain items that are liabilities to be counted as part of the capital base for reporting purposes?

Professor Beckman: 'Reporting is a substantial part of the law. It is too often suggested that there is no link between the law and reporting. This is obviously wrong; in the historical perspective too. I much regret that accountants' current training pays too little attention to the law. Accountants do not learn enough to deal with the rules of law. They also have too little understanding of what the rules of law are. That sounds bold, but the argument holds water. Consider the example I gave at the end of my previous answer.

'Furthermore, a climate has developed in which it is thought that the rules on financial statements set by the legislature do not apply to accountants and companies. Clearly they can draw up their own detailed rules which everyone has to obey. And the more detailed the better! The Act on company financial statements from the early 1970s was thought to be far too detailed. It left no room for interpretation! There was a hue and cry. A new act was desperately needed. It came about in mid-1984, and was even more detailed. Whereupon the old law, which was thought to be so detailed, was praised to the heavens. In 2001, the accountants themselves have shown what is possible. And so we are now getting IAS, which is more detailed than any legislature would dare. But it was "invented here" and so there is no stopping the cheering. They have drawn up their own rules without taking account of the interests of smaller businesses, without taking account of the rules of law, and without taking account of legal systems. In my opinion, not only should this not win any prizes, but it demonstrates a degree of inflated arrogance. A good example are the rules on netting off. The RJ states that items which can be netted off should be netted off in the financial statements. The RJ is overlooking the fact that netting off is a kind of payment, one not involving cash. Without netting off, the separate items remain in place. If they are netted off, the netting works back to the moment when the authority to net off arose. It is quite possible to take the view that if items can be netted off, there is authority to do so. There are other legal systems, however, under which the existence of items which can be netted off means netting off straight away (for example, French and Belgian legislation). The IAS standards make it mandatory to net items off if the authority and a definite intention on netting off or simultaneous settlement exist. This comes from American regulations stating that these provisions create an authority to net off. We now see that the IAS standards make no allowance for continental legal systems under which netting off is immediate and continental systems where netting off can only follow an agreement on netting off (or in the intercompany accounts). The netting provisions are regulatory law and can be excluded or extended contractually. Generally, opportunities for netting off are only available in Anglo-Saxon countries if arranged by contract when they often go far further than is possible in countries with statutory authority for netting off. I have explained this in great detail to show that reporting rules must be anchored in the appropriate legal systems.

'If I return to the question, I think that confusion should not be sown. Debts are debts. And must, therefore, be presented as such. An issue to be recognised, however, is whether certain characteristics of certain liabilities place them in a special category of loan capital, such as generically subordinated liabilities. The same of course applies to limited-term preference shares abroad. They should in fact be generically subordinated during their lifetime.'

Some experts in the reporting field believe that lawyers in fact have too much influence. For example, the 'substance over form' debate. It is argued that 'substance' puts the commercial content into practice; economic reality. 'Form' is the legal structure. This applies not only in the Netherlands, but also internationally. Does this not in fact mean that legal constructions have absolutely no further meaning for reporting? That the legal shell around the business economic kernel is in fact irrelevant since you should look beyond the legal constructions and, in the end, the commercial position is important?

Professor Beckman: 'There is a surprising, and persistent, misunderstanding of the relationship between "substance" and "form" among business economists and accountants with no legal training. So we see rules putting "form" into practice which are given the same footing as "law". "Substance" is put into practice as departures from the rules or what is quite obviously the same: "business economic". There was a call in *Het financieele Dagblad* from someone who said that "form over substance" applied in America because the rules govern there, while "substance" applies in Europe: looking beyond the rules because of the statutory true and fair view. This statement equated those rules with the law – which is obviously nonsense. The American reporting rules from the FASB are not rules of law. Furthermore, the FASB also assumes "substance over form" and the detailed rules arise from the many conflicting interpretations of what "substance" is. The IAS and EU guidelines on annual reporting also work on this basis. Legal certainty means that the subjective insights of any number of individual people should not be given definitive significance. The point is that annual reports are based on facts. This is slightly different from looking beyond legal constructions and putting "economic reality" in their place. I don't yet know what "economic reality" is. If there is a legal construction in the sense of a representation that differs from the facts and what the parties intend, I have no need for quasi-distinctions between "form" and "substance". "Substance over form" is a legal principle, not an economic one or an accounting expression. The requirement on the statutory true and fair view is "substance over form", a legal rule that assists proper interpretation. "Substance over form" does not, therefore, mean primacy of business economics over the form, but that you have to report in a good form and in the right way: what has actually happened must be accounted for properly. That is where the objective and intent of transactions have a real role.

'Departing from the provisions of imperative law has nothing to do with "substance over form". The guidelines of the RJ incorrectly state that short-term investments should be marked to market and this is in conflict with an imperative provision in the Act. It is totally against the law. What is the background to underlying this? Well, securities can be sold just before the balance sheet date, the profit taken and then they are bought back after the balance sheet date. This is a typical example of "substance over form". Even if you have sold with that objective, you should not take the profit. That is the nature of "substance over form".

'How should we regard "substance over form" if soon everything is marked to market, at fair value. Consider the valuation of liabilities: is it acceptable to split a convertible into "debt and equity components"? How do you deal with warrants? The Americans include them in shareholders' equity. Should we do the same, therefore? Does it fit into our continental legal system to do that? Just because it fits the American rules, it does not necessarily fit in here too. Perhaps there is something to say in its favour, but let's think it through carefully rather than just following slavishly. There is also the question of whether you are in conflict with the principle of factuality.

'The use of economic values is not new however. I would point to the considerable literature as early as the beginning of the last century. Those theories are still as solid as a rock. But clearly people like thinking up new things which have been around for a long time; change for change's sake. But are they improvements?'

What do you think of current annual reporting in relation to the usefulness for readers?

Professor Beckman: 'I have indicated several times that financial statements are, or are threatening to become, unreadable. I repeat what I wrote in May 1994 in the corporate law journal *TVVS* (now *Ondernemingsrecht*). Previously I saw two reasons: first, the need to keep items off the balance sheet and, second, modernism in reporting theory.

'The first proved to be highly relevant in 2002, at Enron. Several "special purpose vehicles" were set up with the aim of keeping them out of the consolidation. This was effective, but happened with the knowledge (or approval) of the auditor. In real situations there is nothing against not consolidating, but there is a problem with paper constructions purely for disguising the true financial position, assets and liabilities and income and expenses. The limits of respectable business behaviour and a proper audit opinion are being exceeded. There is deliberate misrepresentation.

'The second point I mentioned in 1994 was modernism in reporting theory. This is even more relevant in 2002. The need to drop the "accounting concept of profit", has become so great that all kinds of things are being thought up to make the financial statements "commercial". Liabilities are sometimes called shareholders' equity, sometimes they are liabilities, I have already mentioned split debt/equity components and all kinds of financial assets and liabilities that suddenly need to be stated at fair value. Under the influence of IAS, there are also wonderful definitions of assets and liabilities, etc. The user is not asked for anything. It seems as if the auditor is assessing what wisdom for the user is. In my opinion, there is nothing for the user in this type of modernism in the primary statements.'

What role do you see for Chapter 9 of the Netherlands Code if IAS is applied soon? Will the law have any significance for listed companies?

Professor Beckman: 'The European Commission is now looking differently at IAS. This is a fundamental change of direction which takes away one of my main objections to IAS. I think it is sensible that they should have a type of public-law status. The draft regulation drawn up by the European Commission in December 2000 states that there will be an endorsement procedure and, in any event, this takes away the private law status. I don't know whether the endorsement procedure will go well, but the European Commission has announced that lawyers will be involved to monitor the quality of the rules.

'Insufficient thought has been given to the fact that the guidelines and standards will be implemented via an umbrella regulation. Certainly now that there is a degree of haste to have consolidated financial statements compiled under the new standards from 2005. That may create a collision with Chapter 9, Book 2 of the Netherlands Civil Code. A regulation takes immediate effect and so Dutch law can be pushed aside. This will need to be looked at again properly. Consequently, I wonder whether the Dutch legislature is being sensible in making IAS compulsory for company financial statements. I have less difficulty with the plans for consolidated financial statements, but company financial statements are something different. They have an important role in the capital protection law, such as with the formation of statutory reserves and the determination of profit distributions.

'All this requires fleshing out. An example: if I take the proceeds from a warrant directly to shareholders' equity, what am I actually doing? I am including something that is deemed by law to be a freely-distributable reserve. But it is not a statutory reserve, as they are listed in the Act and proceeds from a warrant are not among them. It is more in the form of an undistributable reserve. As long as the warrant has not been exercised, it is not freely distributable and is not liquidity. This means Chapter 9, Book 2 of the Netherlands Civil Code should be amended with respect to non-distributability to ensure that this type of item is undistributable.

'In addition, I am wary of the influence of the Americans on IAS. As soon as they want something different, IAS is amended. For example, in the Netherlands we have always written goodwill off against the freely-distributable reserves. Note that I specifically said "freely-distributable reserves", because far too often in practice you see it simply written off against shareholders' equity, while there are no freely-distributable re-serves, sometimes no reserves at all. That is simply against the law. No doubt about it. But OK, it happened until 1984. The legislature then bowed to practice, despite the Fourth EC Directive not allowing goodwill to be written off against freely-distributable reserves, although no-one will put it so bluntly. If you look at the directive you will not find a single clause where this is permitted. The Seventh EC Directive does approve this though; but under strong influence from the Netherlands and the UK, as the rest of Europe did not do this. The Netherlands had a unique position with company financial statements, since valuation at net-asset value – we called it intrinsic value at the time – was a specifically Dutch phenomenon and no other country used it. The UK did not use it either, despite what is often suggested. It was used in consolidated financial statements in the UK, as in the Netherlands, for non-consolidated parti-cipating interests. In the UK, goodwill was only written off against freely-distributable reserves in consolidated financial statements. Then a UK accounting standard changed and prohibited this. The fact that an ac-counting standard in the UK could forbid this approach is a result of a clause in the Companies Act to this effect. There is a statutory basis for such a prohibition.

'And what do we see here? In April 2000, the RJ stated through its chairman that goodwill may no longer be written off against freely-distributable reserves. And that is simply wrong. It is permissible until the law is changed. That is the position even if you don't agree with it.

If the law permits the write off, you cannot forbid it. And you cannot come up with stories about the "statutory true and fair view". It is a specific clause, included in the law and which specifically allows the write off, even in conflict with the Fourth Directive. OK, the proposed legislation currently before the Lower House of the Dutch Parliament will be given the force of law. The aim will be a prohibition, with effect from 1 January 2003. If it succeeds, goodwill will from then on have to be capitalised, amortised and restated at a lower value if it is permanently impaired to below book value. If the cause of the permanent diminution in value disappears, the write-down must be reversed. If we compare that with IAS, we first see that the goodwill has to be computed differently and secondly that there is a different train of thought to be followed: if you have recorded a permanent impairment, you may not reverse it.

'The proposed Dutch legislation I mentioned anticipates the proposals of the European Commission to give the IAS standards a public-law basis by allowing a company, at its option, to apply IAS standards in full during a transition period. As a result, two systems will exist alongside each other. When you see how negative goodwill is treated, you realise that there is a world of difference between what Chapter 9, Book 2 of the Netherlands Civil Code stipulates and what IAS has to say. It is really substantial. But the confusion is still not complete, as the RJ has taken the side of the IASB by adopting what IAS "prescribes" which, to put it mildly, is not entirely in line with our legislation.

'Yes, and then other people get involved. You could read in an article submitted to *Het financieele Dagblad* that KPN is capitalising incorrectly. It was claimed very forcibly that goodwill may only be capitalised if and to the extent that it could be written off against shareholders' equity. In other words if you pay 10 for goodwill and have freely-available reserves of 8, you can capitalise 8. And what happens to the remaining 2? It reduces shareholders' equity of course. This shows the nonsense that this author wrote. *Het financieele Dagblad* did not publish any adverse commentary on this. And there are other examples.

'Moving on, one more thing. I read that in the USA goodwill on acquisitions after 30 June 2001 may not be amortised any more. It was put something like: "New rules in America say that goodwill purchased on all acquisitions after 30 June 2001 must be capitalised. You may not amortise it, you must apply an 'impairment test'. In other words, the company must determine what the goodwill is worth every year. If this creates a fall in value, part of the goodwill is written off. If, later on, the goodwill has risen in value, the company may not return the goodwill to the original amount." End of the summary. What do you achieve with this? Well, the lobby has done its work; it was getting irritating to say each time that the profit figure was before amortisation of goodwill. Now you can simply say "profit". So you can drop the A from EBITDA. That does not have to be done any more, therefore. The rule for negative goodwill is now that, if there is any, it must be written off against all assets until you reach nil. If a little bit is left over, which is almost impossible, you must amortise it. Goodwill other than from acquisitions may no longer be capitalised. And "Pooling accounting" is no longer allowed. What are we doing? Isn't it making a mess big time?'

'Furthermore, the new American rules differ fundamentally from what is usual elsewhere. They do not line up with European Community law or IAS. What is going on? It has been announced that the IASB wants to adapt its goodwill standard to the American one. This is where we see the great American influence.

'The proposed legislation I mentioned earlier anticipates a forthcoming regulation from the European Commission that allows IAS standards to be used as an alternative for the Dutch (that is, European) annual reporting regulations. There may not, however, be a conflict with the Fourth and Seventh Directives. Consequently, the American rules on goodwill, even if incorporated into IAS, may not be applied at the European level until IAS Standard 22 (Business Combinations) – after amendment – has been approved. It is notable that the proposed legislation entirely sets aside the stipulations on statutory reserves in Chapter 9, Book 2 of the Netherlands Civil Code. There is, therefore, serious damage to creditor protection.'

What do you think of the quality of annual reporting in the Netherlands, in particular, directors' reports?

Professor Beckman: 'The quality is in itself not bad and will do. If you compare a Dutch directors' report with an American one, there is much less information. That is true. We do not include three years' figures. Our directors' reports are much shorter. The question is whether there is a need for a detailed report. Personally, I find many American reports quite difficult to read. On the other hand, I make good use of them if I need them in legal cases. But my experience, including at shareholders' meetings, is that shareholders often ask question on subjects which are answered in the directors' report. Questions for the sake of asking.

'In addition, more information is wanted as a result of all the latest developments, such as "fair value", "economic concept of profit" and suchlike. The average shareholder no longer understands it. And no wonder. If we write-down liabilities in favour of the profit and loss account, as happens in America, I can understand that the ordinary shareholder will give up. It may all be fine in theory, but you have to keep practicality in sight. That is, the user-approach that everyone was going on about in the early 1970s. By linking this to fair value, the poor user will be completely uninterested in all this complicated stuff.'

You have referred more than once to valuation at fair value. You don't sound very enthusiastic.

Professor Beckman: 'That's right. I doubt whether valuation at fair value is such a good idea. I am talking about the valuation of financial instruments. A lot has been published on this in recent years which has resulted in detailed American standards from the FASB and a delay to detailed IAS rules. Accountants, more particularly those on such bodies, are clearly keen on this. As, thanks to considerable lobbying, the IAS will also form part of the Community system after an endorsement procedure, the Fourth and Seventh Directives will also need to be amended. This amendment is incorporated in the EU directive of 27 September 2001. The core of the American/IAS rules on valuation of financial instruments at fair value, and on the obligation in this context to provide relevant information has been included. The EU directive requires member states to permit or require valuation of financial instruments and derivatives at fair value. This may be restricted to consolidated financial statements. If valuation at fair value is not made compulsory, the directive requires relevant information to be included in the notes. As an aside: I use the term "fair value", although the Dutch text of the EU directive refers to "open-market value". I regret the Dutch wording. I do not understand why this term, which has a specific meaning in tax legislation in the Netherlands, was suggested. Furthermore, replacement value, for example, is also a market value. It would have been better to use a term such as "actual value", "commercial value" or "market value".

'I think it would be sensible for the Netherlands not to make fair value compulsory for financial instruments, but to permit it as an alternative and, if it is not used, to require information based on fair value to be given in the notes. I think it is a pity that the recent proposed legislation I referred to does not include any stipulations on this. I, therefore, think it would be sensible – to prevent misunderstandings – to avoid the term "open-market value".'

Could significant improvements be made to the quality of the accountancy profession in the Netherlands?

Professor Beckman: 'I think that there needs to be a clear distinction between auditing, the accountant's real duty, and the other work. The quality of reporting can also be assessed by others. It is not something specifically for auditors. The auditors must determine whether the financial statements meet all the substantive requirements. It must be a reliable document. That in particular is the duty of the auditor. You can easily have a difference of opinion on whether something meets the statutory requirements. I am not sure whether an auditor should always aspire to this.'

What do you think of the role of the European Union? The EFRAG is a mechanism for checking IAS.

Professor Beckman: 'I hope that the IAS is looked at seriously. Otherwise we are on the way to disaster. I can understand that people want to check how far things created by the private-law route worldwide meet EU guidelines. And whether the guidelines need to be adapted, therefore, to what has been developed elsewhere. I think that you should, in fact, go a step further and assess whether certain pronouncements can be reconciled with the continental legal systems. I think that we are following the Anglo-Saxon legal systems too easily and that application should once again be in line with Dutch practice.

'I think that the Belgians, French and Spanish will have much more difficulty with this. They have the *plan comptable*, their bookkeeping system which requires detailed records, also for macroeconomic purposes. So I don't think it will be that simple. But this again underlines the distinction to be drawn between company and consolidated financial statements.'

How, in your opinion, should supervision be shaped?

Professor Beckman: 'For supervision you might think of a separate body, outside the accountancy organisations. Plenty of ideas have been put forward on this. Royal NIVRA is far too defensive on this: "We certainly do not feel passed over," says its council. Well, of course you should feel passed over if you cannot convince the outside world that you are sufficiently independent of the business. This is what it is all about.

'Another issue is whether auditors can be expected to investigate things on their own initiative. I do not think so. If the public wants more standards or extensive information, that is for the relevant authorities. If verifiable information is involved, the auditor must deal with it. You should be able to rely on the auditor actually having checked it. In addition, you should be thinking of a body which can have uncertainties submitted to it. I am thinking of the *Commissie Boekhoudkundige Normen* in Belgium which you can approach with questions for proper clarification. The same can be done in the USA, that is, with Staff Accounting Bulletins. We also see interpretations, something that the IASB now does with the SIC, which the Dutchman, van der Tas, is a member of. That body issues interpretations and recommendations which are worth reading and taking to heart.

'I think that is where you should primarily find guarantees. If necessary you should set up a supervisory body to check reporting. But you have to make a choice of principle: should you check every report (limited to listed companies) on your own initiative? Or should you make a rotation list? The latter is probably more practical.

'In any event, separate supervision is not a bad idea, particularly for listed companies. Such a body would need experts in external reporting with both business-economic and corporate law backgrounds. With the business-economic background, I am not thinking only of accountants. An accountant is not an expert in annual reporting merely by dint of qualification. It may well be so, but other examples are business economists and controllers. A corporate law background involves specialist "lawyers".

'Setting up a separate supervisory body raises other questions of course: will the Enterprise and Companies Court continue to operate? A supervisory body could not in fact issue legally-binding judgments. I think that a judge could be very useful for many points of principle. Another question is how expensive would such a body be? It would be yet another institution, a sort of *Pensioen- & Verzekeringskamer* (Pensions and Insurance Supervisory Authority of the Netherlands), a sort of *De Nederlandsche Bank* (Dutch Central Bank). That will create interesting arguments on authority and costs and public-private co-operation.'

What do you think of IAS?

Professor Beckman: 'IAS are not internally consistent. The same applies for the Guidelines for Annual Reporting. Read the piece on Warrants and Options and tie it back to the chapter on financial instruments. You will quickly lose the thread. But I cannot help but say that the Dutch in the guidelines for annual reporting is poor and that does not make it any easier to work out the RJ's intentions. Even worse, as one person reads this into it and another that, you get differences of interpretation and misunderstandings. These documents should be reviewed very critically and the need to justify the positions taken will thus be greater.'

Part VII

External financial reporting and new-economy companies

Chapter 28

The valuation of new economy companies

An interview with Auke de Bos

Auke de Bos

Professor Auke de Bos RA (1965) works within Professional Practice Research at Ernst & Young Rotterdam/London and is attached to the Legal Faculty of Erasmus University Rotterdam as part-time Professor of Business Economics. He is also involved with the postgraduate controller course at this university and with postgraduate courses for lawyers. He is a member of the VERA steering committee on Financial Reporting.

As companies work on the digital highway and their Internet activities expand, many questions are being raised. Where is revenue generated and where should it be booked? How should the new economy companies be valued on the stock market? How should Internet activities be reported? How will this affect regular reporting? Internet companies can be rather innovative with the space available to them in the virtual world. One specific problem area is revenue recognition. Professor Auke de Bos tackles this and other issues concerning the new economy companies.

What, in your opinion, is turnover in Internet activities?

Professor De Bos: 'Turnover is if the client says he or she is satisfied and is prepared to pay for it. It is that simple. With Internet activities, however, it is not always so clear-cut. Dot.com companies often make barter transactions. If one company advertises at another and vice versa, has turnover been generated?

'To answer this question it is necessary to formulate criteria to determine if, in the normal course of events, there also would have been turnover. Otherwise, you run the risk of a potential hand-in-glove situation. Determining turnover requires detailed examination. In the USA, a decision over this issue has already been taken. The EITF No. 99-17 "Accounting for Advertising Barter Transactions" was published there in 1999. According to this guideline, companies can only recognise turnover from barter transactions if they can establish that such a transaction could have also taken place as a cash sale and therefore it was also actually a cash sale. That in itself is easy to determine because the money should then have been transferred by each party. A further criterion is that the companies should have been able to sell the same advertising space to an unrelated party for cash during the past six months.

'The IASB has published an interpretation (SIC 31) which states that such advertising services can only be recognised as turnover if you can provide reliable evidence that similar advertising services have been sold in independent non-barter transactions. In practice, there has been some lack of clarity about this issue and there are some Internet companies, by nature very innovative and enterprising, which also have worked very creatively. They just looked for forms of turnover. Moreover these transactions were sometimes paid in shares; the one company receives no cash consideration, but shares in the other company. When the value of these shares rise or fall, is that really turnover? If the shares double in value, has the turnover then doubled? After much consideration, the conclusion was reached that you can only recognise the price at which you closed the deal as turnover. Then, any upgrading or downgrading which may later occur belongs in the investment portfolio.

'Another issue concerning Internet companies is whether turnover should be recorded gross or net. For example, Amazon.com sells books via the Internet. What is the turnover? Is it the total sale price of the books? Or is it only the profit margin? If you assume a 10% margin, and you sell a book for 100, you have a turnover of 100 in one case and a turnover of 10 in the other. With the foresight that the majority of the new economy companies are valued on their turnover growth, companies have found it advantageous to report turnover gross as much as possible.

'There are still no explicit rules set for the reporting of turnover gross or net in the Netherlands, but this issue has already been addressed in the US. In the Staff Accounting Bulletin on "Revenue Recognition" (SAB 101) further criteria have been established. The most important criterion is whether the company actually was the economic owner of the product and thereby had also assumed the risks of ownership. Thus, if Amazon actually keeps the books in stock and then subsequently delivers them, the turnover is reported gross. However, if the company acts as an agent or broker – the books are owned and kept in stock by a third party and Amazon only orders and delivers them when a purchase order is received – then Amazon can only report the commission. If you read the financial statements and the annual report of Amazon, you see both gross and net turnover. Thus, they make a distinction between the two. For the record, most of the turnover reported is gross. In the Netherlands, we still do not have any rules on this, but they are coming. The Dutch financial reporting standard-setters, the Council for Annual Reporting, has just published a draft guideline for turnover recognition.'

Is conditional sale also a problem?

Professor De Bos: 'Yes, there is the situation when several products are delivered at the same time. For example, an Internet provider sells information via a contract to a client. The client then has the right to that data for five years and receives a software package to get the information off the Internet and to read and interpret that data. This software has a certain cost price. It will be updated in the interim if a new version is needed and subsequently a new computer is also delivered. Now, the question is when is turnover generated? There are three services for one price. Let's say that the price in my example is one million for the five-year rights to information, a software package for which an update is released in the interim and one computer. Is there turnover now for the Internet company or not? Essentially, it's all about identifying the services as much as possible. If the computer is supplied and can no longer be returned, there is turnover because the economic risk has been transferred. But if it is not so clear-cut – if the computer is supplied for five-year use – then the turnover is to be spread over a specific period. Consequently, the basic rule also prevails here: if the client says he or she is prepared to accept the product and not return it and will pay for it, turnover can be reported.

'If we are talking about a total amount of one million and the client pays one half million up front, you cannot report a half million turnover if the client can still reclaim. If certain conditions are not satisfied, you can only report as turnover the part that you can clearly show that you have earned.

'These are some of the issues with regard to the realisation of Internet turnover. It boils down to the problem of Internet companies needing to show investors as much market growth as possible in order to attract new capital. It appears that when there is a lack of clarity regarding the treatment of reporting, the method that leads to showing the highest possible turnover is chosen.'

Internet companies have primarily costs and expenses at start-up. If an investor evaluates an Internet company solely on turnover, does it not really matter what profit or what loss is reported?

Professor De Bos: 'Exactly. Often, Internet companies were inclined to write off costs as fast as possible and capitalise as little as possible because the valuation of such companies was dependent on turnover or some other indicator, such as EBITDA. The more that was booked in the profit and loss account, the better the results that could be shown. Furthermore, the classification of expenses could also be shifted around the various cost categories. If certain costs are ignored, the EBITDA comes out higher. Even alternative EBITDAs were defined. In late 2001, P. T. C. Dekker RA and I did a study on the reporting of performance indicators. The upshot was that almost every company appeared to make use of a different definition of EBITDA and this figure was often used to illustrate the results of the company. Moreover, most companies tended to be creative in the calculation of the EBITDA.'

There is a tendency for Internet companies to book costs for as much as possible in the profit and loss account. Doesn't this lead to a balance sheet which has been stripped naked?

Professor De Bos: 'Yes, that is indeed a characteristic of these companies. They show few assets. Buildings are rented. Expensive cars are leased, as are the computers. The balance sheet of a new economy company does not offer much for scrutiny. There is little or no history, and thus an investor or a creditor has few clues to evaluate such a company.

'That is support for the argument to record intangible assets in the balance sheet as much as possible. An asset is a resource with economic benefits that can be reliably measured. Many intangible assets satisfy this definition and should therefore be eligible for capitalisation. Noteworthy is that the international rules do not allow the capitalisation of intangible assets in all cases. For example, a brand name can be an important intangible asset for a new economy company. The brand name "Yahoo" is well known and is valuable. There are also more examples. If you look at the conceptual framework of the IASB, you see no distinction made between internally generated and acquired intangible assets. Thus, if you create a brand name and thereby incur costs, you should be able to capitalise them on the balance sheet. However, this is not allowed. Internally developed brand names are not recognised as assets. This rule actually contradicts economic reality. Thus, according to the accounting standard setters at the IAS, reliability has precedence over economic reality with respect to intangible assets. It's a pity. From my point of view, brand names belong on the balance sheet. In 2001 a study of the top-100 brand names in the world was conducted by Interbrand. New economy companies were also on the list. Hence, these sorts of brand names are recognised as valuable and this value should be recognised on the balance sheet.'

In addition to marketing costs, the costs for the development of websites and databases are also of importance for Internet companies.

Professor De Bos: 'There are already rules for this. Costs for websites, if they satisfy certain criteria, can be capitalised. The US standard SOP 98-1, "Accounting for the cost to develop or obtain software for internal use", has been adopted by the IASB as SIC 32. Start-up costs for a website – market research for example – cannot be capitalised, but development costs can be capitalised. Furthermore, the various phases have been explicitly specified. There are tables that indicate when you must move over to the capitalisation of such costs.'

Aren't new economy companies confronted with a large value gap?

Professor De Bos: 'Yes, these companies are sharply focused on turnover growth and would rather not capitalise costs. This leads to a value gap, which is defined as the difference between the value of the company (market capitalisation) and the accounting book value of the company (the balance of the assets and the liabilities). In practice, this is seen as rather a problem. In the USA, Professor Baruch Lev has argued for the capitalisation of intangible assets for years. If you recognise the intangible stuff on the balance sheet, you can close the value gap and give a much better picture of the economic reality. In January 2002, the FASB announced the start of a project entitled 'Disclosure about Intangibles'. The aim of this project is to formulate rules regarding the disclosure of intangible assets (brands, client lists, licence agreements and patents) which are not recorded on the balance sheet, but should be available in the case of an acquisition. Thus, the last word has not yet been spoken or written.'

KPN has a market value that is lower than its book value. What does that say about the value gap?

Professor De Bos: 'The value on the balance sheet is a result of what is recognised under assets and what is accounted for under liabilities. The indirect realisable value of the individual assets must be expressed as much as possible on the balance sheet. In other words, if you want to value a patent, then you must first determine its feasibility or saleability. Otherwise, you must approximate the value using an assessment of the indirect revenues. Then you must account for this in the cash flows that relate to the brand. That is an indirect realisable value. Thus, each entry on the balance sheet is in fact a reflection of future cash inflows. If you want to value a company, you are actually talking about the company's cash flows that are not yet attributed to the underlying assets. If you want to assess the economic reality of all kinds of assets and liabilities, than you must approximate each item against the fair value, against the market value, and also against indirect realisable value. That still does not imply by definition that it then also represents the market value or the indirect realisable value of the total company. This is because there is synergy between them: the goodwill that has not yet been deposited and is still an intangible asset. That is the first noteworthy nuance.

'In theory, the value gap, as I have already stated, is the difference between the balance sheet value and the value of the indirect revenues. Furthermore, I assume that all the assets and liabilities are stated at fair value, either the market value or the indirect realisable value. Now, it is possible for the market value to differ from the indirect realisable value. The market value is a question of supply and demand. The relatively low market value of KPN (the leading telecommunications network operator in the Netherlands) is an indication that the acquired goodwill should be written off. (This has since been done to a large degree. In 2001, KPN wrote off an amount of EUR 13.7 billion in goodwill.) Also, the relatively low share price is due to the fact that the share is not very popular at the moment, but that could change at any time. Market value is fickle and dependent on future expectations and sentiments; however, it is not the same as indirect realisable value. A calculation of the cash flows could reveal that the total indirect realisable value is higher than the market value. The opposite can also occur, as we saw with many Internet companies. Their expectations were high, but they were not justified by the underlying values.

'If the indirect realisable value is equal to the market value and this is lower than the balance sheet value, the assets and the liabilities must be devalued. The balance sheet cannot show a higher asset value than the market value, assuming that the market value is equal to the economic value of the company. With Amazon you still see that there is a positive difference between market value and the book value. This is because all sorts of intangible assets are not expressed in the balance sheet. With Microsoft you see a positive difference between the market value and the book value. This is because intellectual capital is not expressed on the balance sheet.

'One of my students did a study on the valuation of Internet companies. He has compared the value of discounted cash flow (DCF) in a company with its market value. For Cisco Systems it emerged that there was a positive difference between its market value and the indirect realisable value, for as far as we could calculate using assumptions. The balance sheet value was even lower. If you take another company, for example Amazon.com, you see that the market value is higher than the DCF calculation. We have picked out a few companies and made comparisons.'

What is your opinion on the valuation of acquired goodwill?

Professor De Bos: 'I believe that you should break down goodwill as much as possible into the underlying intangible assets. For example, if KPN had clearly indicated that licences or brand names were incorporated in the goodwill, the "impairment test" would have been simpler to perform. Now we see just one large amount for goodwill, which makes it difficult to judge whether it has declined in value. It would have been better to have split up the goodwill in underlying intangible assets.'

What is meant by 'channel stuffing'?

Professor De Bos: 'Companies that aren't generating enough turnover sometimes try to jack up their turnover figures at the end of the year.

Sizeable discounts can be offered, especially if software packages or computers which are likely to become outdated soon, are involved. The entrepreneur wants to get rid of the stock as quickly as possible. Consequently, before the accountant begins to depreciate the value of the inventory, it is dumped. The price is low, but that is always better than depreciation of the inventory. Another benefit is that the turnover can be recorded, but of course against the hefty discounts. There is nothing wrong with this. "Channel stuffing" is another story if you are going to deliver to related parties and start working with "side letters" or "tête-à-têtes". In the "creative accounting" of Lernout & Hauspie, a company that develops software packages for voice recognition, deals were made with non-affiliated customers to take back the supplied packages if they were not satisfied. Although it was not yet turnover, it was presented as such. This kind of practice is very difficult for an accountant to uncover.

'Incidentally, ISA 240 of the IFAC, "The auditor's responsibility to consider fraud and error in an audit of financial statements", states that the management should explicitly declare that it is not aware of fraud and that all material information has been provided to the accountant. If "side letters" then surface, the directors of the company have much explaining to do. This standard also states that the accountant must still look actively for fraud. Furthermore, an extensive risk-analysis, directed toward the detection of fraud, is also part of the audit.'

Now that so many new economy companies have gone belly-up, many are asking if the accountant should have issued an unqualified auditor's report. Is this an auditor's duty?

Professor De Bos: 'First off, we are dealing with new developments. New economy companies are different from traditional companies. There is still some lack of clarity regarding turnover, costs for website development, etc. Accountants are expected to be the authority and be on top of the latest developments. Wherever they turn, they are confronted with new phenomena, like "barter transactions". They can act as if it doesn't concern them, but must do something with these swap deals which cannot just be swept under the rug; the accountant must work out whether the company has neatly accounted for the transaction in one way or another in its books. Accountants cannot hide behind a statement that the standards have yet to be set. It is, essentially, all about the economic reality that must be represented. If it's about information that is being withheld, the accountant is in a difficult position. He or she could strap a lie detector to each client, but that goes a little too far. However, if it is about common sense and reliable reporting, the accountant should be the authority. It is his or her duty to convince the client that in the long run poor financial reporting doesn't pay. New economy companies imply both innovation and high risks. The accountant must be very alert, properly analyse the risks and must guide clients. That is his or her duty.'

Book and market value certainly must have something in common with each other, but is financial reporting actually a reflection of the value of the company? Or is it all about volatile value and the feeling for sentiments and such?

Professor De Bos: 'In theory, the accounting concept of profit which is expressed in the balance sheet is not the same as the economic concept of profit which is expressed in the value of the company. Nevertheless, it is very difficult for society to understand and to accept that profit means something different to the accountant than to the business economist and that the balance sheet does not represent the value of the company. Therefore, I believe that we in accounting must connect with the economic value as much as possible. Foremost, information must be useful to the shareholder, in order that optimal decisions can be taken with regard to the allocation of scarce resources. Isn't that the reason the accountancy profession was started in the first place?'

Part VIII

International financial reporting by governments

Chapter 29

IPSAS and financial reporting by the Dutch government

An interview with Aad D. Bac

Aad D. Bac

Professor Aad Bac RA (1943), partner at Deloitte & Touche until 1 November 2001, is Professor of Accountancy, Government Accountancy in particular, at Tilburg University. Since 1 November 2000 he has served as technical advisor to Peter H. E. Bartholomeus RA, the Dutch member of the Public Sector Committee, which is engaged in the development of IPSAS. Bac is a member of the VERA Steering Committee for Government and Non-Profits.

IAS exert their influence not only on the private but also the public sector. The difference is that we call them IPSAS instead of IAS, where the extra letters stand for 'public' and 'sector'. Professor Aad Bac and Peter Bartholomeus are actively engaged on behalf of the Netherlands in creating these international standards for the public domain. We asked Professor Bac about the development of IPSAS and the implications for financial reporting by the Dutch government.

We can distinguish between two phases here. The first is the adaptation of IAS into IPSAS. The second will focus primarily on specific areas of government which are not addressed by IAS. Moreover, the aim is to create a draft framework, in which much more bespoke work is possible for the public sector. Does that apply to the Dutch situation as well?

Professor Bac: 'Yes, and here one must make a clear distinction between the domain of the local authorities and provinces as opposed to the central government. The latter, as concerns its income and expenditure services (for example, agencies), as well as the provinces, local authorities and water boards employ the accrual accounting method – the income and expenditure system – in principle. For central government, all of this has yet to be fully adopted and remains limited for the time being to the agencies and other "income and expenditure services". Given the methods applied, IPSAS could certainly play an important role for local authorities, provinces and water boards in the near future, relatively speaking.

'The rules for financial reporting for the central government have entered a transitional phase. The existing liabilities/cash accounting system is to be abandoned for a modified accrual system. This will presumably take five years. As concerns the designs of the central government as a whole, transition to an income and expenditure system is not on the short-term agenda. Since IPSAS is seen as a totality, its relevance to central government will therefore remain limited for the time being.

'There is no reason why IPSAS – once the income and expenditure system has been fully accepted – should be considered impossible for the government to adopt. These standards comprise few threatening components as concerns financial reporting by local and provincial government.

'There are currently 20 accrual accounting standards in IPSAS. At the end of November 2002 the cash standard was also approved in the FEE Public Sector Committee during a congress in Hong Kong. The IFAC Public Sector Committee has established three steering committees, which are busy elaborating three governmental subjects (non-exchange transactions, social policy obligations and budget reports), which will appear as Exposure Drafts at the end of 2003. The Public Sector Committee is keen to see governments adopt these rules in the future. They will not, however, be able to employ the same method that we, as a professional organisation, have used worldwide in respect of IAS. There are various reasons for this. The original body engaged in the development of IAS (the IASC) – and the

IASB, its legal successor – was in fact a kind of umbrella for professional organisations: one with sole standing and authority. This body was founded upon a charter, which gave it the power to enforce compliance from its members and sometimes even put them under pressure to promote the application of IAS at their clients. It had, however, no way to influence legislation directly. Rather, it operated indirectly via auditors and their clients to obtain a formal status for IAS. As a result, it has been able to influence multiple countries or blocks of countries via the international business community in particular. Thus far, it appears that towards 2005 the EU will be accepting the application of IAS for annual reporting at large enterprises. That alone is quite an achievement.

'Yet this method of gaining acceptance will not work so simply for IPSAS. In most countries, with the exception of those structured according to the Westminster model, the rules on financial reporting by government agencies fall under public law. Changing these rules would automatically mean amending the law, which is different in every country. That is something which a private organisation like the IFAC cannot enforce. At most, it can make propaganda, which it has been doing. As soon as the Public Sector Committee convenes a meeting somewhere, the opportunity is used to establish connections with local and regional government, whose representatives are invited to a seminar or a meeting to cultivate their minds for adoption of the proposed rules for financial reporting. Especially in this connection, much can be expected from international aid organisations such as the World Bank, IMF, OECD and such. Were they to adopt IPSAS as a point of reference for proper reporting in the context of aid programmes, that would certainly break the ice in a push for adopting the standards.

'In the Netherlands, the rules on financial reporting by the central government are part of the Government Accounts Act [*Comptabiliteits-wet*]. If we are intent on seeing IPSAS adopted, that Act will need to be used as the starting point in one way or another. The provinces, local authorities and water boards also have something similar: a Royal Decree has sanctioned these rules by virtue of a provision in the Provinces Act [*Provinciewet*], Local Authorities Act [*Gemeentewet*] and Water Board Act [*Waterschapswet*] respectively. This is therefore also part of public law.'

What exactly is the Westminster model?

Professor Bac: 'That is the administrative model maintained by those countries which were once part of the British Commonwealth of Nations. For instance, New Zealand, Australia, South Africa and the United Kingdom have accounting standards boards which are engaged in issuing accounting standards – for government as well. There government has, more or less yet not completely, privatised legislation in respect of accounting standards. These are authoritative advisory bodies with a much greater professional influence on that legislative process than in the Netherlands. Here, the rules are designed by civil servants at the various ministries – with a leading role played by the Ministry of Finance – in so far as central government is concerned, and by civil servants of the Ministry of the Interior and Kingdom Relations (with advice from civil servants from other governments) as concerns other government bodies. In such cases, auditors in the employ of the government must and will be asked to lend assistance. A number of private professionals will also be consulted, yet to a limited degree, just as has been the practice for many years with respect to local authorities and provinces in particular. Auditors engaged for the local authorities and provinces are consulted about such plans, yet their input has not been institutionalised – unlike that of the accounting standards boards mentioned above. In our system, an amendment to the law is required; there is no particular independent governing authority with legal jurisdiction.'

Will we see any notable differences in IPSAS compared with financial reporting among companies?

Professor Bac: 'That is, in principle, the reason for developing them. The differences which primarily arise in the series of 21 are not so substantial. In fact, these 21 areas were selected for this purpose. The endeavour is to produce a reasonable number of standards as quickly as possible which can be expanded into a complete system. That was a firm condition of the project financers: the World Bank, the IMF, the OECD and the Asian Development Bank. Accordingly, these financiers had a huge say as to the order in which this project would be undertaken. As already said, the more government-specific components will be addressed in the second phase.'

Don't the proposed accounting standards make the government's position look too optimistic? If all manner of assets are estimated at fair value, won't that make us rich in natural parks which, however, we could never lease or sell?

Professor Bac: 'No, then we actually have "tied" capital. That, no matter how great it might be, represents the financial position given steady policy. It could only be converted into cash if there were assets which did not contribute to the government function. Imagine if one were to switch from a cash to an accrual system. That would mean taking stock of and valuing one's assets. According to the laws of accountancy, nothing can be entered on the debit side of the balance sheet without a corresponding entry on the credit side. That is what a balance sheet is all about. So whenever an asset is entered, this necessitates a contra entry in terms of shareholders' equity. On the other hand, if a series of loans were recorded – these are not yet part of the balance sheet, for example, national debt, not to mention future provisions – something would need to be debited from equity. This ultimately leads to a balance which is the general reserve of the relevant government. Incidentally, that balance can even turn out negative in case of particularly high national debt. At any rate, a tremendous amount of capital, which cannot be utilised since it cannot be converted into cash, is no problem.

'In this respect, the most important nascent standard of IPSAS is property plant and equipment, that is, machines, materials, in short all of the customary fixed assets. This offers a choice between two valuation models: historical cost and fair value. Incidentally, historical cost is the benchmark – the first choice, in principle. Fair value is optional.

'There are indeed certain countries which are keen to adopt fair value as the standard. The consequence is that they would need to apply re-valuation with considerable regularity. The difficulties we have encountered, and which remain to be fully resolved, concern cultural heritage, for instance. What would be a reasonable book value for the Arc de Triomphe or a pyramid, the Dutch Parliament or the Louvre? How should we value such things? We no longer know how much was historically spent on their construction, and we can ask ourselves deep down if a fair value can even be placed on them. So now, it has been decided in this respect to take some time attempting to find the best solutions to this problem.

'According to Dutch tradition, replacement value – true fair value – would not stand a chance here. Current regulations allow only historical cost as an accounting principle. This means that we already satisfy that IPSAS benchmark. Incidentally, I believe we have a good reason for it. If fair value is taken as the standard, depreciation will be based on it as well. Accordingly, a substantial amount of depreciation would be isolated from the available resources – in so far as loan capital were used for financing – while repayments would only have to be made on a nominal basis. As such, not every generation would pay for its own costs. But that is merely a side note.'

Will this produce any enormous figures?

Professor Bac: 'No, for as soon as historical cost can be determined, it will form the basis. If it cannot be determined, fair value – according to the rules – would be that price which could be obtained once one starts to assign values. That would be, as it were, the "historical" cost of that asset.'

The most significant changes will be seen in central government, but will things get any easier for the local authorities and provincial government?

Professor Bac: 'I believe so. The Public Sector Committee set this in motion in 1996, but local government in the Netherlands had already started to make changes in this area in the 1980s. During those years we developed the modified cash system for local authorities and provinces and converted it into a full accrual system with the inclusion of all recognisable assets and full recognition of provisions and such – therefore, a complete income and expenditure system. In the 1980s a conscious choice was made to fit government activities of a commercial nature, that is, business-like tasks, in as much as possible with what is now Part 9, Book 2 of the Netherlands Civil Code. In the 1990s we even extended that to all provincial government and local authorities. That does not, however, imply that Part 9, Book 2 of the Netherlands Civil Code – along, informally, with the rules for annual reporting – are applicable without further ado. It cannot be denied that government is clearly different from business in certain areas and that the logic of financial reporting choices made in the world of business certainly do not always fit in with the nature of government.

'So there are differences. I myself often use the adage "harmonisation where possible and differentiation where necessary". Governments which intend to adopt all of Part 9 should therefore enquire of themselves at least once where they will need to deviate by virtue of Article 362, paragraph 4. This article says that one should deviate from the letter of the law when transparency dictates. If it is so imperative to make a distinction, however, the last thing we need is a free-for-all. A better option would be to direct that process oneself. That is the background to the differences which exist between accounting principles for government and Part 9.

'People are presently also busy with a new version of the accounting principles, with even greater streamlining. Yet as concerns the local authorities and provinces, we have in fact more or less done the same thing that the Public Sector Committee is now doing for national government. For the IPSAS are primarily being written for national government.'

Do the IPSAS also go into the truly specific aspects of government, such as measuring aspects of policy (policy evaluation) and non-financial information?

Professor Bac: 'No, that is reserved for the next phase. There, the focus will be on non-transaction-based cash flows, such as tax remittances. The point will be to resolve issues such as: When to account for taxes? How to allocate tax income to different years? Should such allocation be based on the year in which taxes are paid? That can take some time. Or should this be done on the basis of the assessment date, for example? Such choices need to be made. And that requires the development of a consistent policy, where choices can be set down.

'Another topic that needs addressing in the next phase is the budget, especially the way in which it gives direction to financial reporting from that year later. Where structure is concerned, this needs to be a one-to-one relationship. Hopefully, issues such as performance reporting, policy evaluation, measurement of efficiency and effectiveness will also be included. These are presently not part of IAS. Nor should anyone expect to find them there in the future either, for the private sector does not require them to the same degree. Such components will figure into the next phase and that is not the easiest part of the programme.

'To reiterate: the only way to make IPSAS an integral part of government is to convince national governments to allow room for a reference to IPSAS in their legislation and regulations.'

Is there any resistance to IPSAS? How long will it take to introduce them? And are they really necessary?

Professor Bac: 'There are still few countries that apply the accrual accounting method for their government. One country, South Africa, has now declared IPSAS applicable. In order to see IPSAS adopted, one must first make the switch from cash accounting to accrual accounting, which is naturally not "just" a trend. Auditors will be in favour of it no matter what the country. Accrual accounting affords us more and broader possibilities for placing the accounts and financial reporting at the service of tighter management. Yet . . . auditors are not the ones who run the show in government – especially since that would require an amendment to the law. That leaves the administrators to play a role. They truly need to support it and understand the importance of the change in direction. They will want to know the consequences of such change, especially whether it will give them more or less financial elbowroom.

'Thus, there are situations imaginable in which uncertainties may arise as to the consequences for public finance. One might hesitate about whether to create provisions and, if so, which ones. On the other hand, the votes in favour are mounting. As a result, influence will ultimately come from international aid in many countries. Such organisations will wield their influence to ensure that those countries which are dependent on them for support adopt IPSAS as a point of reference for the quality of financial reporting. This will make financial reporting more transparent to them.

'In principle, listed companies should also present their investors with similar annual reports in order for stock exchanges to function properly. That is why IOSCO has been exerting so much influence on the IASB process. Yet governments have no need at all for such harmonisation. Why would we be interested in comparing the financial data of different governments? At national accounting level (encompassing the total economy of a country) this already takes place via the system of national accounts. This does not feature in the discharge process and since there is no such thing as the value of a share in "The Netherlands Ltd", there is no-one who wants to know the value of such a share. So if the discharge process can function properly in a national democracy, that is no reason to switch to a different financial reporting regime. The incentive is therefore lacking. Financial aid organisations which support developing countries, however, are keen on that method. I expect that it will become a matter of pride for the larger countries to avoid being passed up by the smaller ones in this respect. Moreover, "New Public Management" has been in the limelight for years, where extra attention to the quality of the management of government organisations features prominently. There, accrual accounting could be of service. In the meantime, central government has decided to adopt a partial form of the income and expenditure system. Such a system primarily fits in with the European standards which set out more detailed rules than IPSAS for a number of items.'

Part IX

The relationship between management accounting and financial accounting

Chapter 30

Interaction between internal and external reporting

An interview with Ed G. J. Vosselman

Ed G. J. Vosselman

Professor Ed Vosselman (1953) is Professor of Business Economics (with a special focus on Management Accounting and Control) at the Erasmus University, Rotterdam. He administers the registercontroller *programme as its co-ordinator. He was appointed Dean of the Faculty on 1 January 2001.*

Every now and then it's important to take stock of one's position: where do we stand and where are we going? It is therefore also important to know the key theoretical developments in accountancy and the direction in which they are heading. After all, this information is used in policymaking. These are some of the issues with which business economist Professor Ed Vosselman is concerned.

Does the history of accountancy in the Netherlands differ greatly from that in other countries?

Professor Vosselman: 'More in the past than now. Globalisation has given the field an undeniably strong impulse. Naturally, local colour will never fade away, but there is no longer any doubt that we are moving towards more or less international and accepted accountancy. While accountancy in the Netherlands has its own story of creation – as we all know – it should not be overestimated. We have the Amsterdam School of Limperg with areas like cost and profit/loss determination issues, which gradually split into management accounting and financial accounting. Limperg developed his own theories about replacement value in particular. Apart from that, the Rotterdam School came up with various concepts for different kinds of costs. By now, however, we have merged onto the same – internationally recognised – track in both management accounting and financial accounting.

'One of the current issues where financial accounting and management accounting converge in a certain sense lies in the field of measuring non-financial performance. This is expressed in traditional terms like profit and loss. Yet it is becoming ever clearer that profit figures also need to be based on something. That goes for the information that companies provide to outside parties via their annual reports; but it applies just as much to management reporting.

'The issue is to determine the deciding factors of profit and loss. In respect of the latter, I am thinking in terms of analysis tools like the Balanced Scorecard and such. Those generate not only information on profit, but also on the effectiveness of business processes and factors such as a company's delivery time, the reliability of deliveries, innovation and creative ability.

'We have now started a project at Erasmus University, Rotterdam (EUR) in co-operation with COCON. That is an organisation which develops projects with ICES funding, which is used to improve the knowledge infrastructure in the Netherlands. One of these projects targets the tools of the auditor. We are seeing an increasing number of knowledge organisations which maintain networks with each other, and the question is whether auditors and business economists have the proper tools for resolving valuation and management issues in these kinds of networks.

'If that knowledge is applied, how should we arrive at the proper valuation of intangibles? In that respect, we have not come much further than the valuation of goodwill. That is relatively easy to value, to record as an asset, certainly if it concerns goodwill that was actually paid, such as in acquisitions. But things get trickier as soon as we turn to goodwill which has arisen internally. Moreover, maybe the solution would be to use different classifications of intangible assets. If faced with the question of how to control the knowledge in a knowledge-intensive organisation, a division between explicit and tacit knowledge could be handy. Explicit knowledge is available in codified and often documented form. But what about implicit or tacit knowledge? This is what people simply know. It colours their experience, just as their experience also colours their knowledge. Such tacit knowledge is part of an organisation's collective memory. And that naturally represents a certain not-to-be-underestimated value. What is the best way to use and develop this knowledge? And what is the proper way to assign a value to it? I could imagine that such a thing might play a role in corporate acquisitions. Certain capital providers might also be interested in this information. In short, we have questions galore and not enough answers.

'Fortunately, some headway has been made. For example, the Ministry of Economic Affairs recently published its report entitled "Accounting for Knowledge". Yet we still have no real solution to the problem. I think it would be wise to partner experts from academia with the business community to decide how we can develop proper measuring, control and valuation tools for these kinds of intangible assets.'

The Balanced Scorecard is no doubt a handy tool, but are we talking about the functional requirements in a reporting system?

Professor Vosselman: 'Each information system must be suitable or made suitable for the user. Especially now that so many different parties are interested in information and transparency, the point is to design and tailor such tools to this end. Financial figures cover up too much of what is really at play in an organisation. If we truly wish to open this black box, we will need to find other indicators – ones which can be used to fathom the causes behind the economic result. I can imagine that profit is related to customer satisfaction in certain companies. But how can one measure satisfaction in general and customer satisfaction in particular? And is there a relationship to staff satisfaction? After all, a happy employee usually does good work, and that translates into happy customers. And if the customers are pleased, that will spur the staff on to do better work. In short, this creates a positive spiral. A proper analysis of the internal factors that influence profits and which are interrelated in a certain sense is frequently the wish of the enquiring party. That goes not only for outsiders, but also for managers. For they are ultimately the ones responsible for steering the profit-generating process.'

We are familiar with the Balanced Scorecard, Activity Based Costing, Zero Based Budgeting and such, but where is the fundamental theory?

Professor Vosselman: 'I'm not such a great believer in that. Here we need to be pragmatic. Activity Based Costing, the Balanced Scorecard, Value Based Management and Interfirm Cost Management Systems are all relatively new tools, which were developed in and by day-to-day practice before being made available to other organisations. The task of the scholar and the consultant has changed. The Balanced Scorecard was crafted by Kaplan and Norton and others from actual business situations and then spread to and launched at other companies and institutions. That is a brilliant development – people are at least willing to give things a try. It is then up to academics to measure the impact of such instruments – both positive and negative.

'Yet I do not believe in a universal theory. At the end of the day, I find our profession very pragmatic. That is also the big difference from Limperg's era. He was a true doctrinarian, who built a theory without practical elements. That theory was a closed system in which it was always right. Nowadays we are much more apt than in his times to look at the world round us. Unlike him, we are keen to investigate as many practical elements as possible and to incorporate them into our theory.'

We refer increasingly often to MIS-AO rather than traditional AO such as taught by Starreveld. Is this a positive development?

Professor Vosselman: 'Yes. Traditional administrative organisation is outdated. Contemporary, modern businesses are characterised by an advanced application of information and communication technology. That was, naturally, before Starreveld's time. He cannot be blamed, but the world has changed since then. Today's social and financial-economic business context needs to serve as the basis when designing and setting up administrative organisations. And I have the feeling that this is still not happening enough in our field.

'Nor is the relationship between ERP systems and administrative organisation done proper justice. There is a doctoral candidate at Erasmus University, Rotterdam, who is researching the administrative organisation issue at companies, their relationship to modern information and communication technology and their solutions to certain problems. Such research can give us a good idea of what is wrong and how to improve it. What I find unfortunate is that we are so distanced from the rest of the world where AO is concerned. With management accounting and financial accounting we see that internationally-oriented groups of scholars regularly publish in international journals. And here? We are still holding on to the theories of Starreveld; but these are typically Dutch and in dire need of revision.'

MIS-AO and AO used to be the exclusive domain of auditors. We now see other professionals in this field, some of whom are even trendsetters. The trends are coming from the area of system development. Is this enriching the field?

Professor Vosselman: 'Indubitably, people are shaped by their background. Before I came to Erasmus University, Rotterdam, I lectured to engineers at the Eindhoven University of Technology. Engineers are designers, and I learned that skill too during those years. Specifically, I focused on information system design. AO is one such information system which involves the design and conditions for the generation of certain information. An engineer almost always thinks in terms of systems. He or she seeks answers to queries such as what was this designed to do? What is its ultimate purpose? Once this has been answered, it could turn out that the requirements applicable to reliable information need to be sharpened considerably. That can even go for the quality of management information which, although it might not need to be so reliable, still needs to satisfy other functional requirements. Therefore, if an auditor is involved in building an information system, he or she must listen carefully to what other experts have to say.'

Will internal and external reporting grow towards each other in management accounting and financial accounting?

Professor Vosselman: 'I may have been a bit too orthodox in the past. I used to think that each information system had to be designed on the basis of its own objectives. As it turns out, external reporting and internal reporting have different objectives. That would mean designing two – strictly divided – separate systems. But now I see things somewhat differently. One should actually let these two systems "intermingle" where possible – a typical efficiency concept.

'Naturally, the principle of "the design serves the objective" is as vital as ever. Yet where possible – even if it was just to cut costs – a system must be made to perform as many functions as possible. I was once at an insurance company where a consultant had given all sorts of advice on something similar to an Activity Based Costing system. It was a nice thought, yet impractical; the company's accounting system was not suited to it at all. And then we have the requirements of the Insurance Supervisory Board, of which that highly recommended system took no account. I heard that it was granted only a short life.'

Is external reporting useful for today's management?

Professor Vosselman: 'It is hardly useful, if at all. Especially in financial reporting, external reporting is aggregated. Something happens in the organisation, someone drafts a profit and loss account and the profit casts a shadow which outlines, as it were, what happened. But management would never want to follow the contours of a shadow. Instead, their aim is to set sail to cast a nice shadow, that is, to arrange their business activities in such a way that a profit is generated in due course. Management is keen to know what happens on the floor. They want to see figures, but then as process indicators, of work in progress and not of its results. They are more interested in looking ahead than crying over spilt milk.

'Nor does external reporting have much to offer the controller whose aim is to conduct all manner of measurements in the organisation and to propose management models on their basis. The controller will need to support the managers in taking decisions to achieve optimal results, and operate in a pre-external reporting phase. Of course he or she might have something to gain from certain elements of external reporting. That cannot be ruled out; nor should it be. Yet the controller's job is to do his or her best to track, control and optimise the processes in the organisation. Especially in local and network organisations, this is no easy task.

'Another question is whether and, if so, to what extent does management accounting information influence the behaviour and decisions of all of those different managers in all of those different cockpits. The auditor often thinks that the figures reflect reality. Yet let us not forget that figures often construe a certain reality. By measuring things in a particular way, one can provoke and stimulate certain responses.'

Does external reporting pay enough attention to explaining cash flow?

Professor Vosselman: 'I find it a good idea at least to attempt to establish a relationship between cash inflows/outflows and profit/loss.

Management will also be interested in this. But I am against drawing a line between traditional profit and loss accounting, with the risk of creative accounting and profit manipulation, and cash flow reporting, which can be more factual and less prone to manipulation. I sometimes get the impression that one is expected to be for one side and against the other. I will have no part of that.

'I find the profit concept important for determining the business activities and operations to see which economic results they have produced. That can take the traditional route, that is, income less cost, or it can run via cash flows. That only makes things more transparent.'

How is the education at the Dutch universities where reporting techniques are concerned?

Professor Vosselman: 'If I look at the accountancy programme – and let us confine ourselves to this topic – I do not see enough academic research. Just compare that with the field of medicine. How could a physician possibly do a good job without regular input in the form of results from scientific research? Yet in accountancy this is not really the case. It seems as though accountancy as a field draws its learning from day-to-day practice. But is that information properly tested and upgraded via research? The same goes for controllers, incidentally. I have been pleading for extra research for years, because I am convinced that it will improve the quality of the profession. The status of the field depends on it, especially now that the discussion has arisen about the Master's and Bachelor's degrees and the distinction between higher professional and university education.

'I would also like to see more auditors obtain a doctorate and be freed up for research positions. We often get young people who have just completed their studies and who start working on their doctorate straightaway. While they are naturally to be commended, I would rather see them spend some time in the real world after they take their degree. That would give their research an added dimension.

'This is not to say that our accountancy programmes are substandard. On the contrary, I believe that Dutch auditors receive some of the best training in the world. And that goes for *registercontrollers*, too. But there is always room for improvement and for placing our programmes on a higher echelon.'

Part X

Business combination accounting

Chapter 31

A creative approach to mergers and acquisitions

An interview with Jos M. J. Blommaert

Jos M. J. Blommaert

Professor Jos Blommaert (1952) is Professor of Financial Accounting at the University of Tilburg, is affiliated to the Centre for Business Sciences at the University of Leiden as Professor of Business Economics, and lectures at VERA seminars.

The story goes that a French dignitary once said – with all the disdain that comes so naturally to the French – that the Netherlands was 'the fat boy of Europe'. What the French dignitary exactly meant by that is not clear, but we can be sure that no flattery was intended. The Dutchman is well known all over the world as the wilful and wayward little boy who sticks his finger in the hole of a dyke at one moment, only to raise it admonishingly into the air at the next moment. He is self-willed, a know-all and a born contrarian. It is the fate of a waterlogged nation that is unwilling to understand that people elsewhere might not share their views about everything under the sun. It's the same in the world of accounting. There too, the Dutch steer their own lonely course. Jos Blommaert, Professor at Tilburg University and the University of Leiden, expresses his doubts about the artificial Dutch practice of equalising the parent company and consolidated shareholders' equity and profit. But more about that later. Let's first look at what's happening in relation to goodwill.

Are we going in the right direction with goodwill?

Professor Blommaert: 'The growing attention for intangible assets is a good thing in itself. Historically, accountants have exclusively concerned themselves with reporting on trading activities. Pacioli in Venice and Stevin in Antwerp had bookkeeping systems that kept track of goods in stock and nothing else. In the days of the Industrial Revolution tangible fixed assets were the big thing. It took accountants a while to determine how these could best be recorded on the balance sheet. Nowadays we recognise that stocks and tangible fixed assets are less important in the profit-generating process. The significance of such tangible assets has greatly diminished for many companies; particularly those engaged in services. In their case, the key assets are of course human resources, customer base, knowledge and innovative capability.

'Looking at the present accounting system, you see that it has remained somewhat stuck in the days of the Industrial Revolution. You simply won't find the most important assets there. As a consequence, there is a big discrepancy between the value on the balance sheet and companies' worth on the stock exchange or in terms of takeover value.'

Is capitalisation of goodwill in that case the best solution?

Professor Blommaert: 'It could be a step in the right direction, but we still have a long way to go. First of all, the goodwill we are talking about is only purchased goodwill. Internally created goodwill, which is often much greater, has not been taken into account. It has been found that internally generated goodwill accounts for nearly two-thirds of the total value of many companies. In my opinion something more has to be done on that score. Nevertheless, the problem with purchased goodwill could prompt a number of follow-up steps. According to the new guidelines, goodwill has to be capitalised and may no longer be written down against shareholders' equity. But that concerns a goodwill amount very different from the one we were just talking about. Because "goodwill so far" was the difference between the acquisition price and equity value of net assets. The new guidelines state it must be the acquisition price less fair value of net assets. I expect this will result in an amount that is substantially different from the one we've been dealing with so far. Look at the enormous sums of money that KPN paid for E-plus, Getronics for Wang and Ahold for the Argentinean supermarket chain Disco. If you base your calculations on fair value, you end up with totally different figures. What is lacking is the amount of internally created goodwill.

'Once the dust raised by the new rules has settled, I expect new discussions will arise automatically about the various elements that are currently still included in that goodwill. In other words: the "core" goodwill will be capitalised but, unless we're careful, the "other goodwill" will continue to be tacitly written off against shareholders' equity.'

What do you think about the option of not writing down that goodwill?

Professor Blommaert: 'That's a topical issue at the moment in the United States in connection with the new Accounting Standards 141 and 142. The underlying idea is that goodwill does not lose value over time and therefore doesn't need to be written down. So once again I ask the question: what kind of goodwill are we talking about? If it's the goodwill resulting from the synergy that arises from bundling activities and assets, I'm not so sure you can say that its value does not diminish. As for the other "goodwill", if you continue investing in your brand name, in research and development, in schooling, you probably could maintain the value of these assets. And the same applies to other assets. The logical conclusion is that you need not depreciate buildings and machinery either, because with regular maintenance you can maintain their value too. You must keep to consistent rules in this area. What applies to one asset must also apply to the other if it is the same thing from an economic viewpoint.

'Though no definite decisions have yet been taken, the international accounting standards look likely to follow the US rules. This entails replacing the systematic depreciation of goodwill with an annual "impairment test", where the book value of the goodwill is compared with the fair value. If the book value is higher, a special downward adjustment must be applied to the value of that goodwill. This depreciation cannot be reversed in later years. The annual testing of the goodwill value does not only burden the company and its accountants with substantial increase in load, but also introduces an important new source of subjectivity. We're really going back in time. After all, at the start of the last century, depreciation of tangible fixed assets formed part of the profit appropriation and companies would write down as much as the profit could bear. It seems as if something similar could happen with the "impairment test".

How do you see 'purchase and pooling'?

Professor Blommaert: 'I think it's important for goodwill to be capitalised and no longer written down against shareholders' equity. In that sense I think you should also avoid "pooling accounting", as goodwill is not made visible and is implicitly deducted from shareholders' equity. However, I can imagine certain special circumstances where this could be a useful option. Simply forbidding "pooling accounting", as is the case in the new US rules, is going too far in my view.'

Assuming that parties are completely equal and 'pooling' is made restrictive (take ABN AMRO for instance), could you live with 'pooling' in that case?

Professor Blommaert: 'What we see is that the balance sheets of these companies fail to mention many assets that are important to the users and also undervalue the assets that they do recognise. If the intention is to reveal the fair value after such a merger, you would have to apply "purchase accounting". If that's not the intention and you believe that companies need not show a large part of their internally created goodwill value, then you may well wonder whether this should be done in these circumstances. The central issue is not really about valuation of participating interests or consolidation. It's a question of a higher order. What do we want? Do we want companies to show their fair value or not?'

What are your thoughts about stating all balance sheet items at 'full fetched fair value' and putting all (un)realised results on the profit and loss account?

Professor Blommaert: 'The big difference between what we reflect on the balance sheet and what a company is worth on the stock exchange or what is actually paid for it, is really beyond belief. It basically means that the balance sheet is no longer important for making decisions and forming a reliable opinion. That's why I'm a passionate advocate of increasing the relevance of financial statements, which is possible if we start reporting on the basis of something like fair value. This can help to give a more accurate picture of a company's performance and provide a better instrument for making decisions. But not in the same way as we are doing now. Measuring in terms of fair value implies subjectivity in the valuation. To increase the significance of the financial statements in this way, we must first of all develop instruments to measure fair value reliably.'

The criteria for including companies in the consolidation have attracted much criticism. The law provides for exceptions. Are the current arrangements sufficient or do we need new regulations?

Professor Blommaert: 'In the Netherlands we apply certain exceptions concerning the inclusion of companies in the consolidation. I have always wondered what purpose that served since the exceptions are already treated as such in the group concept. In my opinion we're essentially covering the same thing. Dutch law also distinguishes between subsidiaries and group companies, but this distinction is not all that necessary in practice. You usually apply formal legal criteria to decide whether a company is to be consolidated or not. The guidelines are tending towards the same kind of "control concept" that is currently being debated in the United States. For the past 19 years the Americans have been debating whether the consolidation of a subsidiary should depend on "ownership" or "control". Some favour "ownership", but most clearly prefer "control", either on its own or in combination with "ownership". What I would like to see is a discussion about the underlying rationale. What is the function of consolidated financial statements? If you can answer that question, you can also define the term "group" in a more purposeful manner.'

The FASB has introduced a 'consolidation issue' because of the many calamities involving consolidation and 'revenue recognition'. After Lernout & Hauspie in Belgium, similar situations can be seen at Enron in the United States with all sorts of off-balance sheet arrangements and revenue snags. 'Related Parties Transactions' have also created a lot of commotion.

Professor Blommaert: 'We have seen scandals involving "revenue recognition" to affiliated parties, that is, parties that just fell outside the group and therefore didn't need to be consolidated. The question is how to avoid that. I think that manipulation of figures in the context of consolidation at a certain extent is inevitable. Companies becoming involved in this kind of accounting practice will eventually pay the price.

'You do hear calls for new legislation under which companies would only be allowed to recognise the profit once the goods delivered to affiliates have been sold to independent third parties. Time and again you hear that malpractices should be tackled with new and more rules. But if these rules take away the pillars of our profession, new problems and opportunities for manipulation will present themselves. That would be counterproductive. Certain malpractices cannot always be prevented in that way, and therefore these have to be countered with alternative means instead of with more and more rules. Viewed from a purely conceptual perspective: if a certain party does not belong to the group, you must accept that everything delivered to it or received from it is profit for either one or the other. The new guideline states that you must eliminate a proportionate part of the profit when you do business with a non-consolidated company. That "profit" must be charged to the net asset value. That's an odd option because it is in conflict with the "accounting entity". In this case the legal entity and the economic entity are confused with one another. It means bypassing widely accepted principles and I think this will give rise to new and, in many instances, even greater problems.'

Professor Henk Brink RA has observed that it's high time to lay one of the sacred cows in the Netherlands to rest, namely the equalisation of the parent company and consolidated equity and profit. Do you agree with that?

Professor Blommaert: 'Absolutely. People in other countries find it extremely strange that we equalise the equity and profit at consolidated and parent company level. It's difficult to explain the underlying concept, because basically it involves a different way of reporting. But I know there is a lot of resistance in the Netherlands to abandoning this practice. It forms one of the pillars of the administrative and internal controls of companies. Accounting firms have also repeatedly explained to their clients that the equity and profit within consolidated and parent company statements should be equal, because otherwise something must be wrong. If we are going to make a step in the direction that other countries want, it will take us a while to do that, since we have a great deal of explaining to do to a considerable number of people. This is inevitable.

'If we start capitalising goodwill at fair value, it is still possible to equalise the consolidated and parent company equity and profit by artificial means. You will have to recognise the participating interests at fair value and show the fair value in the statements of your participating interest. That would entail a kind of "push-down-accounting" which is not permitted. If we don't do this for that reason, you will see that, just like before, the most important difference in goodwill is underhandedly written down against shareholders' equity in order to equalise the company and consolidated shareholders' equity. It would land us in a very artificial situation. Once again, I was never in favour of equalising the parent company and consolidated shareholders' equity and profit by such artificial means. If you have eliminated profits in the company, how are you to explain that you still have these same profits? What it basically boils down to is that our accounting practices have failed to respect the legal limits concerning parent company financial statements and that we are consolidating these in an artificial manner. And now we have to face the consequences.'

Toward a single global reporting system

Clearly, in view of the introduction of reporting based on IAS, internationalisation is the common theme of all the contributions in this book. In the European Union, the aim is to produce harmonisation of regulations in the field of financial reporting. For a single capital market in the EU, an important requirement is that listed companies use one and the same reporting system; that is, the International Accounting Standards (IAS). The harmonisation goal will considerably improve transparency and comparability of financial statements. In 2005, the point will have been reached where these standards have become generally accepted. The introduction applies to listed companies and all financial institutions with respect to the consolidated financial statements. The proposals also enable member states to extend the IAS reporting obligation to cover both statutory financial statements and the financial statements of unlisted companies. In the Netherlands, Dutch GAAP will gradually fade away and make way for IAS, but may remain in force for particular categories of companies and certain organisations.

The question arises how a worldwide harmonisation of accounting principles can be achieved. It may still take a decade, but US GAAP and IAS will ultimately have to converge. Non-US registrants, which are listed on US stock exchanges, have to comply with US GAAP. Such registrants normally have to comply with multiple systems at the same time; that is, US GAAP and the accounting principles prevailing in the home country. This is an undesirable and inefficient situation, which may easily lead to confusion and additional explanation of the differences between the various systems.

In the political arena we can see how difficult it is to produce worldwide agreement. Consider, for example, NATO's command structure, the establishment of the International Court or decision-making at the United Nations. Nevertheless, evolution is steadily continuing, so the expectation is justified that it will be possible to have one worldwide standard in the field of financial reporting at a future point in time. This would signify attainment of an important milestone in our social order. A lot of work will still have to be done to achieve this. This book mentions bodies that are already active in this field. In the coming period, these bodies will have their hands full with the transition to reporting based on IAS in order to achieve integration with US GAAP at a later stage. The Netherlands, with its long history in the field of accounting and financial reporting, will continue to play a major role in this.

How will we be affected by the introduction of external financial reporting based on IAS? Will the introduction be as flawless as the switch-over to the euro? It was only the business community who benefited from the introduction of the euro. It is difficult to say whether this will be true of the introduction of external financial reporting based on IAS. There used to be a liberal reporting regime in the Netherlands. The Council for Annual Reporting does, however, do everything to ensure that specific Dutch regulations – in so far as they still exist – stay in line with international developments. Our culture of tolerance, consultation and co-ordination – characteristics of the well-known polder model – can also be recognised in our traditional method of financial reporting. A much more businesslike regime, in the Anglo-Saxon manner, will emerge. This is inevitable because of globalisation.

These developments have not kept pace with Dutch legislation. There are a number of rules in Book 2 of the Netherlands Civil Code that do not mesh with the proposed rules for external financial reporting based on IAS. It is well known that the rules of the Council for Annual Reporting lack a legal framework. The sovereignty of accounting circles should eventually be given legal backing. That is why attention must be paid to the solution of this problem.

One of the most important developments is, of course, Fair Value Accounting, the far-reaching consequences of the introduction of which are still insufficiently acknowledged. The concept has still not been fully substantiated. There is still no model for financial statements based on fair value. With the introduction of fair value it is possible to accurately determine a company's financial position. This is a significant improvement compared with the present situation, but it is accompanied by different and new problems for which no adequate answers have yet been formulated. A different interpretation will have to be given to current concepts like transparency, showing a reliable, true and fair view.

An additional comment that can be made is that it is important to keep in mind the aim of financial reporting: it should be transparent and reliable and provide a clear picture of a company's financial state. An abundance of rules and the consequences of valuations based on fair value may, however, obscure the transparency of financial reporting.

The question is often asked whether the accountant in the IAS era will simply become an inspector of rules. There will always have to be an examination to determine whether a company properly applies the prevailing rules for financial reporting. The important thing is that the accountant forms an opinion based on his or her professionalism. External financial reporting based on IAS does not change this. The role of the accountant will become even more important when ascertaining valuations on the basis of fair value. This is a new field for the accountant to master.

Fair value gives the value of a company at the time of testing. The expectation is that volatility will increase, resulting in a feeling of great uncertainty about the interpretation of financial information. That is why a qualitatively sound directors' report, presenting a clear picture of the company and of its future developments, will be required much more than now. Investment analysts will also become more powerful. They will give their opinions about companies with respect to future profitability. The accountant will not and cannot express such an opinion. The public have a greater relish for a picture of the future than for information about the past, and companies' future profitability will be of great interest to them.

What will these developments lead to? Undeniably, the profession of both accountant and controller will be performed differently. But merely recording this fact will not suffice. Financial reporting will become much more complicated. The professional practitioner will have to be able to perform his or her activities properly and honestly. Training and education are the key here. By means of continuing professional education (including that provided by VERA), professional practitioners will be able to adequately formulate an answer to the new challenges that they face.

The Enron affair has caused turmoil in the world of accountants. The end is still not in sight. The lesson to be learned from this affair is that professionalism is a very vulnerable commodity. Six months ago it would have been entirely inconceivable to suggest that one of the Big Five audit firms would no longer exist a year later. This comment apart, the affair has major consequences for the organisation of audit firms. Many firms strived to build up expertise to further expand the total service concept. The question is whether this strategy can still be maintained in the future.

If the sphere of action of the accountant is reduced to mere audit activities, the question arises whether or not just chartered accountants will remain.

This book has provided an insight into the developments that we are confronted with. We hope that you have enjoyed reading the wide range of visions contained within it.

Index